SAINT THÉRÈSE OF LISIEUX

Saint Thérèse of Lisieux
Doctor of the Universal Church

STEVEN PAYNE, OCD

ST PAULS

Alba
House

Library of Congress Cataloging-in-Publication Data

Payne, Steven.
   Saint Thérèse of Lisieux: doctor of the universal church / Steven Payne.
      p. cm.
   Includes bibliographical references.
   ISBN: 0-8189-0923-4 (alk. paper)
      1. Thérèse de Lisieux, Saint, 1873-1897. 2. Christian saints—France—
   Lisieux—Biography. 3. Lisieux (France)—Biography.   I. Title.

   BX4700.T5 P35 2002
   282'.092—dc21

                                                            2002071142

Produced and designed in the United States of America by the
Fathers and Brothers of the Society of St. Paul,
2187 Victory Boulevard, Staten Island, New York 10314-6603,
as part of their communications apostolate.

ISBN: 0-8189-0923-4

Printing Information:

Current Printing - first digit   1   2   3   4   5   6   7   8   9   10

Year of Current Printing - first year shown

2002   2003   2004   2005   2006   2007   2008   2009   2010

ACKNOWLEDGMENTS

The author is grateful to *L'Osservatore Romano* for permission to quote from several articles on St. Thérèse and the doctors of the church that appeared in its pages; to John W. McGee for allowing me to cite his letter that appeared in the *National Catholic Reporter* issue of 31 October 1997; and to Eerdmans for material from *Theological Dictionary of the Old Testament*, edited by G. Johannes Botterweck, Helmer Ringgren, and Heinz-Joseph Fabry, translated by Douglas W. Scott, Copyright © 1997, by William B. Eerdmans Publishing Company, and *Theological Dictionary of the New Testament*, edited by Gerhard Kittel and Gerhard Friedrich, translated by Geoffrey W. Bromiley, Copyright © 1968 by William B. Eerdmans Publishing Company.

Thanks are also due to ICS Publications, 2131 Lincoln Road, NE, Washington, DC, 20002-1199, for permission to quote from *St. Thérèse of Lisieux: Her Life, Times, and Teaching*, edited by Conrad De Meester, Copyright © 1998 by Washington Province of Discalced Carmelites, and for allowing me to cite the following translations of the saint's texts:

Story of a Soul: The Autobiography of St. Thérèse of Lisieux, translated by John Clarke, O.C.D., Copyright © 1975, 1976, 1996 by Washington Province of Discalced Carmelites;

St. Thérèse of Lisieux: Her Last Conversations, translated by John Clarke, O.C.D., Copyright © 1977 by Washington Province of Discalced Carmelites;

Finally, I am deeply grateful to Edmund C. Lane, S.S.P., and Alba House for accepting my manuscript, and to the Carmelite communities of Washington and Nairobi, for their fraternal support during the writing and publication process. This book is dedicated to my father, Lawrence E. Payne, and to the people of sub-Saharan Africa, particularly my Carmelite brothers and sisters there, who taught me by their example what it means to live the "little way" of St. Thérèse in a setting so dear to her missionary heart.

TABLE OF CONTENTS

Table of Contents

PREFACE

One of the more remarkable ecclesiastical developments of 1997 occurred on World Mission Sunday, October 19, in St. Peter's Square, when Pope John Paul II declared St. Thérèse of Lisieux a "doctor of the universal church." This event marked not only the culmination of an unprecedented series of honors bestowed on Thérèse Martin since her death a century earlier, but it also represented a watershed in the evolution of the understanding of this ecclesiastical title. Certainly, at the time of her death in 1897, no one would have guessed that this 24-year-old Carmelite nun, dying unknown in an obscure French Carmel, would soon take the world by storm and go on to become the most popular saint of modern times. Still less would they have imagined that within 100 years this young woman with such a limited education and imperfect literary style, who never wrote a treatise or published an article, would come to be ranked alongside Augustine and Thomas Aquinas as a *doctor ecclesiae*, one of only 33 saints to be so honored.

This short work is a study of the doctorate of St. Thérèse. In the following chapters I will explore the history of the title "doctor of the church," the process by which Thérèse Martin came to be considered for this honor, and some the potential implications of her doctorate for the church in general and theology in particular. My own interest in this topic goes back at least as far as the spring of 1997, when I was contacted by Joseph Baudry,

O.C.D., a member of the Discalced Carmelite commission hurriedly preparing official documents for the canonical process. Father Baudry asked for information on Thérèse's influence in North America and also supplied me with some still unpublished background materials (on the tasks assigned to various committee members, for example, and other matters) to aid my work. Some months later, I obtained a copy of the so-called *Positio*, the resulting large folio-size volume of nearly 1000 pages containing the official texts of the canonical process, including the judgments of seven "theological experts" on Thérèse's suitability for the doctorate. Accompanying this work was a smaller supplementary volume containing the votes of some 31 theological consultors for the Congregation for the Doctrine of the Faith and the Congregation for the Causes of Saints, on the pros and cons of recognizing Thérèse of Lisieux as a *doctor ecclesiae* and on whether she manifested sufficient "eminence of doctrine." Both volumes proved to be a rich source of information on Thérèse, her message, the issues involved in designating her a "doctor of the universal church," the canonical steps by which this came about, and the evolving significance of the title itself in the history of the church.[1]

Although the momentum for bestowal of this title on the Saint of Lisieux had been steadily growing for decades, the declaration itself and the process leading up to it surfaced important theological and pastoral issues, many of them articulated and discussed in the official *Positio* and other ancillary Vatican documents. Questions raised include: What is a doctor of the church as opposed to simply a doctor of theology and who qualifies? How has the concept evolved over time? What counts as "eminence

---

[1] The nature, purpose, and contents of the *Positio* and its supplementary volume are described in greater detail in the opening pages of the third chapter. Doctrinal portions of the *Positio* are available in Spanish translation in *La doctora más joven de la Iglesia: Teresa de Lisieux* (Burgos: El Monte Carmelo, 1998).

of doctrine"? Must a candidate for this title offer an articulated body of theological teaching? Does the choice of Thérèse represent a kind of female "tokenism" or suggest that the standards should be less stringent for women? With John of the Cross and Teresa of Avila already declared doctors of the church in this century, is Carmelite spirituality being unduly favored? If someone like Thérèse can be so designated, why not Ignatius of Loyola, Paul of the Cross, John Vianney and many others? Does the declaration of Thérèse as doctor add anything to the vast influence and authority she has already exerted over the past century? Or does it in fact undercut the "littleness" that is the hallmark of her spiritual doctrine? More generally, by its designation of certain figures as doctors of the church, what role does the church thereby assign them in the theological enterprise? Are these and other saints theological *sources*, and if so, in what sense?

To begin addressing some of these questions, I propose in this work to examine and evaluate the reasons given for and against bestowing on St. Thérèse the title "doctor of the church" and the official explanations of the significance of this action, especially as these are found in the *Positio*, the "vota" of various theologians and consultors, and other Vatican documents. Thus, no attempt will be made here to deal comprehensively with the entire vast and ever growing literature on Thérèse's life and message, to which the words of Ecclesiastes 12:12, "of making many books there is no end," seem peculiarly apt. Instead my focus is narrower, concentrating especially on the *Positio* and related texts. Such a study is all the more needed because these materials are still relatively inaccessible to the broader public, who may wonder why Thérèse is so far the only candidate singled out during the long papacy of John Paul II to join the ranks of the doctors. My analysis will lead in turn to a broader consideration of the place of doctors of the church in particular, and the testimony of the saints in general, within the theological enterprise.

Chapter 1 reviews the historical evolution of the title "doctor of the church" as well as the ongoing discussion of the criteria by which *doctores ecclesiae* are chosen. Here I describe how the concept and role of the "doctor" within the life of the church have significantly broadened over time, and I discuss some of the qualities deemed desirable in candidates today.

Chapter 2 briefly presents the life, writings, and teachings of St. Thérèse insofar as these relate to the question of her doctorate. In this chapter I also retrace the history of efforts to have her named a doctor, beginning already in the first decades of the 20th century and culminating with the declaration of her doctorate in 1997.

Chapter 3 is devoted to a careful reading of the official documents of the canonical process for Thérèse's doctorate. I examine and evaluate the arguments in the *Positio* and "vota" for and against the feasibility of declaring Thérèse a doctor of the church, placing them in the context of broader theological issues.

Chapter 4 discusses, in light of the official documentation, what Pope John Paul II seems to have intended in naming Thérèse a "doctor of the universal church" and the possible theological significance of this declaration. In particular, I briefly consider what she (along with other saints and doctors) may offer to theologians today, especially at a time when many are striving to bridge the gap between spirituality and academic theology, between theology and sanctity. The book ends with some concluding remarks and a select bibliography.

Among the many who helped me in writing this book, I am most grateful to James Wiseman, O.S.B., Elizabeth A. Johnson, C.S.J., and Elizabeth Dreyer, Peter Casarella, Patrick Granfield, O.S.B., and John Welch, O.Carm., whose careful comments have made this study far better than it would otherwise be.

Thanks are due also to Father Kieran Kavanaugh, O.C.D., who first encouraged me to write on this topic and shared with me the fruits of his own research; to Father Jesús Castellano Cervera, O.C.D., for valuable bibliographical leads; to Father John Sullivan, O.C.D., who helped especially with translation difficulties; to Christopher O'Donnell, O.Carm., who courageously offered to read the bulk of the manuscript and made helpful suggestions; and to others who assisted me in tracking down documents otherwise difficult to obtain. Finally, I am grateful to my fellow friars of the Washington Province of Discalced Carmelites for allowing me to pursue this project, to my family for their constant love and support, and to Thérèse herself, for continuing to shed so much light and love upon us all as we enter a new millennium.

Biblical Background

Although the expression "doctor of the church" is found nowhere in the Bible, words related to teaching and learning occur often throughout its pages, as they do throughout the literature of the ancient world.[12] Karl Heinrich Rengstorf notes, for example, that among the Greeks "διδάσκειν is commonly attested from the time of Homer" and "denotes 'teaching' or 'instructing' in the widest sense." It is "the word used more especially for the impartation of practical or theoretical knowledge when there is continued activity with a view to gradual, systematic and therefore all the more fundamental assimilation.... The aim is the highest possible development of the talents of the pupil, but always in such a way that the personal aspect is both maintained and indeed strengthened.... This is important in relation to the transition of διδάσκειν to Jewish soil."[13]

In the Hebrew Scriptures, God is seen as the ultimate teacher.

> In the earliest period he is viewed as the teacher of any special skill. In time, however, this view shifted to one of God as the teacher of the Torah and of all the regulations applying to ethical and cultic life. He was the source of all instruction concerning these vital questions. This also meant, however, that he was the teacher of all wisdom, and was the only one capable of mediating this insight into the heavenly mysteries. Whoever was a

---

[12] Except where biblical texts are included in quotations from secondary sources, all Scriptural passages are quoted from *The Oxford Annotated Bible With the Apocrypha*, Revised Standard Edition, ed. Herbert G. May and Bruce M. Metzger (New York: Oxford University Press, 1965), unless otherwise noted.

[13] Karl Heinrich Rengstorf, "διδάσκω," in *Theological Dictionary of the New Testament*, ed. Gerhard Kittel and Gerhard Friedrich, trans. Geoffrey W. Bromiley, Vol. II: Δ–H (Grand Rapids, MI: Wm. B. Eerdmans Publishing Co., 1968), 135.

limmûd YHWH was instructed by the highest authority and was thus in a position to instruct others as well.[14]

In the Septuagint, words based on the Hebrew root *lmd*, "to teach," are most often translated by some form of διδάσκειν, which seems to assume among Greek-speaking Jews a technical meaning. Rengstorf points out that though not restricted to the religious sphere, "the particular object of διδάσκειν... is the will of God in its declarations and demands."[15] As distinguished from the secular concept of the period, which relates to the development of particular skills and talents, God's teaching "lays claim" to the entire person and thus "has a volitional as well as an intellectual reference."[16] And in the late OT period, with increasing rabbinic attention to the study and correct interpretation of the Torah, διδάσκειν comes to refer especially to "the manner in which, by exposition of the Law as the sum of the revealed will of God, instruction is given for the ordering of the relationship between the individual and God on the one side, and the neighbor on the other, according to the divine will."[17]

The same Greek term διδάσκειν ("teaching") occurs some 95 times in the New Testament, most frequently in the Gospels, and is identified as one of the most characteristic features of the ministry of Jesus. In Luke's description of Jesus' inaugural sermon at Nazareth, for example, Jesus follows the custom of Jewish teachers of his day, reading a passage of Scripture, and then sitting (the traditional posture of an instructor in the Law) to offer an exposition of the text (see, e.g., Lk 4:16ff), whereupon the congrega-

---

[14] A.S. Kapelrud, "lamad," in *Theological Dictionary of the Old Testament*, ed. G. Johannes Botterweck, Helmer Ringgren, and Heinz-Josef Fabry, trans. Douglas W. Scott, vol. 8: lakad—mor (Grand Rapids, MI: Wm. B. Eerdmans Publishing Co., 1997), 9.

[15] Kittel, Vol. II, 137.

[16] Ibid.

[17] Ibid.

tion marvels at his words.[18] Similarly, in Matthew's description of the Sermon on the Mount, Jesus begins his ministry by sitting and "teaching" the people at length (Mt 5:1-7:29). What distinguished Jesus's teaching was not its external form so much as the fact that "he taught them as one who had authority, and not as their scribes," with their lengthy casuistic analyses invoking the expert opinions of past commentators. Jesus' teaching demands decision and total response rather than intellectual debate about the meaning of his words. His teaching (recalling the use of διδάσκειν in the Septuagint) lays claim to the whole person. Meanwhile, the διδάσκειν of the early church will include not only continuing Jesus' proclamation of the reign of God but also rabbinic-style arguments from Scripture that Jesus is indeed the Messiah.

Even more significant in the present context, however, is the use of the term διδάσκαλος ("teacher") in the New Testament. The word appears "58 times in the NT, and 48 times in the Gospels (not counting Jn 8:4). In the Gospels it is used 41 times of Jesus, 29 times in the direct address διδάσκαλε...."[19] Thus "teacher" is one of the titles most frequently given to Jesus in the Gospels, especially when one adds to this the number of times he is addressed as "rabbi," which John 1:38 equates with διδάσκαλος. "The Gospels make it clear point by point that the relation between Jesus and the disciples corresponds to that of rabbinic pupils to their masters, and that the crowd treated Him with the respect accorded to teachers."[20] For the early church, in fact, Jesus is *the* teacher and rabbi, in accord with Mt 23:8: "But

---

[18] Interestingly, the official Vatican medal struck for the doctorate of St. Thérèse shows her seated, holding in her left hand the double image of the Child Jesus and the Holy Face, with a book in her lap and her right hand raised, two fingers extended, in a gesture of teaching or blessing.

[19] Kittel, Vol. II, 152.

[20] Ibid., 153-154.

you are not to be called rabbi, for you have one teacher (διδάσκαλος), and you are all brethren." This helps explain, as Rengstorf says, "why the disciples did not appropriate the name διδάσκαλος after the death of Jesus, although it must have seemed strange that the new leader of a Jewish group so occupied with the study of Scripture as the early Christians should not have been [so] called...."[21]

Nevertheless, when Paul comes to describe the variety of gifts bestowed on the body of Christ, he writes that "God has appointed in the church first apostles, second prophets, third teachers (διδασκάλους), then workers of miracles, then heal-ers, helpers, administrators, speakers in various kinds of tongues" (1 Cor 12:28), and again that "his gifts were that some should be apostles, some prophets, some evangelists, some pastors and teach-ers (διδασκάλους), for the equipment of the saints, for the work of ministry, for building up the body of Christ, until we all attain to the unity of the faith and of the knowledge of the Son of God" (Eph 4:11-13).[22] Though the precise duties and status of these "teachers" is not entirely clear, they appear to hold an important place within the organization of the early Christian community, and it seems reasonable to assume, given the Jewish antecedents, that their responsibilities included instruction in the faith and the interpretation of Scripture.

But the most important link to the later development of the title "doctor of the church" would seem to lie in the fact that the Vulgate translates διδάσκαλος in these Pauline texts as *doctores*

---

[21] Ibid., 156.

[22] Note also that the description in Acts 13:1 of the Antiochene church ("Now in the church at Antioch there were prophets and teachers [διδάσκαλοι]") and the admonition in James 3:1 ("Let not many of you become teachers [διδάσκαλοι], my brethren, for you know that we who teach shall be judged with greater strictness") indicate a growing usage of this term to designate those performing particular service within the community of be-lievers. From the New Testament evidence alone, however, it is difficult to determine to what extent "teaching" was seen as charismatic gift or institutional function (or both).

(while ordinarily translating διδάσκαλος as *magister* when referring to Jesus himself). Thus the church in the West would later be able to find a biblical precedent for the title *doctor ecclesiae* in the Pauline enumerations of the different roles within the body of Christ.

Though brief and incomplete, this sketch of the scriptural background of the title "doctor of the church" sheds important light on its later development. For though the significance of this title has evolved over time, it has retained a biblical and Christological orientation. Indeed, as we shall see, among the official reasons most frequently given for why Thérèse in particular merits the title are that her "doctrine" is rooted in Scripture, that it sheds fresh light upon Gospel truth, and that it points always to Christ, the one she called "the Doctor of doctors."[23]

Patristic and Medieval Developments

During the patristic era the terms "doctor" and "doctor of the church" begin to appear with increasing frequency, alongside "father,"[24] as designations for those regarded as prominent teachers

---

[23] See Sainte Thérèse de l'Enfant-Jésus et de la Sainte-Face, *Manuscrits autobiographiques* (Paris: Éditions du Cerf, 1992), 268 and *Divini Amoris Scientia*, passim. As will be explained in more detail later, the critical edition of *Manuscrits autobiographiques* includes a referencing system to Thérèse's three handwritten manuscripts, used in compiling her "autobiography" after her death. Thus the phrase "le Docteur des docteurs" occurs in Manuscript A on the verso side of leaf 83, usually abbreviated as "Ms A 83v." Unfortunately, this phrase, "the Doctor of doctors," was inadvertently omitted in the Clarke translation of *Story of a Soul*; see *Story of a Soul: The Autobiography of Saint Thérèse of Lisieux*, trans. John Clarke, 3d ed. (Washington, DC: ICS Publications, 1996), 179.

[24] Gherardini traces the analogous evolution of the term "father" in the early church, where the founders of particular Christian communities received "at the same time the title of father and of teacher." Note that the first eight "doctors" officially recognized in the Western church were patristic authors, and thus also "fathers" of the church. See Bruno Gherardini, "Eminence of Doctrine and Holiness of Life," *L'Osservatore Romano*, English language edition, 29 June 1981, 2-3. See also Agostino Trapé, "Community and Peculiarity," *L'Osservatore Romano*, English language edition, 29 June 1981, 4.

of Christian doctrine, though the usage remains fluid for some time. The *Didache* speaks of a church order including "prophets and teachers (διδασκάλων)" along with "bishops and deacons."[25] In the mid-2nd-century *Martyrdom of Polycarp*, St. Polycarp (died c. 155 C.E.) is described as "the teacher (διδάσκαλος) of Asia, the father (πατὲρ) of the Christians" "an apostolic and prophetic teacher (διδάσκαλος)," and a "famous teacher (διδάσκαλος)."[26] Saint Gregory the Great (c. 540-604 C.E.) calls the apostles themselves *doctores sanctae ecclesiae* (doctors of the holy church),[27] while Augustine (354-430) is the first to number a non-bishop, Jerome, among the "fathers," and in a passage underscoring the importance of patristic authorities, speaks of "Irenaeus, Cyprian, Reticius, Olympius, Hilary, Gregory [Nazianzen], Basil, Ambrose, John [Chrysostom], Innocent, Jerome, and the others" as *sanctos doctores egregios atque memorabiles catholicae veritatis* (famous and brilliant holy teachers of the Catholic truth).[28] In his *Commonitorium*, Vincent of Lérins (d. before 450) describes certain patristic authors as "doctors" and "teachers" of the church (*ecclesiarum magistri*).[29] And in the Acts of the Second Council of Constantinople (553) we find: "In these matters we follow in all things also the holy fathers and doctors of the church: Athanasius, Hilary, Basil, Gregory [Nazianzen] the Theologian, and Gregory of Nyssa, Ambrose, Augustine, Theophilus, John CP [Chrysostom], Cyril,

---

[25] *Didache* 15.1, in *The Apostolic Fathers*, vol. 1, Loeb Classical Library (1977), 330-331. See *The Interpreter's Dictionary of the Bible*, s.v. "teacher."

[26] *The Martyrdom of Polycarp* 12.2; 16.2; 19.1, in *The Apostolic Fathers*, vol. 2, Loeb Classical Library (1970), 326-327, 334-335, 336-337.

[27] Gregory the Great, *Hom. in Evang.*, 30, 7; quoted in J. Madoz, "'Doctor Ecclesiae'," *Estudios eclesiasticos* 11 (January 1932): 27. For an English translation of the relevant passage, see Gregory the Great, *Forty Gospel Homilies*, trans. David Hurst, Cistercian Studies Series, no. 123 (Kalamazoo, MI: Cistercian Publications, 1990), 244.

[28] Augustine, *Contra Iulianum* 1, II, c. 37. The English translation here is taken from Saint Augustine, *Against Julian*, trans. Matthew A. Schumacher (New York: Fathers of the Church, 1957), 103. See Madoz, 28.

[29] Vincent of Lérins, *Commonitorium*, 10 and 17.2. Cited in Madoz, 28.

Leo, Proclus, and we accept all those things they expounded in correctness of faith and for the condemnation of heretics."[30]

By the end of the 8th century in the West, however, four of these names had already emerged as preeminent. The first documentary evidence of this is found in Bede the Venerable (d. 735), who writes: "After gathering together the works of the fathers I tried to look... into what blessed Ambrose, Augustine, Gregory the most vigilant (according to his name) apostle of our people, and Jerome the interpreter of sacred history, said; what the other fathers felt about the words of St. Luke."[31] Subsequent authors followed suit in identifying Ambrose, Augustine, Gregory, and Jerome as the church's four great "doctors," a number rich with symbolic significance (paralleling, for example, the number of evangelists).[32]

The first official papal approbation of the title "doctor of the church," however, came during the pontificate of Boniface VIII, "with the decretal *Gloriosus Deus*, published with the bull *Sacrosanctae Romanae ecclesiae* of March 3, 1298."[33] Boniface decreed that the liturgical office for these four saints—"great doc-

---

[30] Act. 3, *Professio fidei*, Mansi, *Sacrorum Conciliorum nova et amplissima Collectio*, Florentiae, 1759, s. IX, 201-202: "Super haec sequimur per omnia et sanctos patres et doctores ecclesiae Athanasium, Hilarium, Basilium, Gregorium theologum, et Gregorium Nyssenum, Ambrosium, Augustinum, Theophilum, Ioannem CP [Chrysostom], Cyrillum, Leonem, Proclum et suscipimus omnia quae de recta fide et condemnatione haereticorum exposuerunt." Cited in Madoz, 28.

[31] *In luc. Evang. Corpus Christianorum*, Series latina 120, 7: "Aggregatis... opusculis patrum quid beatus Ambrosius, quid Augustinus, quid denique Gregorius vigilantissimus (iuxta suum nomen) nostrae gentis apostolis, quid Hieronymus sacrae impres historiae, quid ceteri patres in beati Lucae verbis senserint, quid dixerint digentius inspicere satagi." Quoted in Umberto Betti, "A proposito del conferimento del titolo di Dottore della Chiesa," *Antonianum* 63 (1988): 279, n. 4, and Madoz, 29. The Gregory mentioned here is Pope Gregory I, the Great.

[32] See Madoz, 31.

[33] Betti, "A proposito del conferimento del titolo di Dottore della Chiesa," 279. See the text of this decretal in Aemelius Friedberg, ed., *Corpus Iuris Canonici, Pars Secunda: Decretalium Collectiones* (Leipzig: Ex Officina Bernhardi Tauchnitz, 1922), cols. 1059-1060.

tors of the Church" who with their exalted teaching "revealed the mysteries of the Scriptures, untied knots [i.e., dissolved perplexities], clarified difficulties, and explained what was uncertain" (*scripturarum aenigmata reserat, solvit nodos, obscura delucidat, dubiaque declarat*)—would be celebrated as duplex feasts alongside those of the apostles and evangelists. As Umberto Betti points out, this was not so much a formal declaration of the doctorate as it was a pontifical decision to raise the liturgical rank of these four, already acknowledged for their singular doctrinal importance to the church.[34] Thus "doctor of the church" comes to assume here a significance as much liturgical as doctrinal, in terms of how the church remembers and celebrates its most prominent post-apostolic teachers.

It is worth noting that these first officially recognized "doctors of the church" belonged to the category of "confessors" rather than "martyrs." Indeed, down to the present day no "martyr" in the church's calendar has ever been officially designated "doctor of the universal church," since, at least in liturgical terms, the former title takes precedence. This explains the absence from the church's official list of "universal doctors" of such patristic authors as Irenaeus and Cyprian, who might otherwise seem eminently qualified.

In the meantime, the title "father of the church" had undergone a similar evolution. Trapé observes that "Father meant in turn: teacher, bishop, a bishop writer, an ecclesiastical writer, an orthodox ecclesiastical writer, an ecclesiastical writer risen to the heights of holiness, an ancient ecclesiastical writer approved by the Church."[35] Thus, according to Trapé, an understanding developed that "the characteristic features that distinguish Fathers from other ecclesiastical writers are four, that is: antiquity, ortho-

---

[34] Ibid., 279-280.
[35] Agostino Trapé, "Community and Peculiarity," 4.

dox doctrine, holiness of life, the approval of the Church."[36] Medieval theologians likewise discussed at length the nature of *sacra doctrina* and the kind of authority exercised by the church's ancient "teachers" and "doctors" in theological and doctrinal matters.[37] Still, at this juncture one might have anticipated that any official papal recognition of additional doctors would draw from among those already regarded as "Fathers of the Church."

Post-Reformation Developments

For more than two and a half centuries after the 1298 decretal *Gloriosus Deus*, then, the Latin church remained content with its four "doctors of the universal church." In the Eastern church, fondness for trinitarian symbolism may have partly inspired the similar recognition of their own three great patristic διδάσκαλοι: Basil, Gregory Nazianzen, and John Chrysostom. Pius V incorporated these three, under the "common of doctors," into the 1568 edition of the breviary, revised according to the Council of Trent, and he added the name of Athanasius, thus establishing a symmetry between the four major doctors from the West and the four from the East.

But far more significant additions came with *Mirabilis Deus*, Pius V's bull of April 11, 1567, declaring Thomas Aquinas a "doctor of the church," and with Sixtus V's bestowal of the same title on Bonaventure in the 1588 bull, *Triumphantis Hierusalem*

---

[36] Ibid.

[37] McGinn offers a very useful outline of Aquinas's analogous understanding of the term "doctor" and "how the grace of *doctor* is communicated from Christ to his followers"; see McGinn, *Doctors of the Church*, 9. See also Egan, 155-157, who notes in addition the significance of "the many descriptive titles bestowed by the scholastics," such as *Doctor Angelicus* for Aquinas and *Doctor Seraphicus* for Bonaventure. The evolution of the concept of "doctor" among the scholastics deserves a separate study in itself, but cannot be pursued here, for lack of space.

Gloriam.[38] In effect, these declarations placed two medieval theologians in the same sanctoral and liturgical category as the ancient "fathers and doctors." They thus decisively established as a principle that those to be recognized as church doctors need not be limited to patristic authors, nor must their doctrinal teaching be expressed in the style of patristic texts. Candidates could now be chosen who might resemble the church fathers in their orthodoxy and holiness but lacked the feature of antiquity.

We also see in the choice of these two the beginning of another trend; with the Dominican Thomas elevated by a Dominican pope, and the Franciscan Bonaventure by a Franciscan pope, a view (or desire) arose in some circles that each great religious family should have its own "doctor." It was in this period as well, roughly two months before the proclamation of St. Bonaventure as "Doctor of the Church," that the Congregation of Rites was formally entrusted with examining candidates for the doctorate (by Sixtus V's Apostolic Constitution *Immensa Aeterni Dei*, which organized the Roman Curia). This congregation would continue to oversee the process for nearly 400 years.[39]

---

[38] Here McGinn's chronology is somewhat misleading. He writes that "the first new doctor [from after the patristic era] to be given official papal recognition of his feast as the double feast of a *doctor ecclesiae* in the new edition of the Roman Breviary… was Thomas Aquinas. This was done in 1568 by Pius V…."; see McGinn, *Doctors of the Church*, 13. But although it is true that Pius V *included* Aquinas as a doctor in the Tridentine breviary, he had already formally *declared* him a "doctor of the church" the year before; see °3 of the 1567 bull, *Mirabilis Deus*. For the text of *Mirabilis Deus*, see *Bullarum diplomatum et privilegiorum sanctorum Romanorum pontificum taurinensis editio*, vol. 7 (Naples: Henrico Caporaso, 1882), 564-565. For the text of *Triumphantis Hierusalem Gloriam*, see *Bullarum diplomatum et privilegiorum sanctorum Romanorum pontificum taurinensis editio*, vol. 8 (Naples: Henrico Caporaso, 1883), 1005-1012. The volumes in which these bulls appear are part of a series known collectively as *Bullarium Romanum*.

[39] The text of *Immensa Aeterni Dei* is found in *Bullarium Romanum*, VIII (Turin, 1863), 985 ff. For the history of this Congregation in relation to the causes of saints, see Pietro Palazzini, "I quattrocento anni della Congregazione per le Cause dei Santi," *Divinitas* 35 (1991): 86-92.

The Modern Period

More than a century would pass before further names were added to the list: Anselm of Canterbury in 1720, Isidore of Seville in 1722, Peter Chrysologus in 1729, Leo the Great in 1754, Peter Damian in 1828, Bernard of Clairvaux in 1830, Hilary of Poitiers in 1851, Alphonsus Liguori in 1871, Francis de Sales in 1877, Cyril of Alexandria and Cyril of Jerusalem in 1882, John Damascene in 1890, Bede the Venerable in 1899, Ephraim the Syrian in 1920, Peter Canisius in 1925, John of the Cross in 1926, Robert Bellarmine and Albert the Great in 1931, Anthony of Padua in 1946, Lawrence of Brindisi in 1959, Teresa of Avila and Catherine of Siena in 1970, and Thérèse of Lisieux, the most recent choice, in 1997. A simple glance at these names makes it clear that the kind of candidate chosen for the doctorate has changed over time. Those declared "doctors of the church" before the 19th century were typically renowned for their contributions to a vast array of theological issues, whereas the most recent choices are primarily known for their contributions to spirituality and spiritual theology. Some candidates waited centuries before receiving this ecclesiastical recognition, while others were chosen far more quickly. For example, Alphonsus Liguori, who died in 1787, was declared a doctor only 84 years later, in 1871.

Moreover, as Madoz underscores, the processes by which these candidates were identified and officially recognized were not uniform. Some (e.g., Thomas Aquinas, Robert Bellarmine) were declared "doctors" by solemn Apostolic Constitutions, while others (e.g., the two Cyrils and John Damascene) were included by a simple decree of the Congregation of Rites assigning them the liturgical office of "doctors." Peter Canisius was declared a "Doctor of the Church" in the very decree of his canonization.[40]

---

[40] See Madoz, 33.

When the Congregation of Rites was divided in 1969 into two dicasteries—the Congregation for Divine Worship and the Congregation for the Causes of Saints—it was the latter which continued to oversee the causes of proposed doctors. A further refinement of the process came with Pope John Paul II's 1988 Apostolic Constitution *Pastor Bonus,* which required that the Congregation for the Causes of Saints obtain a vote on the "eminence of doctrine" of potential candidates from the Congregation for the Doctrine of the Faith (CDF).[41]

But perhaps the important development in the modern period was Pope Paul VI's decision to bestow the doctorate on Teresa of Avila and Catherine of Siena in 1970, thus decisively rejecting the opinion that women were excluded from the rank of doctor because of their sex. Some had previously argued, on the basis of Scripture and tradition, that women were not permitted to hold the office of teacher within the church. In his homily at the ceremony proclaiming the doctorate of St. Teresa, Paul VI observed that:

> This has not been done without reference to St. Paul's severe words: "Let women keep silence in the churches" [1 Cor 14:34]. This still signifies today that woman is not meant to have hierarchical functions of teaching and ministering in the Church. Has the Apostle's precept been violated, then? We can give a clear answer: No. In reality, it is not a matter of a title entailing hierarchical teaching functions: but at the same

---

[41] *Pastor Bonus,* art. 73: "Ad Congregationem [de Causis Sanctorum] preterea spectat cognoscere de Doctoris titulo Sanctis decernendo, praehabito voto Congregationis de Doctrina Fidei ad eminentem doctrinam quod attinet." See John Paul II, "Constitutio Apostolica de Romana Curia: Pastor Bonus," *Acta Apostolicae Sedis* 80 (28 June 1988): 878. This new requirement was perhaps intended, at least in part, to address concerns that the title "doctor of the church" was becoming a mere honorific and its doctrinal significance becoming devalued. Indeed, one might naturally expect those officially entrusted with safeguarding church doctrine to be consulted on the question of a candidate's "doctrinal eminence."

time We must point out that this does not in the least signify a lesser appreciation of the sublime mission which woman has in the midst of the people of God. On the contrary, having entered into being a part of the Church through Baptism, woman partakes of the common priesthood of the faithful. This enables and obliges her to "profess before men the faith received from God through the Church" [*Lumen Gentium* chap. 2, no. 11]. So many women have reached the highest summits in such profession of faith, to the point that their words and writings have given light and guidance to their brethren.[42]

In any event, whatever may be said about this sharp differentiation between the "doctorate" and a "hierarchical teaching function," the door was now open for a new range of potential doctors, and Rome began to receive fresh petitions to bestow the doctorate on other women (e.g., Hildegard of Bingen and Veronica Giuliani) as well as other candidates who had already been waiting for a long time (e.g., Bernardine of Siena, Anthony of Florence, Lawrence Giustiniani).[43] In 1972, however, Paul VI suspended further declarations until there could be more thorough study of the requirement of "eminent doctrine."[44] John Paul II's directives to the Congregation of the Causes of Saints in May 1979 and August 1980 stressed that in considering the criteria for the doctorate, they avoid too restrictive an approach to new causes, while at the same time safeguarding the prestige of the title.[45] Some contributions from the congregation's discussion of

---

[42] Paul VI, "Teresa of Avila: The Message of Prayer," *The Pope Speaks* 15 (1970): 221. At this time Paul VI also expressed his desire to declare *many* women doctors.

[43] See Betti, "A proposito del conferimento del titolo di Dottore della Chiesa," 286-287.

[44] Ibid., 287.

[45] Ibid., 287-288. Betti does not cite a source for these papal directives (which apparently have never been published), but simply states that they were given. Betti himself is a consultor for the Congregation for the Doctrine of the Faith.

the criteria were published in 1981.[46] There matters stood until the cause of St. Thérèse's doctorate was formally taken up in 1997.

Criteria for the Doctorate

The classic statement of the prerequisites for recognition as "doctor of the church" appears in *De Servorum Dei Beatificatione et Beatorum Canonizatione* (1734-1738), written by Cardinal Prospero Lambertini (later Benedict XIV) while he served as "promoter of the faith" in the Congregation of Rites: "To become a Doctor of the Church three things are necessary: namely, eminent doctrine; outstanding holiness of life…; and a declaration passed by the supreme pontiff or a legitimately assembled General Council."[47] Though this text is often cited in later documentation, Lambertini makes it clear that he is not inventing these three criteria, but merely summarizing what previous authorities on the subject had said.[48] Indeed, the general assumption has been that these were the standards all previously named doctors had met and to which all future candidates for the doctorate would be held.

The requirement of exceptional holiness has proved relatively unproblematic, since the church has always chosen its doctors only from among those already recognized as saints. Nor has

---

[46] Jesús Castellano also mentions a special document developed at this time for the internal use of the congregation, entitled "Istruzione della Congregazione per le Cause dei Santi sul conferimento del titolo di Dottore della Chiesa." Unfortunately, it has never been published. See Jesús Castellano Cervera, "'Eminens doctrina': un requisito necesario para ser Doctor de la Iglesia," *Teresianum* 46 (1995): 7.

[47] "Ad constituendum porro Ecclesiae Doctorem tria sunt necessaria, eminens scilicet doctrina; insignis vitae sanctitas…; et praeterea summi Pontificis, aut Concilii Generalis legitime congregati declaratio"; see Prospero Cardinal Lambertini, *De servorum Dei beatificatione et beatorum canonizatione*, Book IV, part 2, chap. 11, para. 13 (Prati: Typographia Aldina, 1841), 512.

[48] Ibid., 512-513.

the exclusive authority of popes and councils to declare doctors been seriously challenged, though there have been some differences of opinion on the weight to be given such a declaration. In the formula most recently used, for example, the pope invokes "the fullness of apostolic authority,"[49] and Bruno Gherardini has spoken of the "doctor of the church" as "one whom the Church herself has infallibly proclaimed such."[50] Yet most authors discount the notion that the exercise of "infallibility" is here involved,[51] and it is difficult to see in any case what the object of the allegedly infallible proclamation would be, since no specific dogmatic belief or doctrinal definition is proposed in declaring someone a doctor.

The requirement of "eminent doctrine," however, has proved the most difficult to spell out, and has generated much discussion over the centuries, especially in relation to the choice of new candidates. The Congregation of Rites, for example, formulated the following conclusions, worth quoting at length, from its discussion of March 11, 1871, concerning the doctorate of Alphonsus Liguori:

I. The title of doctor of the church was accorded by universal agreement of the church to those celebrated individuals from ancient times who demonstrated forth holiness of life and by their writings gave light of some sort to the universal church.

---

[49] See the official formula for the declaration of Thérèse's doctorate, quoted in note 3 above.

[50] Gherardini, "Eminence of Doctrine and Holiness of Life," 2.

[51] See Madoz, 40 and Betti, "A proposito del conferimento del titolo di Dottore della Chiesa," 287. Clearly the declaration of someone as "doctor of the church" is not a declaration that his or her writings are entirely free in every part of theological limitations or errors; recall, for example, that Thomas Aquinas opposed the dogma of the Immaculate Conception before it had been officially declared. Likewise, assigning the rank of "doctor" to the liturgical celebration of a particular saint is a matter of church discipline, and can hardly be claimed to involve the deposit of faith. It is worth noting that although Pope John Paul II invoked "the fullness of apostolic authority" in declaring St. Thérèse a "doctor of the universal church," he did not use the words "declare and define."

II. It was not because of themselves that they were called doctors but because of the church to which they rendered illus-
trious service, whether by controversial theological writings
or by explaining the deposit of revelation or by offering
moral directives.

III. The eminence of doctrine (which in some doctors of the
church approached the angelic) was not considered *abso-
lutely* in calling them doctors, but *relative* to some great effect achieved in their own way throughout the church by
their ingenuity, holiness, and doctrine.

IV. Hence if one were to proceed to a comparison of the doctrine of doctors, the degrees would be measured just as major and minor stars are judged in the sky; but all of them have
shed light on the universal church in their own way.

V. The above benefit to the church is the primary reason for
according the title of doctor of the church to some holy man,
and of itself it means this doctrine is eminent and sought
after by the church.

VI. One other conclusion: it is worthless to try to influence the
Holy See to provide a formal declaration of doctor of the
church, unless there is some sort of previous judgment
[*suffragium*] of the church that signifies a true benefit.[52]

---

[52] *Acta Sanctae Sedis* 6 (1870): 317-318: "I. Doctori Ecclesiae titulum illis luminariis, ex
universali veluti Ecclesiae consensu, ab antiquis temporibus fuisse tributum, qui
sanctimonia vitae refulgentes, suis scriptis Ecclesiam universam aliquo modo illustrarunt.
II. Non enim propter seipsos Doctores sunt appellati, sed propter Ecclesiam cui praeclare
inservierunt, sive in confutandis sacris litteris, sive in explanando revelationis deposito,
sive in dirigendis moribus. III. Eminentiam ideoque doctrinae (quae in nonnullis Ecclesiae
Doctoribus fuit prorsus angelica) non fuisse *absolute* consideratam ut Doctores
apellarentur, sed *relative* ad magnum aliquem effectum, quem pro varia Ecclesiae
condicione praeclaro ingenio, sanctimonia et doctrina sunt consecuti. IV. Quare inter
Ecclesiae Doctores, si doctrina absolute considerata inter ipsos comparetur, gradus ita
distinguuntur quemadmodum in firmamento astra maiora et minora; qui tamen omnes
pro rerum condicione universam illuminarunt Ecclesiam. V. Hoc bonum proinde, in
Ecclesiam collatum esse praecipuum argumentum ad Sanctum Virum titulo Doctoris
Ecclesiae decorandum; quod per se aperte significat eam doctrinae eminentiam quae (sic)

Thus the Congregation of Rites acknowledged that the kind of doctrinal "eminence" required may vary and that it is not to be judged by some absolute standard, but relative to the doctrine's impact on, and importance for, the church. It recognized the possibility of "major" and "minor" doctors, but it clearly resisted efforts to treat the doctorate as simply another honor to be given to beloved saints, without regard for the actual benefits of their teaching. In accord with this view, the postulator of the title for St. Francis de Sales indicated that a candidate for doctor of the church should have something truly original to offer when he observed, in 1877, that "a central prerogative of doctors is that they be considered columns and foundations, that their teaching shed new light on the whole church, and that they serve as a new source of doctrine."[53] This same issue appeared again in the preparations for Vatican II, where we find certain misgivings about the modern multiplication of doctors, perhaps exacerbated by some of the declarations that had most recently occurred (e.g., Anthony of Padua and Lawrence of Brindisi). The "votum" of the Catholic University of Angers, for example, asked that "only the saints who have brought renown upon the church with their really eminent doctrine should be awarded the title and honors of the doctor."[54]

More recently, in response to the papal directives mentioned earlier, the Congregation for the Causes of Saints discussed the

---

hac de causa quaerit Ecclesia. VI. Inde pariter colliges: frustra eiusmodi causas penes S. Sedem promoveri ad obtinendam formalem Doctoris declarationem, nisi iam praecesserit aliquod Ecclesiae suffragium quot eiusmodi reale bonum significaverit." Cited by Madoz, 36, and (in part) by Betti, "A proposito del conferimento del titolo di Dottore della Chiesa," 284, n. 19.

[53] *Acta Sanctae Sedis* 10 (1877), 349: "Haec itaque Doctorum intima praerogative est, ut Ecclesiae columnae ac fundamentum habeantur, ut eorum doctrina totius Ecclesiae corpus nova luce perfundatur, ac veluti novus doctrinae fons reseratus fuerit." Cited by Madoz, 37, and by Betti, "A proposito del conferimento del titolo di Dottore della Chiesa," 283, n. 18.

[54] Cited in Betti, "A proposito del conferimento del titolo di Dottore della Chiesa," 284.

criteria for declaring "doctors of the church" in plenary session from March 31 to April 2, 1981, focusing especially on the requirement of "eminent doctrine." Among the contributors, Umberto Betti argues that there are many factors to consider in judging doctrinal eminence, such as "multiple written documentation, duly examined by literary and theological criticism; original contribution at least to some fields of knowledge, such as to offer a real help in deepening study of Divine Revelation, in illustration of the faith, in the illumination and increase of Christian life; its confirmation by use, not occasional but continuous, on the part of scholars in the field of sacred sciences as well as pastors of the Church."[55] The combined presence of these factors, according to Betti, assures that the candidate "is not just a doctor of the Church for his time, but a doctor of the Church of all times, despite the peculiarities of expression characteristic of every cultural era."[56] Indeed, he says, the church turns to the doctors not merely out of antiquarian interest but because of the aid they can offer the present and future church in preserving "authentic teaching" and "the technical formulation of this teaching."

Jean Galot largely agrees, noting that "the doctor is one who has set forth revealed doctrine manifesting deep *understanding* of this doctrine and giving it an *expression* worthy of admiration, so that a special charism of light granted by the Holy Spirit can be recognized in him."[57]

> This requires a certain *personal originality*, so that it is possible to speak of a real contribution to doctrinal development. It is more than a mere retransmission of

---

[55] Umberto Betti, "Preserve the True Meaning of Canonical Requisites," *L'Osservatore Romano*, English language edition, 29 June 1981, 3.

[56] Ibid.

[57] Jean Galot, "Recognize the Charism in its Specific Value," *L'Osservatore Romano*, English language edition, 29 June 1981, 2.

revealed truth. Evidently, this originality cannot be demanded in all fields of theology: it is sufficient that there should be an appreciable contribution in a particular area.

The doctor must have exercised a *considerable influence on the thought of the Church*. It does not seem necessary to me that he should have enjoyed high prestige among his contemporaries....

The doctor must have remained *faithful* to the doctrine of the Church: he must have preserved *orthodoxy*....[58]

And in addition to all of the other criteria, says Galot, one must consider whether bestowing the title on a particular candidate might have definite advantages in light of the contemporary needs of the church and world.

There are, in fact, two distinct problems: whether for his doctrinal activity a saint deserves the title of doctor, and whether it is opportune to proclaim him doctor, for the good of the Church and the propagation of the Christian faith. The second problem calls for an analysis of the present situation of the Church from the doctrinal point of view: the proclamation of a doctor must be considered in the general development of Christian culture....

It is possible that certain "signs of the times" may indicate the conferral of the title of a doctor when the doctrine of a saint is such as to meet important intellectual needs of an age.[59]

Bruno Gerhardini stresses that "by eminence of doctrine is meant not only perfect orthodoxy together with immunity from

---

[58] Ibid.
[59] Ibid.

error, much less the mere scientific nature or methodological rigour of a given treatise, but a set of objective data which can be specified as follows: dogmatic certainty, persuasiveness and power of demonstration, originality of the whole production or at least a part of it, a part which is not of secondary importance and is plainly of interest to the whole Church."[60] But he adds a note of caution: "It will be really difficult, however, to prove this eminence in one who was, for example, a great preacher and nothing more, or in one who does not present writings worked out on a consistent basis, or in one whose work, although of unquestionable value, does not reveal a global knowledge and mastery of the sacred sciences."[61] Agostino Trapé underscores this point even more emphatically in reviewing the list of those already named doctors. Though all of them are undoubtedly great saints, "they are of very different stature, importance, and significance," and the qualifications for eminence of doctrine have gradually become so broadened that "one would think, none among the saints who have taught and written, would be unable to enter."[62]

In this connection it seems necessary to make some distinctions. It is necessary to distinguish between a man of action, a sacred speaker, a promoter of a particular devotion, a pious writer, and a theologian. In the first cases a saint may acquire enormous merits in the Church and with regard to her, but he does not for this reason deserve, in my judgment, the title of doctor. Only in the last case (theologian) does this title come into question. So neither action, however vast and effective, nor the promotion of particular devotions, however useful and fruitful, nor pious writings, however multiple and widespread, are sufficient.

---

[60] Gherardini, "Eminence of Doctrine and Holiness of Life," 2.
[61] Ibid., 3.
[62] Trapé, "Community and Peculiarity," 2.

But even in connection with theology some necessary distinctions must be made. It is not a question merely of theology set forth, but of theology illustrated, deeply studied, and defended. I mean that the theologian, to be worthy of the title of doctor of the universal Church, must have not only repeated, however excellently, what others had said, but must have contributed something of his own, with his writings and in an outstanding way, to the progress of the sacred science.[63]

In short, there is general consensus that doctors should not be multiplied indiscriminately lest the title be devalued, and that candidates should evidence a truly profound, original, and lasting theological contribution to the church, not merely repeating, however excellently, what has been said before. At the same time, however, there is a recognition that declarations of the doctorate do not occur in a theological and historical vacuum and that developments within the church, along with its intellectual and pastoral needs in light of the "signs of the times," may call for new and different kinds of candidates today. As we shall see in the next chapter, all of these issues will come to the fore in discussions of the possible doctorate for St. Thérèse. While recognizing her outstanding holiness, the theological consultors discuss at great length whether such a proclamation is opportune, and whether she manifests the necessary "eminence of doctrine," particularly since, as Pope John Paul II himself concedes, she "does not have a true and proper doctrinal corpus."[64] Before turning to the particular case of St. Thérèse, however, a few preliminary observations are in order about the significance of the doctorate in light of the history we have just outlined.

---

[63] Ibid.

[64] John Paul II, *Divini Amoris Scientia*, no. 8.

Reflections

First, as we have seen, the notion of "doctor of the church" has certain biblical antecedents, and arises within a Christian tradition which acknowledges a hierarchical teaching function, one which sees the perennial value of certain officially recognized authorities within the tradition who can offer reliable guidance to the interpretation of Scripture and the understanding of revelation. Thus those Christian denominations which have no hierarchy, discount arguments from tradition, and acknowledge no higher authority in the correct interpretation of Scripture than that of the individual Christian immediately confronting the text, would seem to have no obvious place for "doctors." This does not mean, however, that Catholicism ascribes to the "doctors of the church" an independent "magisterium," or that it sees them as adding new truths to the "deposit of faith." Rather, in continuity with the Old and New Testaments, the Catholic tradition acknowledges God as the ultimate teacher, the source of all knowledge and wisdom, and Jesus as the very incarnation of this supreme knowledge and wisdom, both the teacher and the teaching itself. Subsequent Christian "teachers" and "doctors," then, are not replacements or substitutes for Christ the teacher. Rather, through the work of his Holy Spirit, they are granted a share in his ministry of teaching, extending it in time and space under the guidance of those entrusted by office with safeguarding the church's fidelity to revealed truth. They assist the "magisterium" in expounding the faith and are authenticated by it. "Doctors and teachers" help to deepen the church's grasp of what has already been given in Christ, at least implicitly, and to spell out its implications for Christian thought and action. Thus the "eminent doctrine" of a doctor of the church, however much it may be cast in the language and thought patterns of another era, must always in some way be eminently useful, directly or indirectly, for the church's deeper understanding and exposition of divine revelation. Vast and novel intellectual accomplishments alone, however influential, do not by themselves constitute "eminent doctrine." A certain "originality" is one of the qualities demanded of candidates, but this cannot mean an originality so radical that it attempts to add to, or take away from, the *depositum fidei.*

Second, designating someone as a "doctor of the universal church" obviously has several facets. In particular, it is directed both to the past and to the future, simultaneously creating a new reality and acknowledging a reality that already exists. To proclaim someone a "doctor of the church" is in some sense to recognize that they are already a "doctor" *in* the church, that is to say, someone whose doctrine, by its depth, excellence, originality, and fidelity to the Gospel has exerted a profound influence on the life and teaching of the church. But it is also to give his or her teaching new weight, to invest it with "the fullness of apostolic authority," and to recommend it to the church of the present and future as a reliable guide for the interpretation of God's word and will. There would be little point in bestowing the doctorate on those whose teaching, however brilliant in its day, is now merely of antiquarian interest. Rather, their theological contribution must have some lasting or even permanent value. As Betti emphasizes, candidates are meant to be "doctors of the church" not merely for their own times, but for all time.[65]

Third, it seems important to remember that the official use of the title "doctor of the universal church" has liturgical origins and retains liturgical significance. This observation in itself indicates that the title is bestowed not just for the benefit of professional theologians nor merely as a reward for intellectual excellence, but that it has implications for the whole worshipping com-

---

[65] See Betti, "A proposito del conferimento del titolo di Dottore della Chiesa," 282.

munity. These figures are presented and celebrated in the church's liturgical cycle as eminent and reliable teachers for *all* the faithful. In fact, as Betti notes, the liturgical renewal following Vatican II has created something of a paradox, for while the Congregation of Rites had continually insisted that the dignity of the doctors of the church be safeguarded by a degree of liturgical celebration distinguishing them from less important saints, and that candidates not be chosen unless they warranted such honors, the revision of the calendar has reduced many of the doctors to the rank of an "optional memorial."[66] In any case, one might argue that saints already popularly celebrated especially for their teaching, such as St. Thérèse with her "little way," might be appropriate candidates for recognition as a doctors. At least this would be one consideration favoring such a declaration.

Fourth, the liturgical background of the title may explain in part the insistence on the criterion of holiness of life. If the title of "doctor" were simply a recognition of scholarly excellence, or of deep and lasting influence on the church, candidates would not necessarily need to be recognized saints; Tertullian and Origen, for example, made vast contributions to Christian theology despite the fact that they later were condemned as heretics, and one can profitably study the *Summa theologiae* without realizing the sanctity of its author. In fact, there would be no reason in principle why the list could not be extended to include important authors about whose lives we know virtually nothing (e.g., the writer known as Pseudo-Dionysius). But the insistence on orthodoxy and holiness of life insures that what candidates offer is not merely intellectual brilliance but a lived doctrine, and that there is a conformity between what they preached and practiced. For those more recent "doctors of the church" best known for their spiritual teaching this is especially the case, since their "doctrine"

---

[66] Ibid., 285-286.

arises out of a Spirit-guided theological reflection on personal experience in the light of Scripture and the church's tradition. At the same time, however, holiness of life is obviously not in itself sufficient for the title, unless we are willing to declare *all* saints "doctors of the church" because of what they taught by their example.

This leads, in the fifth place, to a point raised by Trapé, namely, that it seems clear from the choice of candidates that the interpretation of the criteria for declaring someone a "doctor of the universal church" has considerably broadened in modern times. Even before the case of St. Thérèse arose, the list of the previous 32 doctors included some whose works today are scarcely read (e.g., Lawrence of Brindisi), whose doctrinal contributions are scarcely known (e.g., Anthony of Padua), or who offer scarcely anything resembling a "doctrinal corpus" in the traditional sense (e.g., Catherine of Siena).[67]

Moreover, Rome has found itself increasingly deluged with doctoral petitions that seem to have more to do with the desire of a particular region or religious group to heap further laurels on their favorite saint than on any evidence of "eminent doctrine." That is why the relevant Vatican congregations have been so insistent that although a saint may have been a tireless catechist or preacher, a great ascetic and servant of the poor, or the primary promoter of an important religious movement or devotion, this is not in itself sufficient to warrant declaration as a "doctor of the universal church." It goes without saying, one supposes, that any potential candidate must have left behind significant liter-

---

[67] St. Anthony of Padua is widely known and loved within the church, but not primarily as a *teacher*. St. Catherine of Siena's teaching has exerted considerable influence, but she is not a systematic theologian in the traditional sense (though, interestingly, it is she, and not Anthony of Padua or Lawrence of Brindisi, who is quoted in the *Catechism of the Catholic Church*). This is not to denigrate these saints or their declaration as doctors, but just to acknowledge that they are a different kind of doctor than Augustine or Aquinas.

ary remains, as a vehicle through which his or her teaching can be conveyed. But neither is sheer quantity of writing a qualification, even if it is on theological or devotional subjects. The teaching must represent a profound and "original contribution at least in some fields of knowledge, such as to offer a real help in deepening study of Divine Revelation, in illustration of the faith, in the illumination and increase of Christian life," and be confirmed by "use, not occasional but continuous, on the part of scholars in the field of sacred sciences as well as pastors of the Church."[68]

Finally, given the requirement of "eminent doctrine," a certain historical and theological evolution in the understanding of the doctorate and in the kind of candidates chosen seems inevitable, since "eminence" is not judged purely on the basis of qualities intrinsic to the teaching itself, but involves an evaluation of its "reception" in the church.[69] Among patristic authors, for example, it is relatively easy to identify those whose teaching helped shape the church's fundamental dogmatic formulations and credal statements. Among medieval authors, it is likewise easy to single out the great systematizers of entire fields of theology. Later authors cannot reasonably be expected to play such a foundational or systematizing role. The church now has different intellectual and pastoral needs, and thus may require new kinds of "doctors." The saints of modern times whose teachings (and not simply their example) have made the greatest impact were rarely professional scholars. In particular, while the door is now open to women "doctors of the universal church," given earlier academic restrictions

---

[68] See Betti, "Preserve the True Meaning of Canonical Requisites," 3.

[69] In a recent article, Christopher O'Donnell briefly touches upon the question of "reception" in relation to Thérèse's doctorate. See Christopher O'Donnell, "Thérèse Among the Doctors of the Church," *Milltown Studies* 45 (2000): 128. This article also includes very extensive and useful bibliographical data.

placed upon them there will be few if any potential candidates from before the 20th century that could be considered "systematic theologians" in the traditional sense, though they may offer a "teaching" which has proved enormously influential in the church's intellectual and pastoral life. At a time of a "turn toward experience" in theology, when Catholic theologians are broadening their approaches and recognizing diverse methodologies, attempting to integrate theory and praxis and to incorporate the voices of women and the insights of popular religion into their work, perhaps the declaration of St. Thérèse as "doctor of the church" (a young woman of modest education whose "little doctrine" has nonetheless influenced scholars and popes) is particularly opportune.[70]

---

[70] For further discussions of the history of the title "doctor of the church" and the requirement of "eminence of doctrine," see Jesús Castellano Cervera, "'Eminens doctrina': Un requisito necesario para ser Doctor de la Iglesia," *Teresianum* 46 (1995): 3-21. The "Reflections" in the final section of this chapter roughly parallel those of Castellano, although they were written independently of his treatment.

Chapter Two

How Thérèse Martin Became a "Doctor of the Church"

Though the final ecclesiastical preparations in 1997 for the proclamation of Thérèse's doctorate took place very quickly—some would even say *too* hastily—serious efforts to have her declared a "Doctor of the Church" go back many decades, at least to the 1930's. The present chapter traces the evolution of these efforts, and begins with a brief overview of the life and legacy of this saint, on which assertions of her "outstanding holiness" and "eminent doctrine" would later be based.

Sources

Millions of pages, of varying quality and in nearly every language, have been written on the life of this popular saint. The primary source for biographical information is, of course, Thérèse herself, especially in her autobiographical manuscripts and letters.[1]

---

[1] The best and most complete edition of her works currently available in French is the *Nouvelle Édition du centenaire: Édition critique des oeuvres complètes (Textes et dernières paroles) de Sainte Thérèse de l'Enfant-Jésus et de la Sainte-Face*, published in 1992 in Paris by Éditions du Cerf and Desclée de Brouwer, in a boxed set of eight volumes. This edition will be cited as NEC. Most of these texts are also available in popular editions from the same publishers. ICS Publications is currently completing an English translation of

Also important is the information provided by those who knew her. Besides the *Derniers entretiens* (known in English as *Her Last Conversations* and discussed below), there are her mother's letters,[2] the testimonies given in the beatification and canonization process,[3] the recollections of her blood sisters and novices,[4] and various other documents published over the years in the Lisieux journals *Annales de Sainte Thérèse* and *Vie thérèsienne*, all of which are utilized in the ample notes and textual analyses included in the current critical French edition of Thérèse's works.

Those in the saint's social milieu were inveterate "savers," so that virtually every line written by or about Thérèse during her lifetime has been preserved.[5] Moreover, because Thérèse died so

---

the *Édition critique*, minus some of the more technical apparatus. Jean-François Six, a critic of NEC, has also published his own edition of the Thérèsian writings in three volumes, presenting her texts in strict chronological order but leaving out the *Derniers entretiens*, which he considers largely unreliable; see *Thérèse de Lisieux par elle-même*, ed. Jean-François Six, 3 vols. (Paris: Bernard Grasset and Desclée de Brouwer, 1997). Crucial for the development of modern Thérèsian studies was the publication of the 1956 facsimile edition of the autobiographical manuscripts used in *Histoire d'une Âme*; see *Manuscrits autobiographiques de Sainte Thérèse de l'Enfant-Jésus*, ed. François de Sainte-Marie, 3 vols. plus facsimiles (Lisieux: Office Central de Lisieux, 1956), hereafter cited as MA1956. More recently, Thérèsian scholar Conrad De Meester has published his own critical edition, entitled *Histoire d'une Âme de Sainte Thérèse de Lisieux selon la disposition originale des autographes novellement établie par Conrad De Meester* (Moerzeke, Belgium: Carmel-Edit, 1999).

2   Zélie Martin, *Correspondance familiale 1863-1877* (Lisieux: Carmel de Lisieux, 1958).

3   *Procès de béatification et canonisation de Sainte Thérèse de l'Enfant-Jésus et de la Sainte-Face*, 2 vols. (Rome: Teresianum, 1973-1976). A selection of the testimonies from the beatification process have been published in English in *St Thérèse of Lisieux by Those Who Knew Her*, trans. Christopher O'Mahony (Dublin: Veritas, 1975).

4   See especially Céline's *Conseils et souvenirs*, first published in Lisieux in 1951 and later translated into English as *A Memoir of My Sister St. Thérèse* (New York: P.J. Kenedy & Sons, 1959). A revised French edition appeared more recently as *Conseils et Souvenirs*, publié par Soeur Geneviève (Paris: "Foi Vivant," Éditions du Cerf, 1973). See also the substantial excerpts from Marie of the Trinity's recollections in Pierre Descouvemont, *Thérèse of Lisieux and Marie of the Trinity: The Transformative Relationship of St. Thérèse of Lisieux and Her Novice, Sister Marie of the Trinity* (Staten Island, NY: Alba House, 1993).

5   The current edition of her *Correspondance générale*, for example, includes "266 letters from Thérèse, 202 from her correspondents, and a large number of other letters concerning St. Thérèse directly (in which she is a co-recipient of a letter) or indirectly (in

young and was canonized so quickly, many who had dealt with her were still available to be interviewed as her popularity grew. The result is that, despite the brevity and "ordinariness" of her life, and the "hiddenness" of her vocation, we perhaps know more day-by-day biographical details about Thérèse than about any other saint. Gradually, as the relevant documents have been published in more reliable editions, the sometimes overly hagiographic or melodramaticThérèsian biographies of an earlier era, suited to the tastes of the times, have given way to more balanced and accurate presentations.[6]

Though some aspects of Thérèse's life-story remain obscure, and sentimental and polemical biographies still continue to appear,[7] most Thérèsian specialists now agree on the basic facts, as

---

which she is mentioned in passing or at length)"; see Saint Thérèse of Lisieux, *General Correspondence*, trans. John Clarke, 2 vols. (Washington, DC: ICS Publications, 1982-1988), 5. In references to this edition, "LT" indicates a letter written by Thérèse, "LC" a letter to Thérèse, and "LD" a letter about Thérèse; thus "LT 27" refers to the twenty-seventh surviving letter Thérèse composed, written to her sister Pauline in the Lisieux Carmel on October 8, 1897.

[6] Piat's works on the Martin family, written with the collaboration of the Lisieux Carmel, are still useful; see especially Stéphane-Joseph Piat, *The Story of a Family: The Home of The Little Flower*, trans. by a Benedictine of Stanbrook Abbey (New York: P.J. Kenedy & Sons, 1947). A very important and influential biography, despite its sometimes tendentious tone, is Ida F. Goerres's *The Hidden Face: A Study of St. Thérèse of Lisieux* (New York: Pantheon, 1959); this massive book was one of the first scholarly biographies of the saint to utilize the 1956 facsimile edition of her manuscripts, and to set Thérèse in the broader context of her time and culture. For more recent biographical studies in English incorporating the most up-to-date information on Thérèse's life, see especially Guy Gaucher's *The Story of a Life: St. Thérèse of Lisieux* (New York: HarperCollins, 1993) and *The Passion of Thérèse of Lisieux* (New York: Crossroad, 1990); Pierre Descouvemont and Helmuth Nils Loose's *Therese and Lisieux* (Toronto: Novalis, 1996); Patricia O'Connor's *Thérèse of Lisieux: A Biography* (Huntington, IN: Our Sunday Visitor, 1983); and *Saint Thérèse of Lisieux: Her Life, Times, and Teaching*, edited by Conrad De Meester (Washington, DC: ICS Publications, 1997).

[7] For example, Monica Furlong's widely distributed *Thérèse of Lisieux* (New York: Pantheon, 1987) is replete with small errors of fact and portrays Mother Marie de Gonzague as "sado-masochistic" (p. 85), while at the other extreme Jean-François Six's *Light of the Night: The Last Eighteen Months in the Life of Thérèse of Lisieux* (Notre Dame, IN: Notre Dame University Press, 1998) tries to rehabilitate the reputation of Marie de Gonzague by demonizing Mother Agnès and attacking other authors who have treated her favorably. See also Jean-François Six, *La véritable enfance de Thérèse de Lisieux: névrose et sainteté*

outlined in the biographical section of the *Positio* for her doctorate and presented here.[8]

The Life of Thérèse Martin (1873–1897)

The Early Years

Marie-Françoise-Thérèse Martin was born on January 2, 1873, in the small town of Alençon, in Normandy, France, where her parents, Louis Martin (1823-1894)[9] and Zélie Guérin (1831-1877), had met and married in 1858. She was the youngest of their nine children, only five of whom—Marie (born 1860), Pauline (born 1861),[10] Léonie (born 1863),[11] Céline (born 1869),[12] and Thérèse herself—survived infancy. Louis and Zélie were both devout Catholics, and both had at one time considered entering religious life. A successful watchmaker and jeweler, Louis Martin sold his shop in 1870 in order to assist his wife at home in her

---

(Paris: Éditions du Seuil, 1972); idem, *Thérèse de Lisieux au Carmel* (Paris: Éditions du Seuil, 1973). Six is a prolific Thérèsian scholar who has made valuable contributions to the knowledge of the saint's life and times, but his works tend to be argumentative and tendentious.

[8] A short biography and a chronology of Thérèse of Lisieux can be found in chapters three and five, respectively, of the first part of the *Positio*, which contains the *Informatio* presented to the congregations involved in bestowal of the doctorate. See Congregatio de Causis Sanctorum (Prot. N. 2168), *Urbis et Orbis. Concessionis tituli Doctoris Ecclesiae universalis S. Teresiae Iesu Infante et a Sacro Vultu, moniali professae Ordinis Carmelitarum Discalceatorum (1873-1897)* (Cabellione: Rogeri Rimbaud, 1997), 59-88, 93-117.

[9] For the life of Louis Martin, see Joyce R. Emert, *Louis Martin: Father of a Saint* (Staten Island, NY: Alba House, 1983).

[10] For a recent biography of Pauline, see Jean Vinatier, *Mère Agnès de Jésus: Pauline Martin, soeur aînée et "petite Mère" de sainte Thérèse de l'Enfant-Jesus* (Paris: Éditions du Cerf, 1993).

[11] For further information on Léonie, who was one of the earliest "converts" to Thérèse's "little way" and in recent years has attracted a devoted following of her own, see Marie Baudouin-Croix, *Léonie Martin: A Difficult Life* (Dublin: Veritas, 1993).

[12] For a biography of Céline, see Stéphane-Joseph Piat, *Céline, Sister Geneviève of the Holy Face: Sister and Witness of Saint Thérèse of Lisieux*, trans. Carmelite Sisters of the Eucharist (San Francisco: Ignatius Press, 1997).

profitable lacemaking business. The five daughters grew up in a relatively comfortable middle-class environment, imbued with the simple but profound Catholic piety of their parents; all of them would eventually enter religious life. In fact, with the exception of Léonie, the perpetual "outsider" who would ultimately join the Visitandines like her Guérin aunt, Sr. Marie-Dosithée, all of the sisters would eventually enter the Lisieux Carmel.

At the time Thérèse was born, however, her mother was already suffering from a serious tumor of the breast, and feeding problems forced Zélie to entrust her daughter for over a year to a wet nurse, Rose Taillé, who had cared for several of her previous children. When the 15-month-old Thérèse finally returned home, she was at first troubled by the separation from Rose but quickly readjusted. A far more traumatic separation occurred in August 1877, when Zélie finally succumbed to her inoperable cancer. Thérèse was a precocious four-and-a-half-year-old child far more aware of surrounding events than her elders realized. "All the details of my Mother's illness are still present to me" (Ms A 12r) she would later recall, and "God granted me the favor of opening my intelligence at an early age and of imprinting childhood recollections so deeply on my memory that it seems [the events she recounts] happened only yesterday" (Ms A 4v).[13]

Thérèse identifies her mother's death as the beginning of the second and most painful phase of her life:

---

[13] As explained below, the work known as *Story of a Soul* was originally edited by Mother Agnès out of three "autobiographical" manuscripts (known as A, B, and C) that Thérèse had written in her later years. Unless otherwise noted, all quotations from these manuscripts are taken from *Story of a Soul: The Autobiography of St. Thérèse of Lisieux*, trans. John Clarke, 3d ed. (Washington, DC: ICS Publications, 1996); the quotations here appear on pages 33 and 16-17, respectively. This third ICS Publications edition incorporates the French system of annotation, which identifies quotations according to the manuscript and page on which they appear in the autographs. (Thus "A 4v" indicates that the quoted passage can be found on the verso side of leaf 4 in Manuscript A, the initial memoir written at Mother Agnès's command.) All italics and capitalizations are from the printed texts, unless otherwise noted.

> This period extends from the age of four and a half to that of fourteen, the time when I found once again my *childhood* character, and entered more and more into the serious side of life. I must admit… my happy disposition completely changed after Mama's death. I, once so full of life, became timid and retiring, sensitive to an excessive degree. One look was enough to reduce me to tears, and the only way I was content was to be left alone completely. I could not bear the company of strangers and found my joy only within the intimacy of the family. (Ms A 13r)[14]

She had become particularly attached to her older sister Pauline, whom she spontaneously chose as her "second 'Mama,'" just as Céline had chosen Marie.

Before year's end, at the urging of the family of Zélie's brother, the pharmacist Isidore Guérin, Louis retired from business and moved with his daughters to Lisieux,[15] to a secluded property known as "Les Buissonets."

> Les Buissonets was like an enclosed garden. They knew no one except the Guérins. The family, deprived of the mother's dynamic presence, depended entirely on the father. He took no active part in the town but lived quietly on his savings and investments. He took charge of the garden, spending his days reading, meditating, and praying in the belvedere, a spacious piece of land on the highest part of their property. It overlooked the town. He liked to take walks with his youngest daughter. They

---

[14] *Story of a Soul*, trans. John Clarke, 3d ed., 34-35.

[15] For a photographic glimpse of Lisieux at the end of the 19th century, see Jean-François Six, *Lisieux au temps de Thérèse*, preface by Yvette Roudy (Paris: Desclée de Brouwer, 1997). For the social and political milieu of Lisieux, and its development as a pilgrimage site after Thérèse's death, see Matthew James Dowling, "The Evolution of a Modern Pilgrimage: Lisieux, 1897-1939" (Ph.D. diss., Yale University, 1995).

would go fishing.... The oldest girls, with the help of maids and nurses, were responsible for the house and education of the two youngest children, Céline and Thérèse.[16]

Thus Thérèse's social circle, always limited, became even more restricted. She immersed herself in pious activities and in reading, especially lives of the saints.

> When reading the accounts of the patriotic deeds of French heroines, especially the *Venerable* JOAN OF ARC, I had a great desire to imitate them.... I considered that I was born for *glory* and when I searched out the means of attaining it, God inspired in me the sentiments I have just described. He made me understand my own *glory* would not be evident to the eyes of mortals, that it would consist in becoming a great *saint*! This desire could certainly appear daring if one were to consider how weak and imperfect I was, and how, after seven years in the religious life, I still am weak and imperfect. I always feel, however, the same bold confidence of becoming a great saint because I don't count on my merits since I have *none*, but I trust in Him who is Virtue and Holiness. God alone, content with my weak efforts, will raise me to himself and make me a *saint*, clothing me in His infinite merits. (Ms A 32r)[17]

At eight-and-a-half Thérèse began attending the nearby Benedictine school, where she did well in her courses (except writing and arithmetic) but was ill-equipped to deal with the often boisterous other children. She confided to her beloved Pauline

---

[16] Guy Gaucher, "Childhood in Lisieux," in *Saint Thérèse of Lisieux: Her Life, Times, and Teaching*, 39.

[17] *Story of a Soul*, 72.

that she "would like to be a hermit and go away with her alone to a faraway desert place" (Ms A 25v); Pauline had replied off-handedly that she shared the same desire, and would wait for her. Thérèse was therefore stunned to learn soon afterward, from an overheard conversation between her two oldest sisters, that Pauline was planning to join Carmel, and thus that "she *would not wait for me* and I was about to lose my second *Mother!*" (Ms A 25v).[18] Pauline tried to console Thérèse by explaining the Carmelite vocation to her, and Thérèse, upon reflection, decided that she too was called to Carmel, "not for *Pauline's sake*," however, "but for *Jesus alone*." Nonetheless, this new separation came as a profound shock to her already delicate system. For over two months in 1883 she slipped into a "strange sickness" that kept her bedridden, baffled the doctors, and alarmed her family, who wondered if she would ever recover. Whatever the physiological or psychological etiology of this disease (a topic on which much ink has been spilled), it was apparently triggered by her uncle Isidore's remarks one evening about her dead mother and lasted until Pentecost of 1883 when, during a particularly bad episode, she finally looked upon the family's statue of Mary and saw the *"ravishing smile of the Blessed Virgin"* (Ms A 30r)[19]; the young girl who had so often experienced painful separation from the maternal figures in her life had found at last a mother who would never abandon her. Her first communion in May 1884 brought a profound experience of union with Christ in love, "as a drop of water is lost in the immensity of the ocean" (Ms A 35r).[20] Her older sisters Pauline (now Sr. Agnès of Jesus) and Marie had prepared her well, as they did again for her confirmation in June of that same year.

---

[18] Ibid., 57-58.
[19] Ibid., 66.
[20] Ibid., 77. She adds: "I *felt* that I *was loved*."

Nevertheless, even after her "miraculous cure," Thérèse remained timid and oversensitive despite her best efforts. Marie, whose practical guidance at home had helped her youngest sister weather serious bouts of scruples, now also departed for the Carmel of Lisieux. Bereft once again, Thérèse turned to the four siblings who had died before her birth, asking them to care for her as her living sisters had always done and to give her peace of mind. "The answer was not long in coming, for soon peace came to inundate my soul with its delightful waves, and I knew then that if I was loved on earth, I was also loved in heaven" (Ms A 44r).[21] But a far more profound change came with the 1886 "grace of Christmas," when she found herself suddenly and unexpectedly able to fight back tears after an impatient comment by her father as they returned home from midnight Mass. The incident itself was small, but for Thérèse it heralded a new stage in her life:

> I was really unbearable because of my touchiness.... I really don't know how I could entertain the thought of entering Carmel when I was still in the *swaddling clothes of a child!*
>
> God would have to work a little miracle to make me grow up in an instant, and this miracle He performed on that unforgettable Christmas day. On that luminous night which shed such light on the delights of the Holy Trinity, Jesus, the gentle, *little* Child of only one hour, changed the night of my soul into rays of light. On that *night* when He made Himself subject to *weakness* and suffering for love of me, He made me *strong* and courageous, arming me with His weapons. Since that night I have never been defeated in any combat, but rather walked from victory to victory, beginning, so to speak, *"to run as a giant!"*

---

[21] Ibid., 93.

...It was December 25, 1886, that I received the grace of leaving my childhood, in a word, the grace of my complete conversion.... Thérèse had rediscovered once again the strength of soul which she had lost at the age of four and a half, and she was to preserve it forever! On that *night of light* began the third period of my life, the most beautiful and the most filled with graces from heaven. The work I had been unable to do in ten years was done by Jesus in one instant, contenting himself with my *good will* which was never lacking.... I experienced a great desire to work for the conversion of sinners, a desire I hadn't felt so intensely before.

I felt *charity* enter into my soul, and the need to forget myself and to please others; since then I've been happy! (Ms A 44v–45v)[22]

An opportunity to exercise this new-found zeal for sinners soon came when she "heard talk of a great criminal, just condemned to death for some horrible crimes; everything pointed to the fact that he would die impenitent" (Ms A 45v).[23] His name was Henri Pranzini, and he had been convicted of the brutal murder of three women in Paris. While the press and French society in general joined in vilifying Pranzini as a scoundrel and monster, Thérèse took it upon herself to pray and offer Masses for his salvation, asking if possible for some sign that her prayers had been heard. When she learned that, at the last moment before his execution, Pranzini had kissed a crucifix offered to him, she saw in this the sign she had requested, and she was confirmed in her commitment to spend her life interceding for sinners.

Viewing Carmel as the ideal place to devote herself to this vocation, she now began in earnest to seek admission. At every

---

22 Ibid., 97-99.
23 Ibid., 99.

turn, however, her way seemed blocked because of her age; she was still only 14 years old. Yet she managed to obtain her father's consent, and with him appealed to the Bishop of Bayeux (Mgr. Hugonin) and ultimately to Pope Leo XIII, during an audience with a large group of French pilgrims from the Bayeux diocese (including Louis, Céline, and Thérèse) who had come to Rome for the golden jubilee of the pontiff's ordination to priesthood. Leo XIII's disappointing (but perhaps prophetic) response was simply: "You will enter if God wills it" (Ms A 63v).[24] Meanwhile the trip itself, which included many of the clergy, awakened Thérèse to the need to pray for priests (something the Discalced Carmelite nuns have traditionally seen as an important element in their vocation), and fired her desire for martyrdom, like the early Christians who had died in the Roman persecutions. Yet despite disappointing delays upon her return to Lisieux, and the objections of the ecclesiastical superior of the Carmel, Canon Delatroëtte, the tide had turned in her favor. On April 9, 1888, the 15-year-old Thérèse entered the enclosure door of the Lisieux Carmel and joined the large community of 26 nuns (twice the ideal number that Teresa of Avila had originally envisioned for the Discalced Reform).

Life in Carmel

Thérèse would later write: "*Illusions*, God gave me the grace *not to have* A SINGLE ONE when entering Carmel. I found the religious life to be *exactly* as I had imagined it." "And yet," she admitted, "my first steps met with more thorns than roses" (Ms A 69v).[25] She fought the temptation to depend overmuch on her energetic and charming but often imperious and unpredictable prioress, Marie de Gonzague, who treated Thérèse severely dur-

---

[24] Ibid., 135.
[25] Ibid., 149.

ing her first years but was one of the first outside the Martin family to recognize her true value. Thérèse likewise resisted any pampering or special treatment by her elder sisters, Pauline and Marie. She was regarded as unskilled and slow at the ordinary household chores that she had always been spared at home. In this spartan environment she suffered from the cold and poor food and began to experience ongoing aridity in prayer for the first time. One of her greatest challenges was simply living in such close daily proximity with the other nuns, some of whom amply displayed "a lack of judgment, good manners, touchiness in certain characters; all these things which don't make life very agreeable" (Ms C 28r).[26] Unable because of her health to practice the severe physical mortifications and penances of the great ascetics, she dedicated herself instead to an unbroken discipline of patience and charity within the community, trying to fulfill all her ordinary tasks with extraordinary fidelity and love.

Thérèse was to live in Carmel for nine years. Upon her entry, Mother Marie de Gonzague gave her the religious name she had long hoped to receive: she would henceforth be known as "Sr. Thérèse of the Child Jesus." When she received the habit on January 10, 1889, she added the further subtitle, "of the Holy Face," recalling a favorite devotion within the Martin family.

For Thérèse, this twofold new name was no mere matter of words but signified the mystery of her own particular vocation and spirituality.[27] As with so much else in her life, Thérèse developed

---

[26] Ibid., 246. Indeed, some of the nuns in the Lisieux Carmel with Thérèse later had to leave the community for psychological reasons.

[27] Her sister Céline would later write: "Devotion to the Holy Face was, for Thérèse, the crown and complement of her love for the Sacred Humanity of Our Lord. This Sacred Face was the mirror wherein she beheld the *Heart* and *Soul* of her Well-Beloved. Just as the picture of a loved one serves to bring the whole person before us, so in the Holy Face of Christ, Thérèse beheld the *entire Humanity* of Jesus. We can say unequivocally that this devotion was the burning inspiration of the Saint's life." She continues: "Furthermore, in our appraisal of her devotional life at Carmel, we must recognize, in the interests of objective truth, that her devotion to the Holy Face transcended—or more

her own distinctive approach to both the Divine Infancy and the Holy Face, themes already deeply rooted within the Carmelite tradition. In contrast to the obligations imposed on members of the popular Archconfraternity of the Holy Infancy of Jesus in her own day—a movement which had grown out of a series of private revelations to a nun of the Beaune Carmel, Sister Marguerite of the Blessed Sacrament (1619-1648)[28]—Thérèse did not emphasize the multiplication of vocal prayers and external practices but the imitation of Jesus's childlike abandonment to the Father. Although the focus of popular devotion to the face of the suffering Jesus, as it developed within the Archconfraternity of the Holy Face of Tours, was on reparation to God for blasphemies and the profanation of Sunday,[29] Thérèse instead pondered the Holy Face as the image of Christ's unimaginable love for humanity, the same love which had first brought him to earth in the Incarnation. For Thérèse, sentimental approaches to the Infant Jesus could not be separated from the suffering of the Passion, nor the crèche divorced from the Cross.

---

accurately embraced—all the other attractions of her spiritual life," even her devotion to the Child Jesus, with which she is more closely identified in the popular imagination. "All her writings—the *Autobiography*, the *Letters* and the *Poems*—are impregnated with the love of this same Adorable Face." See Geneviève of the Holy Face, *A Memoir of My Sister St. Thérèse*, 111-112.

[28] See Descouvemont and Loose, *Thérèse and Lisieux*, 160-161; and Raymond Darricau, "Margaret of the Most Holy Sacrament (Margaret Parigot, 1619-1648)," in *Saints of Carmel*, ed. Louis Saggi (Rome: Carmelite Institute, 1972), 187-194. It should be noted that St. Teresa of Avila had a deep devotion to the Child Jesus, and that Cardinal Bérulle, who had such a profound impact on French spirituality in general and the French Carmels in particular, wrote at length on identification with the interior state of the Divine Infancy. The Carmel of Lisieux was also well acquainted with devotion to the Infant of Prague. See also Descouvement and Loose, *Thérèse and Lisieux*, 128-135, 156-157.

[29] Devotion to the Holy Face, in the form that the Martin family knew it, had arisen from a series of private revelations to Marie de Saint-Pierre (1816-1848), a Discalced Carmelite nun of Tours, and had been eagerly promoted by Leo Dupont (1797-1876), whom his contemporaries called "the holy man of Tours." For further information on the history of this devotion, see Descouvemont and Loose, *Thérèse and Lisieux*, 136-140; *The Golden Arrow: The Autobiography and Revelations of Sister Mary of St. Peter*, ed. and trans. Emeric B. Scallan (New York: William-Frederick Press, 1954).

Moreover, the ordeal of her father's progressive paralysis, mental breakdown, and institutionalization soon after Thérèse's entry into Carmel (which many were whispering was due to the anguish of losing his youngest daughter to the convent) gave her at last the key to an unsettling childhood experience in the summer of 1879 or 1880, during one of Louis's frequent business trips away from home, when she thought she had seen him in the garden, his head "covered with a sort of apron" (Ms A 20r).[30] Since her ill father had begun veiling his face, Thérèse now saw the experience of 14 years earlier as a premonition, linked to the mystery of the Holy Face, suffering with love for humanity. "Just as the adorable Face of Jesus was veiled during His Passion, so the face of His faithful servant had to be veiled in the days of his sufferings in order that it might shine in the heavenly Fatherland near its Lord, the Eternal Word" (Ms A 20v).[31] Once again the painful circumstances of her own life became the springboard for a deeper meditation on the mystery of God's infinite love. The noble face of her earthly father, which for Thérèse had always served as a kind of window onto the benevolent face of the Divine Father, now also recalled for her the "hidden face" of the Suffering Christ, and her desire to be "hidden" with him.

Thérèse had entered Carmel still afire with her childhood ideal of becoming "a great saint" (LT 52, 80).[32] During her postulancy she wrote: "I would so much like to love Him!... Love Him more than He has ever been loved!... I would like to convert *all* the sinners of this earth and to save all the souls in purgatory!" (LT 74). In a letter she carried on her heart at her profession she asked for "love, infinite love without any limits other than

---

[30] *Story of a Soul*, 46.

[31] Ibid., 47.

[32] See *General Correspondence*, 1: 433, 520. As explained above, "LT" indicates a letter written by Thérèse, and is followed by a number indicating its enumeration in the French critical edition and the Clarke translation.

Yourself," and for the grace to die a martyr "of heart or of body, or... both" and "to save very many souls" (Pri 2).[33] She realized that in her own case these high aspirations could not be matched by the heroic deeds that marked the lives of her heroes, such as St. Joan of Arc. In their place, she reasoned, she would offer all the tiny daily sacrifices and sufferings she experienced, not letting a single opportunity pass. She quotes with approval the words of the family confessor, Father Pichon: "Sanctity! We must conquer it at the point of the sword; we must *suffer*... we *must agonize!*" (LT 89). Suffering beyond all her expectations soon came, as we have seen, with her father's illness. "At that time I was having great interior trials of all kinds, even to the point of asking myself whether heaven really existed" (Ms A 80v).[34] Helpless, she could only take refuge in the face of the suffering Christ "on fire with love for us" (LT 87). But a chance interview in 1891 with the community's retreat director, the Franciscan Alexis Prou, "launched me full sail upon the waves of *confidence and love* which so strongly attracted me," when he reassured her that the countless involuntary failings about which she was so concerned *"caused God no pain"* (Ms A 80v).[35]

As she entered her twentieth year, then, she had weathered the worst of the storm, and had been humbled by her own weakness. Her father was released and was able to visit Thérèse one final time. Her sister Pauline—Agnès of Jesus—was elected prioress in February 1893, and Thérèse was soon asked to assume a more prominent role in the community. Following custom, Mother Agnès appointed her predecessor (and sometime rival),

---

[33] *The Prayers of Saint Thérèse of Lisieux*, trans. Aletheia Kane (Washington, DC: ICS Publications, 1997), 38-40. "Pri" is the abbreviation used for the "Prières" in NEC, of which this ICS volume is the translation; thus "Pri 2" refers to the second prayer. This same text also appears in an appendix to *Story of a Soul*, 275.

[34] *Story of a Soul*, 173.

[35] Ibid., 174.

Marie de Gonzague, as the new novice mistress but made Thérèse her "assistant," thus putting the youngest member of the community in a most delicate position, which she handled with remarkable maturity and discretion. Mother Agnès likewise passed on to Thérèse her previous role as community "playwright," and the latter would eventually compose eight dramatic pieces for community feasts and special occasions, beginning with a "pious recreation" on Joan of Arc. Other sisters began asking her to write devotional poems for them, or to paint.

New vocations were entering, including the irrepressible Marie of the Trinity who would become her close friend, ardent disciple, and among the most important witnesses after Thérèse's death. Likewise her blood sister and childhood companion Céline finally entered in September 1894, a few months after the death of the father whom she had been nursing, and despite strictures against several nuns of the same family in the same Carmel. So many of Thérèse's deepest hopes had been fulfilled, beyond all expectation.

Still, she was beginning to feel the first symptoms of her illness, and after six years as a Carmelite her goal of conquering holiness at sword's point seemed ever more distant. Reevaluating her situation, she had begun to seek "a means of going to heaven by a little way, a way that is very straight, very short, and totally new."

> I have always wanted to be a saint. Alas! I have always noticed that when I compare myself to the saints, there is between them and me the same difference that exists between a mountain whose summit is lost in the clouds and the obscure grain of sand trampled underfoot by passers-by. Instead of becoming discouraged, I said to myself: God cannot inspire unrealizable desires. I can, then, in spite of my littleness, aspire to holiness. It is impossible for me to grow up, and so I must bear with my-

self such as I am with all my imperfections.... I wanted
to find an elevator which would raise me to Jesus, for I
am too small to climb the rough stairway of perfection. I
searched, then, in the Scriptures for some sign of this elevator, the object of my desires, and I read these words
coming from the mouth of Eternal Wisdom: *"Whoever
is a LITTLE ONE, let him come to me."* And so I suc-
ceeded. I felt I had found what I was looking for. But
wanting to know, O my God, what you would do to *the
very little one* who answered Your call, I continued my
search and this is what I discovered: *"As one whom a
mother caresses, so will I comfort you; you shall be carried
at the breasts, and upon the knees they shall caress you."*
...The elevator which must raise me to heaven is Your
arms, O Jesus! And for this I had no need to grow up,
but rather I had to remain *little* and become this more
and more. (Ms C 2v–3r)[36]

Here was Thérèse's "great discovery," which she would continue to proclaim and practice for the remainder of her short life,
and which after her death would be identified as the core of her
"doctrine" and would come to be known as "the little way of spiritual childhood."[37] She now realized that what ultimately mattered

---

[36] Ibid., 207-208.

[37] For a masterful study of the evolution of Thérèse's "little way," see Conrad De Meester, *The Power of Confidence: Genesis and Structure of the "Way of Spiritual Childhood"* of St. *Thérèse of Lisieux*, trans. Susan Conroy (Staten Island, NY: Alba House, 1998). More popular presentations of the same material can be found in Conrad De Meester, *With Empty Hands: The Message of Thérèse of Lisieux* (Washington, DC: ICS Publications, 2002); and Conrad De Meester, "The Discovery of the Little Way," in *Saint Thérèse of Lisieux: Her Life, Times, and Teaching*, 147-153; my own presentation here closely follows De Meester's. Surprisingly, though she does write of her "little way," in her extant autographs Thérèse never uses the precise phrase "little way *of spiritual childhood*." This latter formula, which has become so closely identified with her, first appears only with the 1907 edition of *Histoire d'une Âme*, in Mother Agnès's edited account of a conversation with the saint. It seems likely, therefore, that Mother Agnès herself was its source. Nonetheless, most commentators have adopted the formula, since it so succinctly summarizes the focus of Thérèse's "little way." See De Meester, *The Power of Confidence*, 3-8.

were not her own arduously acquired virtues or sufferings but those of Christ, not her acts of love for God but God's boundless merciful love toward her and toward all "little ones." It is worth noting that she had attained this insight not by immediate intuition or private revelation but through a typical process of meditation upon Scripture and informal "theological" reflection upon her own experience in the light of revelation.

Reflecting further on those holy people who offer themselves as "victims" to satisfy divine justice, she noted how much God's overflowing *love* is likewise disdained, and so felt inspired on June 9, 1895 (Trinity Sunday), to make her famous "Act of Oblation to Merciful Love," which reads in part:

> O my God! Most Blessed Trinity, I desire to *Love* You and make You *Loved*, to work for the glory of Holy Church by saving souls on earth and liberating those suffering in purgatory. I desire to accomplish Your will perfectly and to reach the degree of glory You have prepared for me in Your Kingdom. I desire, in a word, to be a saint, but I feel my helplessness and I beg You, O my God! to be Yourself my *Sanctity!*...
>
> In the evening of this life, I shall appear before You with empty hands, for I do not ask You, Lord, to count my works. All our justice is stained in Your eyes. I wish, then, to be clothed in Your own *Justice* and to receive from Your *Love* the eternal possession of *Yourself*....
>
> In order to live in one single act of perfect Love, I OFFER MYSELF AS A VICTIM OF HOLOCAUST TO YOUR MERCIFUL LOVE, asking You to consume me incessantly, allowing the waves of *infinite tenderness* shut up within You to overflow into my soul, that I may become a *martyr* of Your *Love*, O my God!... (Pri 6)[38]

---

[38] See *Prayers of Saint Thérèse of Lisieux*, 53-55; an extensive commentary follows the text, on pages 55-74. This text also appears in *Story of a Soul*, 276-277.

A few days later, while making the stations of the cross, she suddenly felt "seized" by a consuming fire of love for God, a rare "mystical moment" in her life which left her convinced that her self-offering had been accepted.

Meanwhile, at the behest of the prioress (her sister Pauline), Thérèse had already begun transcribing her childhood memories. As Mother Agnès would later testify in the diocesan process:

> At the beginning of the year 1895, two and a half years before the death of Sister Thérèse, I was with my two sisters (Marie and Thérèse) one winter evening. Sister Thérèse was telling me about several incidents in her childhood, and Sister Marie of the Sacred Heart (my older sister Marie) said: "Ah, Mother, what a pity we don't have this in writing; if you were to ask Sister Thérèse to write her childhood memories for you, what pleasure this would give us!" I answered: "I don't ask anything better." Then turning to Sister Thérèse, who was laughing because she thought we were teasing, I said "I order you to write down all your childhood memories."[39]

At first Thérèse was nonplussed by the command, wondering what she could tell her sisters that they did not already know. But she soon found her theme:

> It is not, then, my life, properly so-called, that I am going to write; it is my *thoughts* on the graces God deigned to grant me. I find myself at a period in my life when I can cast a glance on the past; my soul has matured in the crucible of exterior and interior trials....
>
> It is with great happiness, then, that I come to sing the mercies of the Lord with you, dear Mother. It is for

---

[39] See *Story of a Soul*, xv.

you alone I am writing the story of the *little flower* gathered by Jesus. I will talk freely and without any worries as to the numerous digressions I will make. A mother's heart understands her child, even when it can but stammer.... (A 3r-v)[40]

This text, now generally known as Manuscript A, was written down in free moments in an inexpensive copybook, and given to Mother Agnès for her feast day on January 20, 1896, though the latter did not read it for some weeks.

Meanwhile Pauline had entrusted to Thérèse a "missionary-brother," a 21-year-old seminarian who had written to the Carmel asking for a sister who would help him by her prayers and sacrifices. So began Maurice Bellière's brief but rich correspondence with the delighted Thérèse, who herself felt drawn to the missionary vocation and had always desired a priest-brother. Thérèse would later be entrusted with a second missionary, Adolphe Roulland, as if in compensation, as she saw it, for her two older blood brothers who had died in infancy. In her letters to both young men she was able to explain her thoughts on martyrdom, eternal life, the apostolic dimension of the contemplative vocation, and the nature of mission, while recommending to them her way of "confidence and love" in the face of their fears regarding divine judgment.[41]

On Holy Thursday night, 3 April 1896, Thérèse underwent her first hemoptysis, when blood came "like a bubbling stream" to her lips (Ms C 4v).[42] The experience was repeated the next evening. Thérèse rejoiced at this undeniable sign that her "en-

---

[40] Ibid., 15.

[41] In addition to the letters found in the two volumes of her General Correspondence, see also Patrick Ahern, *Maurice and Thérèse: The Story of a Love* (New York: Doubleday, 1998).

[42] *Story of a Soul*, 210.

trance into eternal life was not far off," but a few days later, ironically, at the beginning of the Easter season, she was plunged into
a great inner darkness. The nature of this "trial of faith," which
for many commentators makes Thérèse particularly "modern," has
been much debated: whether she worried that science might one
day be able to explain everything away, whether she was tempted
to doubt the existence of God or only of heaven, whether this
corresponded to the "passive night of the spirit" described by her
mentor, John of the Cross, or whether it was some superadded
share in the redemptive suffering of Christ. What is certain is that
this ordeal would last up until the time of her death, with only a
few brief interruptions, and that Thérèse accepted it as a way of
identifying with sinners and unbelievers of her day, whose lack
of faith, she admits, she had previously never understood.[43]

> Your child, however, O Lord, has understood Your
> divine light, and she begs pardon for her brothers. She
> is resigned to eat the bread of sorrow as long as You de-
> sire it; she does not wish to rise up from this table filled
> with bitterness at which poor sinners are eating until the
> day set by You. Can she not say in her name and in the
> name of her brothers, *"Have pity on us, O Lord, for we
> are poor sinners!"* Oh! Lord, send us away justified. May
> all those who were not enlightened by the bright flame
> of faith one day see it shine. (C 6r)[44]

Some months later, in September 1896 as she began what
was to be her final retreat, Sister Marie of the Sacred Heart, her

---

[43] See especially Ms C 5r-7v, *Story of a Soul*, 211-214. For recent discussions of Thérèse's
"trial of faith," see Frederick L. Miller, *The Trial of Faith of St. Thérèse of Lisieux* (Staten
Island, NY: Alba House, 1998); and Emmanuel Renault, "Thérèse in the Night of Faith,"
in *Saint Thérèse of Lisieux: Her Life, Times, and Teaching*, 223-234. Compare also
Gaucher's *The Passion of Thérèse of Lisieux* and Six's *Light of the Night*, mentioned above.
[44] *Story of a Soul*, 212.

godmother and oldest sibling, asked her for a "short note" on the "secrets" that Jesus was revealing to her. Thérèse replied with a brief text which has come to be known as Manuscript B, perhaps the jewel and centerpiece of all her writings. In it she explains to Marie "'*my little* doctrine,' as you call it" (Ms B 1v)[45] and, addressing Jesus, famously describes the discovery of her true vocation:

> To be Your *Spouse*, to be a *Carmelite*, and by my union with You to be the *Mother* of souls, should not this suffice me? And yet it is not so. No doubt, these three privileges sum up my true *vocation: Carmelite, Spouse, Mother*, and yet I feel within me other vocations. I feel the *vocation* of the WARRIOR, THE PRIEST, THE APOSTLE, THE DOCTOR, THE MARTYR....
>
> O Jesus, my Love, my Life, how can I combine these contrasts? How can I realize the desires of my poor *little soul?*
>
> Ah! in spite of my littleness, I would like to enlighten souls as did the *Prophets* and the *Doctors*. I have the *vocation of the Apostle*. I would like to travel over the whole earth to preach Your Name and to plant Your glorious Cross on infidel soil.... (Ms B 2v)[46]

Once again following her typical "method," and searching the Scriptures for an answer, she came upon Paul's First Letter to the Corinthians, and the passage on charity as the "more excellent" way and gift.

> I finally had rest. Considering the mystical body of the Church, I had not recognized myself in any of the

---

[45] Ibid., p. 189. Note that it is on the opening page of this text, Manuscript B, that Thérèse speaks of the "science of love," the phrase adapted as the title of *Divini Amoris Scientia*, the Apostolic Letter for her doctorate.

[46] Ibid., 192.

members described by St. Paul, or rather I desired to see myself in them *all*. *Charity* gave me the key to my *vocation*. I understood that if the Church had a body composed of different members, the most necessary and most noble of all could not be lacking to it, and so I understood that the Church *had a Heart and this Heart was BURNING WITH LOVE. I understood it was Love alone* that made the Church's members act, that if *Love* ever became extinct, apostles would not preach the Gospel and martyrs would not shed their blood. I understood that LOVE COMPRISED ALL VOCATIONS, THAT LOVE WAS EVERYTHING, THAT IT EMBRACED ALL TIMES AND PLACES.... IN A WORD, THAT IT WAS ETERNAL!

Then, in the excess of my delirious joy, I cried out: O Jesus, my love... my *vocation*, at last I have found it.... MY VOCATION IS LOVE!

Yes, I have found my place in the Church and it is You, O my God, who have given me this place; in the heart of the Church, my Mother, I shall be *Love*. Thus I shall be everything, and thus my dream will be realized. (B 3v)[47]

Then by means of the striking parable of a poor little bird, she describes how every soul could be drawn into "the burning abyss of this Love" if only "it abandoned itself with total confidence to Your Infinite Mercy" (Ms B 5v).[48] After reading this text, Marie marveled at its depths and described her sister as "possessed by God," while expressing regret that she herself was not as holy and did not share Thérèse's desire for martyrdom, which God would surely credit to her "as works" (LC 170). Thérèse responded quickly but with great theological and spiritual delicacy and insight:

---

[47] Ibid., 194.
[48] Ibid., 200.

How can you ask me if it is possible for you to love God as I love Him?...

My desires for martyrdom *are nothing;* they are not what give me the unlimited confidence that I feel in my heart. They are, to tell the truth, the spiritual riches that *render one unjust,* when one rests in them with complacency and when one believes they are *something great....* These desires are a *consolation* that Jesus grants at times to weak souls like mine (and these souls are numerous), but when He does not give this *consolation,* it is a grace of *privilege....* Dear Sister, how can you say after this that my desires are the sign of my love?... Ah! I really feel that it is not this at all that pleases God in my little soul; what pleases Him is *that He sees me loving my littleness* and *my poverty, the blind hope that I have in His mercy....* That is my only treasure, dear Godmother, why would this treasure not be yours?...

Oh, dear Sister, I beg you, understand your little girl, understand that to love Jesus, to be His *victim of love,* the weaker one is, without desires or virtues, the more suited one is for the workings of this consuming and transforming Love.... The desire alone to be a victim suffices, but we must consent to remain always poor and without strength, and this is the difficulty.... Ah! let us remain then *very far* from all that sparkles, let us love our littleness, let us love to feel nothing, then we shall be poor in spirit, and Jesus will come to look for us, and *however far* we may be, He will transform us in flames of love.... It is confidence and nothing but confidence that must lead us to Love.

...Oh, dear little Sister, if you do not understand me, it is because you are too great a soul ... or rather it is because I am explaining myself poorly, for I am sure that God would not give you the desire to be POSSESSED by *Him,* by His *Merciful Love* if He were not reserving this favor for you... or rather He has already given it to you, since you have given yourself to Him, since you *desire* to be consumed by Him, and since God never gives desires that He cannot realize.... (LT 197)

Thérèse had moved far beyond the calculus of virtues and merits that characterized the religious environment of her youth and the French Victorian piety of most of the nuns with whom she lived. This became all the more apparent in "last words" that Pauline and others began to record as Thérèse's health deteriorated rapidly. Among many reminiscences, spiritual reflections, astute observations, wry comments on her condition, and cries of pain, she repeatedly resisted any suggestion that she could now trust in her own sanctity.

At the beginning of June in 1897, realizing that Thérèse's death could not be far off, and that she had so far written little about her experiences in Carmel, Mother Agnès deftly persuaded the recently re-elected prioress, Mother Marie de Gonzague, to order Thérèse to resume her memoirs, so that there would be additional material for her obituary notice. Accordingly, in a text addressed to her prioress which has come to be called Manuscript C, Thérèse once again took up the thread of her own story to "finish *singing* with you [i.e., this time Marie de Gonzague] the *Mercies of the Lord*" (Ms C 1r).[49] In it she speaks especially of her discovery of the "little way," her "trial of faith," her novices and missionary brothers, and the concrete practice of fraternal charity. Within a month, however, her weakness forced her to discontinue her memoirs with the well-known closing words:

> Yes, I feel it; even though I had on my conscience all the sins that can be committed, I would go, my heart broken with sorrow, and throw myself into Jesus' arms, for I know how much he loves the prodigal child who

---

[49] Ibid, 205. The notation "[5vo]" at the top of page 205 in the ICS edition is a misprint.

returns to Him. It is not because God, in His anticipating Mercy, has preserved my soul from mortal sin that I go to Him with confidence and love.... (Ms C 36v–37r)[50]

Because Thérèse was determined to participate in the ordinary convent routine as long as she could, few of the nuns realized the seriousness of her disease. Because she usually kept her own counsel except when called upon to speak or write, few as well realized the depths of her spirituality. From this point on, however, Thérèse's tuberculosis progressed rapidly, with only some brief remissions. She was moved to the infirmary on July 8. Some in the community openly wondered what there would possibly be to say after her death about this simple and unassuming nun. Thérèse used her waning strength to encourage others with an occasional poem or letter, or a cheerful word or smile when she was able to manage it. Meanwhile her physical sufferings, without the relief of painkillers, became excruciating. After a terrible two-day agony, she died on September 30, 1897, at about 7:20 P.M., holding and gazing at her crucifix, and speaking her final words: "Oh! I love Him!... My God, I love you!" At the last moment, her face had taken on a look of ecstasy before she closed her eyes and passed away. A mysterious smile remained on her lips. She was buried in the Carmel's new plot in the town cemetery on October 4, 1897, with only 30 mourners attending. Most assumed she would soon be forgotten.

The Publication of Thérèse's Writings

Like many religious communities, the Discalced Carmelite nuns have the custom of publishing an obituary "circular letter" after the death of a community member. These documents could occasionally be quite lengthy, going into great detail about the

---

[50] Ibid., 259.

sister's childhood, the discovery of her call, her favorite devotions and memorable sayings, etc. Thus, paradoxically, Carmelite women sometimes received in death the public recognition they had been taught to avoid in life, out of humility.

After Mother Agnès learned the shocking news that her youngest sister was dying, her thoughts naturally turned to the question of the obituary. She had been deeply impressed upon belatedly reading the autobiographical memoir of childhood graces that, during her term as prioress, she had commanded Thérèse to write. As we have seen, she also skillfully proposed to her successor in office, Mother Marie de Gonzague, that Thérèse be ordered to continue the account of her life, so that they might have additional material for the circular letter.

In the meantime, as her death approached, Thérèse had a growing sense of a posthumous mission, and a conviction (using one of her favorite arguments) that God would not inspire such desires without intending to fulfill them. Though Thérèse had at first laughed at Céline's suggestion that her childhood recollections be published,[51] it began to occur to her that these writings might be precisely the instrument through which her mission would reach a "multitude of little souls." In her final months she gradually warmed to the idea of their eventual publication, apparently discussing the matter in some detail with Mother Agnès, advising her on how to proceed, and delegating her to make any necessary corrections or changes (a task for which Thérèse no longer had the strength). Thus when later asked during the beatification process "if the Servant of God had any suspicion that what she was writing would be published some day, or would at least be used in her obituary circular," Pauline testified:

---

[51] See Gaucher, *The Story of a Life*, 146: "Céline was the first reader as her sister filled each little book. One day, she said to her 'enthusiastically': 'It will be printed! You will see that it will be useful later!' Thérèse, finding the remark ridiculous, just laughed heartily: *I am not writing to produce a literary work, but through obedience.*"

She had no such suspicion when writing the first part, which was chiefly about her childhood and youth. She thought she was writing it just for me and our two sisters, Marie and Céline, who were with us in Carmel. In fact, that was what we thought ourselves at the time. The same is true of [Manuscript B]; her sister Marie had asked her for this, and it was written exclusively for her. But when Mother Gonzague asked her to write about her life in Carmel, I hinted to her that this might give edification to many people, and that its publication might well be the means that God would use to realize her ambition to do good on earth after her death. She accepted this quite simply. I also told her that Mother Prioress was liable to burn the manuscript. "That wouldn't matter," she said; "it would mean that God did not wish to make use of that means but there would be others."[52]

And Pauline (Mother Agnès) added:

One day she said to me: "I don't know what I'm writing." Another day, after she had been interrupted several times, she said: "I am writing about charity, but I have not been able to do it as well as I should have liked to; in fact, I couldn't have done it worse if I'd tried. Still, I have said what I think. But you must touch it all up, for I assure you it is quite a jumble." And another time: "Mother, whatever you see fit to delete or add to the copy-book about my life, it is I who have added or deleted it. Remember that later on, and have no scruples about it."[53]

---

[52] Testimony of Mother Agnès of Jesus, O.C.D., in *St Thérèse of Lisieux by Those Who Knew Her*, 35. Pauline spoke less categorically about Thérèse's thoughts regarding possible publication of Manuscript B in her testimony before the Apostolic Process; see MA 1956, 1:64 and *Procès de béatification et canonization de Sainte Thérèse de l'Enfant-Jésus et de la Sainte-Face* (Rome: Teresianum, 1976), 1: 202.

[53] Ibid., p. 34.

Moreover, in her record of Thérèse's "last conversations," Mother Agnès recalls Thérèse saying to her: "After my death, you mustn't speak to anyone about my manuscript before it is published; you must speak about it only to Mother Prioress. If you act otherwise, the devil will make use of more than one trap to hinder the work of God, a very important work!"[54]

Whatever Thérèse had in mind, Pauline certainly took this delegation to heart. After her youngest sister's death she proposed to the prioress that, in place of the usual obituary letter, a book-length work be compiled out of the various autobiographical manuscripts Thérèse had left behind. Mother Marie de Gonzague agreed, provided the texts be adjusted to make it appear that they were all addressed to herself.

Pauline immediately set to work, writing a first draft and then a second copy. "She divided the three manuscripts into eleven chapters, and composed a twelfth, in which she related Thérèse's last months and death. The [work] concluded with some extracts from her letters, a good number of her poems, and the testimony of her novices."[55] Mother Gonzague passed the second copy along to a good friend of the monastery, the Norbertine priest Godefroy Madelaine, who made further suggestions "in blue pen-

---

[54] St. Thérèse of Lisieux, *Her Last Conversations*, trans. John Clarke (Washington, DC: ICS Publications, 1977): 126 (1 August 1897, no. 1).

[55] Pierre Descouvemont and Raymond Zambelli, "Thérèse's Universal Influence," in *St. Thérèse of Lisieux: Her Life, Times, and Teaching*, 255. Rather than following the chronological order of the three manuscripts, Mother Agnès placed an edited version of Manuscript A first (the one originally addressed to herself, describing Thérèse's childhood), followed by her revision of Manuscript C (originally addressed to Mother Gonzague, and dealing in more detail with her life in Carmel). Then followed the bulk of Manuscript B (originally written for her sister Marie, and describing Thérèse's discovery of her vocation to be "love in the heart of the church"), in the eleventh chapter, before the description of Thérèse's death in chapter 12. Thus Manuscript B was an integral part—indeed, the climax—of the first published version of *Histoire d'une Âme*, and not an "appendix," as O'Donnell suggests, though chronological order of the texts was restored after the facsimile edition of the manuscripts was published in 1956. See Christopher O'Donnell, *Love in the Heart of the Church: The Mission of Thérèse of Lisieux* (Dublin: Veritas, 1997), 12.

cil," obtained the bishop's imprimatur, and wrote a preface. Father Madelaine also suggested that the otherworldly title proposed by the nuns, *A Canticle of Love or the Passing of an Angel*, be replaced by *Histoire d'une Âme* (Story of a Soul). When completed, the first edition came to 475 printed pages; its title page bore, along with a Carmelite seal and the publication data, the words *Soeur Thérèse de l'Enfant-Jésus et de la Sainte Face, Religieuse Carmélite, 1873-1897: Histoire d'une Âme, Écrite par elle-méme, Lettres—Poésies*.[56] Two thousand copies were printed by the Imprimerie de Saint-Paul at Bar-le-Duc a year after Thérèse's death, and the Lisieux nuns wondered how they would ever dispose of them.[57]

To everyone's surprise, however, the book was an almost instantaneous success, as copies were passed among clergy and religious and shared with their friends. The Carmelite nuns soon found themselves deluged with expressions of appreciation for Thérèse, accounts of favors received, and requests for more information about her. *Story of a Soul* sold out quickly, and had to

---

[56] For information on the evolution of this famous text, in addition to other cited works, I am relying especially on *Manuscrits autobiographiques*, vol. 1: *Introduction*, ed. François de Sainte-Marie (Lisieux: Carmel de Lisieux, 1956); Sainte Thérèse de l'Enfant-Jésus et de la Sainte-Face, *La première "Histoire d'une Âme" de 1898* (Paris: Éditions du Cerf, "Nouvelle édition du centenaire," 1992); Sainte Thérèse de l'Enfant-Jésus et de la Sainte-Face, *Manuscrits autobiographiques*, édition critique (Paris: Éditions du Cerf, "Nouvelle édition du centenaire," 1992); and *Histoire d'une Âme de Sainte Thérèse de Lisieux selon la disposition originale des autographes*, ed. Conrad De Meester (Moerzeke, Belgium: Carmel-Edit, 1999). Hereafter the 1898 edition of *Histoire d'une Âme* will be indicated as "HA 1898," and Conrad De Meester's recent edition as "DM 1999." François de Sainte-Marie's facsimile edition of the autobiographical manuscripts will be designated as "MA 1956," and the current NEC edition as "MA 1992."

[57] Although most studies claim that the book was published on September 30, 1898, precisely one year after Thérèse's death, Conrad De Meester shows that it actually came out several weeks later, on October 19 or 20. See Conrad De Meester, "De la cellule de Thérèse de Lisieux—l'atelier de l'imprimeur: Le tout début de l'*Histoire d'une Âme*," in *Thérèse et ses théologians: Colloque organisé par l'Institut Catholique de Toulouse et les Carmes de Toulouse*, ed. Joseph Baudry (Versailles: Éditions Saint-Paul; Venasque: Éditions du Carmel, 1998), 50; and DM 1999, 13.

be reprinted every year thereafter.[58] "The first translation was made into English (1901), and there followed translations into Polish (1902), Italian and Dutch (1904), and German, Portuguese, Spanish, Japanese and Russian (1905)."[59] By 1914, the year that Pius X signed the introduction of her cause, the Lisieux nuns were receiving an average of 400 letters a day concerning Thérèse (a number which more than doubled during the years of her beatification and canonization).[60] "By 1915, the Carmel had sent out 211,515 copies of *Histoire d'une Âme*, 710,000 of *Vie abrégée* (*Abridged Life*), and 110,000 copies of *Pluies de roses* (*Shower of Roses*)."[61] In less than two decades following her death, this young French nun who had lived and died in utter obscurity had become known and loved by millions around the world.[62]

Thus the public was first introduced to the writings of St. Thérèse in a heavily edited version. Unfortunately, neither of Pauline's original two drafts has survived intact, so it is difficult to attribute precise responsibility for each alteration in what Thérèse had originally written. Certainly Mother Gonzague was ultimately responsible for those changes required by her insistence that the texts be altered to appear as if addressed to her. Father

---

[58] Subsequent editions sometimes included revisions and additions likewise overseen by Mother Agnès. More letters were added in later editions, for example, as well as accounts of favors received; the famous phrase "little way of spiritual childhood" commonly used to describe Thérèse's "doctrine" first appeared only in the 1907 edition of *Histoire d'une Âme* (see note 36, above).

[59] Gaucher, *Story of a Life*, 208.

[60] Descouvemont and Zambelli, "Thérèse's Universal Influence," in *Saint Thérèse of Lisieux: Her Life, Times, and Teaching*, 257.

[61] Gaucher, *Story of a Life*, 211. *Pluies de roses* is the general title of a series of anthologies of the letters sent to the Lisieux Carmel describing favors attributed to Thérèse's intercession; seven volumes appeared between 1911 and 1926. Gaucher also notes, on page 211, that "between 1898 and 1925, 30,328,000 pictures [of Thérèse] had been distributed."

[62] For a popular account of Thérèse's posthumous career, see Bernard Gouley, Rémi Mauger, and Emmanuelle Chevalier, *Thérèse de Lisieux ou La grande saga d'une petite soeur (1897-1997)* (Paris: Fayard, 1997).

Madelaine had also played a significant role; in the Ordinary Process of 1910-1911 he remembered that "I studied the manuscript for about three months. I divided it into chapters [sic], and made a few little corrections, just a few literary touches, nothing affecting the substance."[63] He then went on to quote from his letters to Marie de Gonzague at that time:

> I must read it again. I shall then mark with blue pencil what I think should be omitted from the published edition. All of it, absolutely all of it, is precious for *you*. But there are some details that are so intimate and out of the ordinary, that it would be better, I think, not to print them for the public. There are also slight mistakes in grammar and style; these… can easily be made to disappear. Finally, we have also noticed a certain repetitiousness; for the public it would be better to suppress some of these repetitions. I shall mark them…. But, Mother, I can scarcely tell you the pleasure and spiritual delight with which I read those pages, so totally permeated by the love of God.[64]

Yet the bulk of the changes clearly seem attributable to Mother Agnès; just as she had done years before when tutoring her youngest sister at Les Buissonnets, Pauline once again edited Thérèse's words freely, correcting her mistakes, polishing her style (as she thought), modifying or deleting passages that seemed too

---

[63] Testimony of Godefroy Madelaine, O. Praem., in St Thérèse of Lisieux by Those Who Knew Her, 273. In fact, Father Madelaine seems to have misremembered his role regarding the division into chapters. The one surviving fragment of the manuscript he corrected is headed "Chapter XIV" and contains some of Thérèse's poetry, indicating that the text was already divided into chapters when he received it, though he may have helped in determining the chapter headings. See De Meester, "De la cellule de Thérèse de Lisieux," 42-43.

[64] Testimony of Godefroy Madelaine, O. Praem., in St Thérèse of Lisieux by Those Who Knew Her, 273.

personal or that might embarrass those who were still living. In her own testimony during the same Ordinary Process, when asked "if the published edition [of Thérèse's writings] corresponded to the original manuscript, so that one could take the former for the latter with complete security," Mother Agnès said:

> There are some changes, but they are unimportant and do not affect the substance or general meaning of the account. These changes are (a) the suppression of some very short passages which relate intimate details about our family life during her childhood; (b) the suppression of one or two pages that I thought would be of little interest to readers outside of Carmel; (c) the manuscript is made up of three parts: one addressed to me, the second to her sister Marie, and the third (chronologically, that is) to Mother Marie de Gonzague, the then prioress. Since Mother Gonzague supervised the publication, she demanded some little changes in the parts addressed to the Servant of God's sisters; in order to give the whole work a greater unity, she made it look as if it was all addressed to herself.[65]

After hearing this testimony, the tribunal judges demanded an exact copy of the manuscripts for the official record, and satisfied themselves that Thérèse's thoughts had not been substantially altered. Nonetheless, once the general public discovered that the published versions of *Histoire d'une Âme* were not identical with what Thérèse had actually written, there were increasing demands for the release of the texts in their original form. By the time the official authorization for this came in 1947, however, the aging Mother Agnès was already too weak to undertake such a daunt-

---

[65] Testimony of Mother Agnès of Jesus, O.C.D., in *St. Thérèse of Lisieux by Those Who Knew Her*, 36-37.

ing project, which she entrusted to Céline. Céline in turn assisted François de Sainte-Marie, O.C.D., the Carmelite scholar, in publishing the first "critical" edition of the "autobiographical manuscripts," as they were called, including three volumes of notes and analysis along with Manuscripts A, B, and C in facsimile. This 1956 publication represented a turning point in Thérèsian scholarship, showing clearly that the editing behind the original edition of *Histoire d'une Âme* had been far more extensive than the responses of Mother Agnès and Father Madelaine had suggested. By François de Sainte-Marie's count more than 7000 textual changes had been introduced. Critics saw this as conclusive proof of what some had long suspected: that the Martin sisters, and especially Pauline, had distorted and even falsified both the image and the message of Thérèse to fit popular notions of sanctity, in order thereby to promote her possible canonization.[66]

A sober comparison of *Histoire d'une Âme* with the *Manuscrits autobiographiques*, however, helps to moderate some of these charges. Many of the changes introduced by Pauline are simple corrections of spelling and grammatical style; given Thérèse's limited training in composition and the difficult circumstances under which she wrote (often without rereading), it is hardly surprising that there should be many small errors in the manuscripts that any reasonable editor would be expected to correct. Moreover, at the time the first edition of *Histoire d'une Âme* was published, Thérèse was still unknown, and simply reproducing her texts without some attempt to weave them together into a whole would only have provoked ridicule; there was as yet no great cry for the *ipsissima verba* of a favorite saint.

---

[66] See, for example, Etienne Robo, *Two Portraits of St. Teresa of Lisieux*, rev. and enl. ed. (Westminster, MD: Newman Press, 1957). For a description of the controversies, and a response to the criticisms, see Peter-Thomas Rohrbach, *The Search for Saint Thérèse* (Garden City, NY: Hanover House, Doubleday & Co., 1961). For a more recent example of the continuing attack on Mother Agnès, see Six, *Light of the Night*.

Other small alterations were presumably made to spare embarrassment to those still living, and especially to the Lisieux Carmel. This perhaps explains, for example, why in Thérèse's famous description of the nun whose noise-making disturbed Thérèse's mental prayer, Pauline changed the other sister's "strange habit" from clicking her teeth to rattling her rosary beads (Ms C 30v).[67]

Far more significant were the extensive cuts, "almost one third of the whole text."[68] François de Sainte-Marie's listing of passages from the autographs omitted in the 1898 *Histoire d'une Âme*—limiting himself only to those over one line long!—comes to some 30 pages of fine print.[69] Most of the deleted sections are from Manuscript A, dealing with Thérèse's intimate childhood memories. In some cases Pauline may have considered the details too personal or trivial; in other cases the omission may have been needed to preserve the fiction that the text was addressed to Mother Gonzague.

Pauline often amended Thérèse's wording, "both flattening Thérèse's tone and gilding it with her own flowery style."[70] In some cases the changes and emendations tended to "angelize" her youngest sister and to obscure suggestions of childhood failings and neuroses. For example, she changed her mother's description of Thérèse from a "nervous" to an "exuberant" child.[71] Mother Agnès also added material, including further extracts from her mother's letters, pious anecdotes, or clarifications of points

---

[67] Compare *Story of a Soul*, 249 with the sixth paragraph from the end of chapter 10 in HA 1898.

[68] Rohrbach, *The Search for Saint Thérèse*, 14.

[69] See MA 1956, 1:99-129. At the same time, Mother Agnès apparently fought to preserve some passages that Father Madelaine would have preferred to see cut; see De Meester, "De la cellule de Thérèse de Lisieux," 36-38.

[70] O'Connor, *Thérèse of Lisieux: A Biography*, 146.

[71] See Robo, *Two Portraits of St. Teresa of Lisieux*, 52.

Thérèse's wording left obscure.[72] It was Mother Agnès rather than Thérèse, for example, who inserted a reference to the latter's use of "virtue beads" as a child to tally her "sacrifices," a practice that seems far removed from her later discovery of the "little way" and her desire to go to God "with empty hands."[73] At the same time, all of the important Thérèsian events and themes are preserved in recognizable form: the death of her mother, her mysterious illness and cure, her "Christmas conversion," the prayer for Pranzini, her appeal to the pope, the discovery of her "little way" and her vocation to be "love in the heart of the church," her "Oblation to Merciful Love," her "trial of faith."

All of this has led most recent Thérèsian scholars to a paradoxical conclusion. On the one hand, Mother Agnès in effect "rewrote" Thérèse's texts. No doubt Thérèse herself had encouraged her editorial efforts, and, as Conrad De Meester has recently argued, Mother Agnès may well have regarded *Histoire d'une Âme* as Thérèse's *biography* rather than *autobiography*—thereby setting aside the need to slavishly follow her youngest sister's wording. Still, it would be pointless to try to reconcile Pauline's changes with modern critical standards.[74] And yet, on the other hand, nothing truly essential was lost. Thérèse's true spiritual portrait is still discernable beneath the pious overlay, as was her physical portrait beneath Céline's idealized paintings and retouched photographs.[75] Through Pauline's version Thérèse's message of utter

---

[72] See, for example, the long passage from *Histoire d'une Âme* quoted in *Story of a Soul*, 19, note 8.

[73] Compare *Story of a Soul*, 25, note 19 with the "Oblation to Merciful Love," Ibid., 277.

[74] See MA 1956, 1: 78.

[75] The history of the visual representations of Thérèse is similar to that of her texts. Céline had been trained as a painter, and brought with her into Carmel the camera used to take most of the surviving photographs of Thérèse. After Thérèse's death, Céline took charge of the production and distribution of images of her late sister, just as Mother Agnès took charge of the texts. Some heavily retouched photographs were circulated, and throughout the remainder of her life Céline continued to paint portraits of Thérèse, which

childlike confidence in a God of merciful love found its intended audience of "little souls" in a way that might well not have occurred through unedited publication of her texts in their original state. Pauline had adapted Thérèse to the needs and tastes of the time.

A similar verdict has been rendered on the early published versions of other texts in the Thérèsian "corpus." As indicated by the original subtitle, Mother Agnès had included some of Thérèse's letters, along with 39 poems and thirteen verse fragments from her "pious recreations," in an appendix to the original version of *Histoire d'une Âme*, material that was amplified in later editions.[76] From 1907 onward, the Lisieux Carmel also published the poems in a separate volume. Once again, however, Mother Agnès had exercised a heavy editorial hand, most often "correcting" Thérèse's imperfect poetic style, but sometimes marring the thought as well. Likewise, in working on the first separate volume of Thérèse's letters, published in 1948, Abbé André Combes, one of the first theologians to undertake a systematic study of Thérèse, was only partially successful in persuading Céline

---

became ever more idealized as she grew older. These paintings were highly regarded in their day by the Carmelites of Lisieux; photography was still in its infancy and often considered mere mechanical reproduction, incapable of capturing the "truth" of the person only accessible through the painter's art. Nonetheless, most of Céline's portraits would be considered excessively sentimental by today's standards. When a complete annotated edition of the unretouched photographs was finally published in 1961 (by the same Father François de Sainte-Marie responsible for the facsimile edition of the autobiographical manuscripts), many were shocked, and accused Céline of having falsified the "true face" of Thérèse just as Mother Agnès was accused of having falsified her texts. A more balanced assessment, however, would suggest that Céline's retouched photographs and pious portraits were not intended to deceive but to present Thérèse according to the tastes of their time, and that Thérèse is still recognizable beneath the sentimental veneer. See François de Sainte-Marie, *Visage de Thérèse de Lisieux*, 2 vols. (Lisieux: Office de Lisieux, 1961). This was translated into English as *The Photo Album of St. Thérèse of Lisieux*, commentary by François de Sainte-Marie, trans. Peter-Thomas Rohrbach (New York: P.J. Kenedy & Sons, 1962).

76 See NEC *Poésies*, 277.

to allow a "strictly authentic edition."[77] Finally, Thérèse's "last words," those sayings recorded during the 18 months before her death by Mother Agnès and others, and used in the composition of chapter 12 in *Histoire d'une Âme*, proved most problematic of all. Here is where we find some of Thérèse's most famous statements, such as "I will spend my heaven doing good on earth" and "I will let fall a shower of roses." Yet in this case there were no texts in Thérèse's own hand, but only the sometimes unreliable (or convenient) memories of her listeners. Mother Agnès recopied and reedited her notes several times, with numerous alterations, and not all of her versions have survived. It was only in 1922 that she compiled her most complete collection, the famous "Yellow Notebook," used in the 1927 anthology, *Novissima Verba*. "Certainly these texts were not taken down on a tape recorder," notes Guy Gaucher, "and they bear the stamp of Mother Agnès of Jesus.... We cannot give these sayings the same weight as the writings of St. Thérèse herself, but to deprive ourselves completely of them would diminish our knowledge of Thérèse as sick, human, suffering, jovial, praying, poor, and at times sublime in her complete simplicity. Mother Agnès would not have been able to invent many of the lines recorded."[78]

Such controversies over the texts could have easily derailed any efforts to have Thérèse declared a "doctor," since one could

---

[77] See *General Correspondence*, 1:44-55. As explained in this introductory section, part of the difficulty was that Combes wanted to include Manuscript B among Thérèse's letters (since it was indeed a "letter" addressed to Marie of the Sacred Heart), but to have reprinted the original of Manuscript B at that time would have made evident the discrepancies between Thérèse's words and Mother Agnès's version in *Histoire d'une Âme*. Perhaps even more surprising, the Postulator of the Cause for Thérèse, Mgr. de Teil, had apparently indicated to the Martin sisters early on that they would not be required to turn over any of the letters whose originals had been destroyed by the time of the official examination of Thérèse's writings. Hence a number of letters considered too personal or childish were destroyed, while others were cut up for relics, leaving behind at best only second-hand (and sometimes edited) copies of the originals. See ibid., 25-39.

[78] Guy Gaucher, "The Last Conversations," in *St. Thérèse of Lisieux: Her Life, Times, and Teaching*, 239.

scarcely make the case for the "eminence of her doctrine" without a clear sense of what she had actually said and written. Otherwise there was always the danger that what passed as her teaching would turn out to be a corporate effort of the surviving Martin sisters themselves along with other Thérèse enthusiasts. Fortunately, after the death of Sr. Geneviève (Céline) in 1959, the way was finally opened for a critical reexamination of all the archival materials. Soon work began on a "centenary edition" of Thérèse's writings, prepared by a committee including such reputable scholars as Bernard Bro, O.P., and Guy Gaucher, O.C.D., as well as Sr. Cécile, O.C.D., of the Lisieux Carmel. In this series of "critical" texts, the volumes *Derniers entretiens* and *Dernières paroles* appeared in 1971, the two-volume *Correspondance générale* in 1972 and 1974, the two-volume *Poésies* in 1979, the *Récréations pieuses* in 1985, and *Prières* in 1988. In 1992 these works were reprinted, together with the original *Histoire d'une Âme* and an updated edition of the *Manuscrits autobiographiques*, in a boxed eight-volume set known as the "Nouvelle édition du centenaire" (NEC). Members of the same team have also published an annotated collection of all of Thérèse's scriptural references[79] and, more recently, a massive general concordance of her works.[80] The providential result of so many earlier disputes, which NEC carefully tries to resolve, is that students of Thérèse now have more reliable texts and better critical tools than are available for many of the other "doctors of the universal church." Certainly all of this scholarship and the further studies it has generated, played a crucial role in paving the way for Thérèse's own "doctorate," enabling

---

[79] *La Bible avec Thérèse de Lisieux*, ed. Soeur Cécile, O.C.D., et Soeur Geneviève, O.P. (Paris: Éditions du Cerf, 1979).

[80] *Les mots de Sainte Thérèse de l'Enfant-Jésus et de la Sainte-Face: Concordance générale*, établie par Soeur Geneviève, O.P., de Clairefontaine, Soeur Cécile, O.C.D., du Carmel de Lisieux, et Jacques Lonchampt (Paris: Les Éditions du Cerf, 1996).

readers more easily and clearly to follow the evolution and structure of her principal ideas.

On the Way to the Doctorate

But perhaps the strongest indication that Pauline's editorial overzealousness, however regrettable, had not in fact "betrayed" her younger sister, is that, decades before the critical texts became available, Thérèse's teaching was already being carefully studied and her doctorate proposed in terms very similar to those later articulated in the official *Positio*. Admittedly, many of the early writings on Thérèse were uncritically devotional and hagiographic, as one might expect in the first flush of enthusiasm for this attractive "servant of God" to whom so many favors were being attributed. But even apart from her role as intercessor, Thérèse was regarded from the beginning as someone with a particular *message*. In his preface to the first edition of *Story of a Soul* in 1898, Père Madelaine had already praised Thérèse's "theology which the most beautiful spiritual books only rarely attain to such a high degree."[81] Pius X had called her "the greatest saint of modern times"; in 1910, after being shown a letter of Thérèse encouraging frequent communion, he had expressed his pleasure at her teaching and the rapid progress of her cause. In 1921, in his allocution on the occasion of the decree of the heroicity of Thérèse's virtues, Benedict XV characterized her "way... of spiritual childhood" as "the secret of sanctity," and praised her "ample treasure of doctrine." During 1923, in connection with the approval of the miracles required for Thérèse's beatification and the beatification itself, Pius XI spoke at length of her message and described her as

---

[81] See Sainte Thérèse, *La première "Histoire d'une Âme" de 1898*, 16.

the "star" of his pontificate, a "teacher" (*Maître*), and even "a word of God"! In his homily at the canonization in 1925, the same pope said, in part:

> St. Thérèse had learned thoroughly this teaching of the Gospels [i.e., "Unless you be converted and become as little children, you shall not enter the kingdom of heaven"] and had translated it into daily life. Moreover, she taught the way of *spiritual childhood* by word and example to the novices of her monastery. She set it forth clearly in all her writings, which have gone to the ends of the world.... In her catechism lessons she drank in the pure doctrine of Faith, from the golden book of *The Imitation of Christ* she learned asceticism, in the writings of St. John of the Cross she found her mystical theology. Above all, she nourished heart and soul with the inspired Word of God on which she meditated assiduously, and the Spirit of Truth taught her what He hides as a rule from the wise and prudent and reveals to the humble. Indeed, God enriched her with a quite exceptional wisdom, so that she was enabled to trace out for others a sure way of salvation.[82]

It is worth noting that by speaking of her "exceptional wisdom," her attention to Scripture, her widespread influence, and so forth, a pope was *already* indicating in the 1920's that Thérèse fulfilled the major criteria according to which the 1997 consultors would later be asked to judge her "eminence of doctrine" (see below).

Likewise worth noting is that the year of Thérèse's canoni-

---

[82] This excerpt is from Thomas Taylor's rendering of the canonization homily delivered on May 17, 1925, and is found in his 1927 revised translation of *Histoire d'une Âme*; see *Saint Thérèse of Lisieux, the Little Flower of Jesus*, trans. Thomas Taylor (New York: P.J. Kenedy & Sons, 1927), 272-273.

zation also marked the publication of "the first *doctrinal* study dedicated to the spiritual experience of St. Thérèse": *Un renaissance spirituelle*, by Hyacinthe Petitot, O.P.[83] This Dominican philosopher and theologian credits Thérèse with developing "a wonderful and a new pattern of heroic sanctity," accessible to all, and known popularly as the "Way of Spiritual Childhood." Recalling the words of Piux XI, he goes on to say that "the adequate understanding of the saint's spirituality, her virtuous example, and the graces she has obtained for her disciples have already inaugurated 'the reform and renewal of Catholic life.'"[84] Other authors were quick to follow suit, nearly always mentioning what Thérèse had called her "little way," which her sisters had dubbed "the little way of spiritual childhood." Thérèse was celebrated for having rediscovered for our times the Gospel precept to "become like little children," not relying on our own accomplishments or despairing over our failures but abandoning ourselves with complete trust into the arms of Jesus, surrendering totally to a God who is Merciful Love. For her, this recognition of God as Merciful Love became, we might say, a hermeneutical principle in the light of which all other doctrines were interpreted.

The impact of her seemingly simple message was so immediate and profound that, not long after her canonization, various parties were already informing the Lisieux Carmel of their interest in having Thérèse declared a "doctor of the church."[85] Dom Obrecht, the abbot of Gethsemani Abbey in Kentucky, said as much during a 1928 visit to the Carmel; when the astonished sisters objected that such a novelty seemed impossible, he replied

---

[83] Hyacinthe Petitot, *Sainte Thérèse de Lisieux, Une renaissance spirituelle* (Paris: Desclée, Éditions de la Revue des Jeunes, 1925). See Conrad De Meester, "Le dominicain Hyacinthe Petitot et sainte Thérèse de Lisieux," in *Thérèse et ses théologiens*, 67-71.

[84] Hyacinthe Petitot, *Saint Teresa of Lisieux: A Spiritual Renascence*, trans. Benedictines of Stanbrook Abbey (New York: Benziger Brothers, 1927), xx, xxiv.

[85] These early efforts are recounted in detail in Paul Droulers, "Le doctorat de Sainte Thérèse de Lisieux proposé en 1932," *Ephemerides Carmeliticae* 24 (1973): 92-100.

that the times were changing and that if women could now be doctors "in the human order," why not also in the church?[86] In 1929, two Mexican Jesuits proposed bestowing the title "ascetical doctor" (*doctoresse ascétique*) upon her, in part to preserve her message and example from the sometimes banal presentations it had too often been given.[87] In 1930, the bishop of Taubaté, Brazil brought to Rome his own request for Thérèse's doctorate, in which he raised and refuted the objection that such a title would contravene Paul's strictures against women teaching publicly in the church.[88] The same year, from Argentina, a professor of logic and mathematics, Emilio-G. De la Calle, wrote that Thérèse clearly seemed to fulfill the requirements of outstanding holiness and eminent doctrine, and argued that calling her a "word of God," as Pius XI had done, was already tantamount to calling her a "doctor of the church." In 1931, De la Calle and the auxiliary bishop of Buenos Aires published several articles in support of Thérèse's doctorate.[89] Other letters were sent to the Lisieux Carmel, independently, from Austria, Poland, Japan and elsewhere, asking that she be named a doctor.

Credit for organizing the first official petition, however, is usually given to the Jesuit P. Gustave Desbuquois (1869-1959), noted director of the "Action Populaire," who at the first Thérèsian Congress in 1932, held in the crypt of the new basilica in Lisieux, created a sensation by arguing in detail why she should be named a "doctor."[90] He mentioned, for example, her timely and acces-

---

[86] Ibid., 93.

[87] Ibid., 94-95.

[88] Anticipating what other theologians would later conclude, the bishop pointed out that Thérèse had taught "privately" by her example and writings, which had only become "public" after her death; see ibid., 96, note 15.

[89] Ibid., 95-98.

[90] See ibid., 86-92; Guy Gaucher, "Le père Desbuquois et le doctorat de Thérèse," *Carmel* no. 87 (1988): 42-53.

sible retrieval of the traditional biblical themes of "spiritual childhood," hope, and "Merciful Love," her emphasis on what we now describe as "the universal call to holiness," her broad appeal and enormous influence, and the fact that Pius XI, in his many statements on Thérèse, had already characterized her as a great Christian teacher and a "word of God" for our times. Desbuquois's proposal was enthusiastically endorsed by the congress participants, including some bishops and cardinals. News of this development spread quickly, garnering support from around the world. In Portugal, for example, 57,000 signatures were collected and forwarded to the future Pius XII, Cardinal Pacelli, then the Vatican's Secretary of State. With the endorsement of her local ordinary, Mother Marie of the Incarnation, an Ursuline of Trois Rivières in Canada, began writing to all of the bishops around the world, and within a year had obtained 342 episcopal signatures. Clearly the desire at the time to have Thérèse declared a doctor was deep and widespread, not simply a vain idea promoted by the Martin sisters to further glorify their youngest sibling. Moreover, far from wanting to use a Thérèse doctorate to impose on women an outmoded 19th century model of the feminine, Desbuquois and many of his supporters felt that bestowing the title on Thérèse would represent part of a progressive effort by the church to encourage a greater recognition of the role of women and endorse the modern efforts toward their emancipation.

Soon, however, the process ground to a halt. Cardinal Pacelli, writing to Mother Agnès on behalf of Pius XI in response to her report on the Thérèsian Congress of 1932, indicated that it was better not to speak any more of the doctorate for Thérèse, "even if her doctrine did not for that reason cease to be a sure light for souls seeking to know the Gospel spirit."[91] The precise

---

[91] See Droulers, "Le doctorat de Sainte Thérèse de Lisieux proposé en 1932," 117–121, and page 51 in the *Informatio* section of the *Positio*.

reasons for this decision were never stated, but it has often been suggested that this pope who so often praised Thérèse's teaching was simply unprepared to bestow the doctorate on a woman. Already some years earlier, when the procurator general of the Discalced Carmelite friars, who was also provincial of the Milan province, had proposed Teresa of Avila as a doctor, Pius XI had succinctly replied "obstat sexus," though he "left the entire question to the decision of his successor."[92] And so the matter was dropped for decades. Nonetheless, succeeding pontiffs continued to recommend Thérèse's *teaching* to the faithful. Pius XII himself, while still the legate of Pius XI, had declared that "she had a mission" and "she had a doctrine." Paul VI called her "an incomparable guide to the ways of prayer."[93] John Paul II has praised her message repeatedly, especially during his own pilgrimage to Lisieux in 1980. Her name appears fifteen times in the synodal *Acta* of the Second Vatican Council,[94] and she is cited six times in the *Catechism of the Catholic Church* (where only nine doctors of the church are cited more often).[95]

Thérèse's teaching had also continued to attract the interest of theologians and other scholars. The Dominican theologian Marie-Michel Philipon expressed the opinion that Carmel had given the church "three doctors" of the first rank: Teresa of Avila,

---

[92] See ibid., 121-122, 127; Jesús Castellano Cervera, "El doctorado de Santa Teresa del Niño Jesús: Memoria histórica y significado eclesial," *Revista de Espiritualidad* 57 (1998): 78-79.

[93] See the quotations compiled by Guy Gaucher in "'Je me sens la vocation de docteur' (Ms B, 2vo)," in *Thérèse de l'Enfant-Jésus: Docteur de l'Amour*, ed. Centre Notre-Dame de Vie (Venasque: Éditions du Carmel, 1990), 29.

[94] The interventions mentioning Thérèse at Vatican II are quoted in the *Informatio* section of the *Positio*, 371-373. Interestingly, many of them are from missionary bishops, suggesting that Thérèse be cited in the Decree on the Church's Missionary Activity, *Ad Gentes Divinitus*, not only as co-patroness of the missions but as a prime example of the apostolic dimension and missionary fruitfulness of the contemplative life.

[95] See the table in Appendix 3 of Bernard McGinn, *Doctors of the Church* (New York: Crossroad, 1999), 188-189.

John of the Cross, and Thérèse.[96] The Jesuit philosopher Erich Przywara argued that Thérèse, who during her "trial of faith" maintained hope in the face of her own nothingness, offered the perfect response to the modern nihilism of Nietzsche.[97] Abbé André Combes composed a series of groundbreaking studies of Thérèse's doctrine based on scrupulous attention to her texts, and delivered them first as courses at the Institut Catholique in Paris.[98] The great ecclesiologist Yves Congar, O.P., spoke of the influence of Thérèse on his own life and thought, and responded very positively to the idea of declaring her a "doctor of the church."[99] Even more significantly, Hans Urs von Balthasar devoted a book and several articles to the analysis of Thérèse, whom he insisted "was directly entrusted with a mission to the Church," one of only two "perfectly evident instances during the nineteenth century of a primarily theological mission."[100] The list could be extended indefinitely.

Not surprisingly, then, efforts to have Thérèse declared a "doctor of the universal church" were taken up again in earnest after 1970, when Paul VI decisively overcame any objection on

---

[96] See Droulers, "Le doctorat de Sainte Thérèse de Lisieux proposé en 1932," 126, note 94, as well as Marie-Michel Philipon, *The Message of Thérèse of Lisieux*, trans. E.J. Ross (Westminster, MD: Newman Press, 1954).

[97] See Eva Maria Faber, "Chemin de kénose: la réponse de sainte Thérèse—l'héroïsme de ses contemporains d'après le Père Erich Przywara, SJ," in *Thérèse et ses théologiens*, 95-108.

[98] See Claude Langlois, "L'abbé Combes, théologien et historien de Thérèse," in *Thérèse et ses théologiens*, 133-160.

[99] See "Lettre du Père Yves Congar—Mgr. Gaucher," *La Documentation Catholique* 2040 (15 December 1991): 1088.

[100] Hans Urs von Balthasar, *Two Sisters in the Spirit: Thérèse of Lisieux and Elizabeth of the Trinity* (San Francisco: Ignatius Press, 1992), 28. The other example, according to von Balthasar, is John Vianney, especially for his insights on the sacrament of penance. See also Hans Urs von Balthasar, "The Timeliness of Lisieux," in *Carmelite Studies I: Spiritual Direction*, ed. John Sullivan (Washington, DC: ICS Publications, 1980): 103-121. Other shorter articles by von Balthasar are mentioned by Virginia Raquel Azcuy, "La 'théologie vécu' de Thérèse de Lisieux: Interprétation et réception dans l'oeuvre de H.U. von Balthasar," in *Thérèse et ses théologiens*, 211-227.

the basis of sex alone by bestowing the title on Teresa of Avila and Catherine of Siena. During 1973, the centenary of Thérèse's birth, Cardinal Garrone petitioned Rome for her doctorate, as did the postulator general of the Discalced Carmelites in 1974, but they were reminded that all further concessions of the doctorate had been suspended by the pope in 1972, until the whole matter could be studied further.[101] Nevertheless, the petitions kept increasing, not only from the General Chapter of the Discalced Carmelites but from bishops' conferences all over the world and from many individual members of the hierarchy. The partial listing given in the *Positio* mentions formal petitions from 43 conferences of bishops and six cardinals, along with petition signatures from 250,000 priests, religious, and laity.[102]

What was happening, meanwhile, in the Vatican congregations?[103] Already on 31 August 1992, the Congregation for the Causes of Saints, in accordance with the required procedure, had requested from the Congregation for the Doctrine of the Faith the necessary opinion on the eminence of Thérèse's doctrine. Four years later there was still no vote, but the CDF had formulated its "norms and criteria" for evaluating doctrinal eminence, which Pope John Paul II approved on 10 November 1996.[104] In this document, to be discussed more fully in the next chapter, six requirements are mentioned: (1) an "ecclesial discernment of the existence of a charism of wisdom, conferred by the Holy Spirit"; (2) a

---

[101] See *Positio*, 51-52, and Umberto Betti, "A proposito del conferimento del titolo di Dottore della Chiesa," *Antonianum* 63 (1988): 287.

[102] See *Positio*, 606 ff.

[103] For a detailed description of the final stages of the process, see Jesús Castellano Cervera, "El doctorado de Santa Teresa del Niño Jesús: Memoria histórica y significado eclesial," 77-111; and the "Presentation du Rapporteur" in the opening pages of the *Positio*, iv-v.

[104] See *Positio*, iv. The one-page document, in Italian, is entitled "Norme di procedure e criteri dottrinali per il giudizio circa la 'Eminens Doctrina' dei santi propositi come 'Dottori della Chiesa'."

teaching which "excels ('eminet')[105] by the quality of the writings, the height and profundity of the doctrine, by a mature sapiential synthesis, and by the impact of the positive influence exercised"; (3) a message at the service of "Catholic doctrine and Christian life"; (4) a doctrine drawn from "the pure sources of the Word of God, Tradition, and the Magisterium of the Church"; (5) a "large diffusion, positive reception, and particular beneficial influence among the people of God"; and (6) a "secure message of lasting value."[106] Though these criteria obviously require further elaboration, and had not necessarily been designed only with Thérèse in mind, they certainly helped to overcome hesitations regarding the cause of her doctorate, as we shall see. For one could make a strong case, as many of the theological consultors in the canonical process later did, that she had met all of these six requirements: that she had drawn upon the Scriptures and classic Christian sources, for example, that she clearly offered an excellent spiritual doctrine, that it had been widely diffused, that her message was relevant and of lasting value, and so on.

In December of 1996, presumably because the centenary year of Thérèse's death was about to begin, the Vatican Secretary of State asked for a progress report on Thérèse's doctorate from the Congregation for the Causes of Saints. At the beginning of February 1997—only about eight months before the actual declara-

---

[105] The Latin word "eminet" (in parentheses and quotation marks) is interpolated here in the original Italian text of the "Norme di procedure" presumably to make explicit the connection with the traditional requirement that a candidate demonstrate "eminens doctrina." Recall that in his apostolic letter for Thérèse's doctorate, Pope John Paul II will repeat the term in saying: "Her teaching not only conforms to Scripture and the Catholic faith, but excels (*eminet*) for the depth and wise synthesis it achieved." See *Divini Amoris Scientia*, no. 7.

[106] See *Informatio*, pp. 588-603. These "Norms and Criteria" have not yet been officially published, but they are often referred to, directly or indirectly, in the published documents related to the doctorate of Thérèse. A careful reading likewise shows that they provide the structure for much of *Divini Amoris Scientia*, the Apostolic Letter for the declaration of Thérèse as "doctor of the universal church," as we will indicate in chapter 4 below.

tion—members of the two congregations finally met to plan the remaining stages in this difficult and complicated doctoral process. The CDF promised a vote on her doctrinal eminence for April, while the Congregation for the Causes of Saints asked the Postulator General of the Discalced Carmelites, Father Simeon Fernandez, to start pulling together as soon as possible the required background material, a charge the latter then presented to the Discalced Carmelite Definitory. Camilo Maccise, General of the Discalced Carmelite Friars, next appointed a committee to compose and compile the necessary materials outlining the case for Thérèse's doctorate, to be examined by the appropriate Roman dicasteries.[107] On 8 March 1997, the first official document of the cause, the *Supplex libellus*, was submitted to the Congregation for the Causes of Saints, over the signatures of Fathers Simeon and Camilo and the bishops of Bayeux-Lisieux (Mgr Pierre Pican and his auxiliary, Guy Gaucher); though brief, it represented "an anticipation of the main lines of the *Positio* and contained a summary explanation of the reasons urging the request for the doctorate."[108] A few days later Daniel Ols, O.P., was named "relator" of the cause.

At the beginning of April, under a strict deadline, a committee of Discalced Carmelite experts on Thérèse somehow managed to draft the *Informatio*, which now comprises some 800 pages

---

[107] Aside from Father Loys de Saint Chamas of the Notre-Dame de Vie secular institute (founded by the late Marie-Eugène of the Child Jesus, a Discalced Carmelite) this committee was composed entirely of Discalced Carmelite clergy, including Guy Gaucher (auxiliary bishop of Bayeux-Lisieux), Camilo Maccise (General of the Discalced Carmelites), Jean Sleiman (member of the Discalced Carmelite Definitory), Simeón de la Sagrada Familia (Postulator General of the Discalced Carmelites), Jesús Castellano Cervera (president and professor of the *Teresianum*, the Discalced Carmelites' pontifical school in Rome), François-Marie Léthel and Mario Caprioli (professors at the *Teresianum*), Conrad De Meester, Joseph Baudry, Philippe Hugelé, and Antonio Fortes. See Jesús Castellano Cervera, "El doctorado de Santa Teresa del Niño Jesús: Memoria histórica y significado eclesial," 80.

[108] Ibid., 81. This text of this *Supplex libellus* can be found on pages 1-14 of the bound red volume of the *Positio*.

of the published *Positio*, in little more than a week. This *Informatio* section, presenting a case for the "eminence" of her doctrine, includes among other things a biography of Thérèse; a history of her causes of beatification, canonization, and the doctorate; an overview and analysis of her writings and doctrine; a huge bibliography; a long listing of all the petitions received; and a list of the many saints, blesseds, popes, cardinals, bishops, theologians, religious congregations and others who have acknowledged her influence.[109]

This *Informatio* was then forwarded to the congregations for their study. However, since the Congregation for the Doctrine of the Faith had not managed to hold their promised vote by April, a compromise procedure had to be devised with the pope's approval, which involved several joint meetings to consider the further input of various theological consultors and to vote on the question.[110] It was not until the end of May that their work was done.

Regarding the theological input, as we will see in more detail in the next chapter, the Congregation for the Doctrine of the Faith designated 5 theological experts, and the Congregation for the Causes of Saints 2 theological experts, to submit their opinions on the question of whether to grant the title "doctor of the

---

[109] The material in the *Informatio* section, as we shall see, includes: the history of Thérèse's causes of beatification and canonization (chapter 1); the history of her doctorate (chapter 2); a biography of Thérèse (chapter 3); her personality (chapter 4); a chronology (chapter 5); an examination of her writings and their history (chapter 6); a general overview of her doctrine (chapter 7); a study of her theology (chapter 8); an examination of her sources (chapter 9); a review of the reception and use of Thérèse's doctrine by the Magisterium (chapter 10); a listing of the persons, movements, and events she has inspired or influenced (chapter 11); the relevance of her doctrine for the contemporary church and world (chapter 12); and conclusions (chapter 13). The *Informatio* closes with a partial listing of petitions for Thérèse's doctorate, and a bibliography of more than 130 folio pages.

[110] See Jesús Castellano Cervera, "El doctorado de Santa Teresa del Niño Jesús: Memoria histórica y significado eclesial," 86-87.

church" to Thérèse; of these, 6 were favorable and only 1 opposed. These 7 theological opinions, together with the original *Informatio*, were then forwarded by the respective congregations to a host of theological consultors, all of whom likewise received a one-page copy of the "norms and criteria" as well as the NEC version of Thérèse's writings. In the case of the CDF, 19 consultors voted in favor, 2 more were affirmative "iuxta modum" (that is, with certain reservations), and 1 was against. In the case of the Congregation for the Causes of Saints, 7 consultors voted in favor, 2 more were affirmative "iuxta modum," and 3 were negative. Thus when the numbers were added together, there were 26 consultors in favor, 4 more in favor with some reservations, and only 4 out of 34 against. With this kind of majority, it was easy for the subsequent consistory on June 17 to unanimously approve the doctorate. The heads of both congregations then reported the results to the pope, who, a few weeks later, on World Youth Day (August 24), announced his intention to declare Thérèse a "doctor of the universal church."

Reflections

Because of the obvious differences between Thérèse and previously named doctors, it is easy to dismiss her official inclusion among their ranks as a foolish or cynical gesture, the result of pressure tactics by pious devotees or Vatican efforts to reimpose the spirituality and female role models of the past.[111] Those familiar

---

[111] See, for example, William C. Graham, "Is There a Case Against Saint Thérèse as Doctor of the Church?" *Sisters Today* 67 (January 1995): 56-58. For a reply to this article, and Graham's response, see John F. Russell, "St. Thérèse of Lisieux: Doctor of the Church?" *Sisters Today* 69 (January 1997): 7-12; and William C. Graham, "My Response to Father Russell," *Sisters Today* 69 (January 1997): 13-14. Graham's objections and Russell's responses will be discussed at greater length in chapter 4.

only with Mother Agnès's recast versions of her youngest sister's writings, or the kitsch associated with much pre-Vatican II devotion to Thérèse, are likely to be dubious, perhaps seeing the attention to Thérèse's "message" as akin to all the "deeper meanings" projected onto the sentimentalized Princess Diana following her tragic death. There is, in fact, much in Thérèse's story that belongs irretrievably to a bygone bourgeois French Victorian Catholic milieu and era.

Yet the history we have surveyed in this chapter indicates that the impetus behind Thérèse's doctorate is neither recent nor superficial. No doubt the Lisieux Carmel, and especially the Martin sisters, did what they could to generate interest in their youngest sibling and tailored her image somewhat according to the tastes of the time, which were their own as well. But there are many examples of similar but unsuccessful efforts by religious communities to promote the cause of one of their own who died young "in the odor of sanctity."[112] Whatever the Martin sisters' ambi-

---

[112] The cases of two Discalced Carmelite nuns mentioned earlier, of whom Thérèse would have known, are illustrative. Sr. Marguerite of the Blessed Sacrament (1619-1648), of the Carmel of Beaune, who died at the age of 29, received apparitions of the Child Jesus, who encouraged her to found an association in his honor; this movement was later established with papal approval as the Archconfraternity of the Holy Infancy of Jesus. The decree of the heroicity of her virtues was promulgated in 1905 under Pius X, but her cause has not advanced, and the archconfraternity she helped establish seems largely inactive. See Descouvemont and Loose, *Thérèse and Lisieux*, 160-161; and Raymond Darricau, "Margaret of the Most Holy Sacrament (Margaret Parigot, 1619-1648)," 187-194. Similarly, the cause of the somewhat older Marie de Saint-Pierre (1816-1848), whose revelations regarding the Holy Face eventually led to the establishment of the Archconfraternity of the Holy Face (to which Thérèse belonged) has not progressed at all. See Descouvemont and Loose, *Thérèse and Lisieux*, 136-140 and *The Golden Arrow: The Autobiography and Revelations of Sister Mary of St. Peter*. Yet both devotions were strongly promoted in the Carmels of France during Thérèse's lifetime, and as we know, she was herself deeply devoted to the Infant Jesus and the Holy Face. Moreover, even the name under which her autobiographical manuscripts have come to be known, *Histoire d'une Âme*, was shared with other pious biographies of the time. Conrad De Meester mentions, for example, L. Laplace's *Histoire d'une Âme: La servante de Dieu Mathilde de Nédonchel* (Lyon-Paris: Vitte Lecoffre, 1895), fourth edition of a biography of a young

tions, Thérèse would obviously not have reached the renown and influence she achieved had her life and message not found its responsive audience. In a way beyond all expectations, the story of the joys, struggles, and insights of this unknown 24-year-old nun struck a profound chord with theologians and simple believers alike and seemed to them somehow to address the spiritual needs of the 20th century. More than three decades after the Second Vatican Council, it is hard to appreciate just how "revolutionary" was Thérèse's emphasis on "ordinary holiness" and confidence in God's merciful love, in the face of the residual Jansenism and the heroic model of sanctity still prevalent in her own day. But the critical editions of Thérèse's writings and more careful studies of her thought have only underscored the ways in which she deepened and moved beyond the limitations of the theology and spirituality she had inherited.

Moreover, as we have seen, arguments favoring Thérèse's doctorate came early; they originated not with the Lisieux Carmel but with scholars and members of the hierarchy and were based on the importance of her *teaching,* not merely on nostalgia or a desire to further "gild the lily" with additional titles. The intent was far from reactionary. In most cases those endorsing her doctorate viewed it as in part a way for the church to raise the level of discussion, promote a truly contemporary spirituality, and embrace the modern movement toward women's emancipation. Indeed, the popes of the 20th century had already in effect all but called her a "doctor," and seem to have held back so long from this final step primarily out of a now outmoded reservation about the teaching role of women within the church.

"apostle of the Sacred Heart" who wanted to enter Carmel and died at the age of twenty-four and a half. See DM 1999, 14, n. 7. If sheer industry in promoting a cause were enough to ensure canonization, one could have expected Marguerite of Beaune, Marie de Saint-Pierre, and Mathilde de Nédonchel, for example, to have been raised to the altars long ago.

In any case, having now reviewed the major stages leading up to the doctoral declaration for St. Thérèse, let us now turn to the *Positio* and the views of the theological consultors, whose input formed one of the final parts of the process. For, whatever the reasons given *in the past*, these "vota" reveal some of the theological opinions given *today* on the appropriateness and meaning of the bestowal of the title.

Chapter Three

THE *POSITIO* AND THE OPINIONS OF THE THEOLOGICAL CONSULTORS

t the time of the declaration of Thérèse's doctorate in 1997, the Congregation for the Causes of Saints released the official documentation in two very unequal volumes. The first is a large, red, clothbound, folio-size volume of nearly 1000 pages, containing the background material submitted to the theological consultors to assist them in voting on the suitability of declaring Thérèse a doctor. The second is a light gray paperback folio volume of 160 pages, containing the actual texts of their written votes. Despite their differences, these two books clearly belong together, since they bear the same protocol number (Prot. N. 2168) and essentially the same title: *Urbis et Orbis: Concessionis Tituli Doctoris Ecclesiae Universalis S. Teresiae a Iesu Infante et a S. Vultu, Moniali Professae Ordinis Carmelitarum Discalceatorum in Monasterio Lexoviensi.*[1] Both are sometimes called collectively the *Positio*, though this term applies more strictly to that material in the red volume presented to the con-

---

[1] To be more precise, the title page of the gray volume abbreviates "Ordinis Carmelitarum Discalceatorum," to "O.C.D.," and adds Thérèse's dates (1873-1897) at the end of the subtitle. But it is clearly intended to be a supplement to the red volume, even though it was printed by a different publisher. Hereafter we will refer to the red volume as the *Positio*, and the gray volume as the *Positio* supplement.

sultors as a kind of "position paper." The present chapter will ex-amine this documentation in more detail.

The *Positio* for the doctorate of St. Thérèse, along with the supplementary volume that contains the "vota" of the theologi-cal consultors, belongs to a peculiar literary genre. Like *Story of a Soul* itself, it was not composed as a single work but compiled out of a series of documents written at various times, to various audi-ences, for various purposes, with no assurance till the end of the process that any of them would ever be published. The contents are a mix of the canonical and theological, the historical and hortatory.

Moreover, again like *Histoire d'une Âme*, it is not always im-mediately apparent to which hand various passages may be attrib-uted. In this case, following Vatican custom, nothing except the nine-page prefatory "Présentation du rapporteur" and the four-teen-page *Supplex libellus* is signed, though some of the other con-tributors can be identified by other means. The "anonymity" of the theological consultors, in particular, is presumably intended in theory to spare them undue pressure or embarrassment and ensure their impartiality. But it does hinder students of the pro-cess from being able to interpret a particular theological "vote" in light of that consultor's other published theological opinions. In addition (and perhaps intentionally), it can obscure the possi-bly "inbred" character of some aspects of the process, where a coauthor of the *Informatio*, for example, might also be one of the theologians asked to vote, in light of the same *Informatio*, on the suitability of bestowing the doctorate on Thérèse[2] or where con-

---

[2] For example, as the texts indicate, Jesús Castellano Cervera, O.C.D., is one of the com-mittee members who helped to write the *Informatio* and also one of the theological con-sultors for the CDF "vota" on whether the *Positio* established the case for Thérèse's doc-torate. Similarly, the two theologians whose expert opinions were solicited by the Con-gregation for the Causes of Saints for inclusion in the background material submitted to that congregation's consultors for a vote, also *cast* a vote in that congregation's "special congress." This is not to question their objectivity or honesty, but just to note some of the peculiarities of the process which could have some influence on the outcome.

sultors could perhaps be arguing from papal allocutions or other ecclesiastical documents that they helped to "ghostwrite."

Despite these limitations, however, the *Positio* and the published "votes" of the theological consultors contain a wealth of interesting material on the reasons for and against declaring Thérèse a doctor, along with reflections on the significance of the doctorate itself (not only what it has meant in the past, but what it could mean for the church of the future). Before examining the votes of the theologians, a brief outline of the contents of the *Positio* should prove helpful, to see more precisely the specific material and questions to which the consultors were responding.[3]

Preliminaries: The "Presentation du Rapporteur" and *Supplex Libellus*

After the title page and a list of the committee members who helped with the writing and editing, the *Positio* begins with the "Presentation du rapporteur," a seven-page introduction by the "relator" or promoter of the cause, Daniel Ols, O.P., dated 25 April 1997. Though brief, this text includes some important data not mentioned elsewhere in the pages that follow. Ols starts out by noting the unusual circumstances of the present case: (1) that it is the first since Paul VI suspended concessions of the doctorate in 1972; (2) that it is thus the first to follow the new requirement, established in 1988 by the Apostolic Constitution *Pastor Bonus,* of a vote on "eminence of doctrine" from the CDF (though in this case the process had to be adapted, with papal approval, to meet the time constraints); and (3) that those involved were given

---

[3] Among the few articles so far written that discuss the *Positio* in any detail, see Jesús Castellano Cervera, "El doctorado de Santa Teresa del Niño Jesús," *Revista de Espiritualidad* 226-227 (1998): 81-85; Jean-Gabriel de l'Enfant-Jésus, "L'éminence de la doctrine de Thérèse dans la *Positio*," *Carmel* 87 (1998): 69-86.

so little time to develop the *Positio*.[4] Nevertheless, after describing the quick succession of final steps in the process, Ols declares that, despite the limitations of the *Positio*, it offers "material of the first order" for answering the question ("dubium") of whether to concede the title of doctor of the church to Thérèse.[5]

The "relator" then goes on to state very frankly some further concerns to be taken into account before naming Thérèse the first "doctor of the universal church" since Paul VI put such declarations on hold. First, he says, with a multiplication of doctors comes a certain "devaluation" of the title, as shown in the fact that apart from the traditional eight "great doctors," only ten others merit even an "obligatory memorial" in the Roman calendar.[6] Second, declaring Thérèse a doctor could open the door to various other requests. Ols notes that the process for Bernardine of Siena has been completed for some time and lacks only a papal declaration, that the CDF has already been asked for a vote regarding the "doctrinal eminence" of Veronica Giuliani, Gregory Narek, John Bosco, and Juan de Avila, and the Congregation for the Causes of Saints has dossiers on possible doctorates for Irenaeus of Lyons, Cyril and Methodius, Hildegard of Bingen, Gertrude of Helfta, Bridget of Sweden, Julian of Norwich, Lawrence Giustiniani, Antoninus of Florence, Thomas of Villa-

---

4   "Présentation du rapporteur," in *Positio*, iii.

5   Ibid., vi. According to Ols, time did not allow the provision of an *Informatio* in the traditional sense, which would have been a relatively brief synthesis of the information and arguments in the *Positio*; instead, in this case the voluminous background documentation furnished by the drafting committee became the *Informatio*. Likewise, the votes of the theological consultors for the CDF, given on 5 May 1997, would ordinarily have been bound together with the rest of the *Positio* before everything was handed on to the Congregation for the Causes of Saints. However, as we know, in order not to delay the process further these votes were printed separately later as a supplement (i.e., the folio-size gray volume).

6   Ibid., vi. Ols notes that one can respond to this "devaluation" of the title in at least two ways: (1) by arguing that the concessions should be stopped or slowed; or (2) by arguing *a fortiori* for further concessions ("If Anthony of Padua and Lawrence of Brindisi are doctors, why not X?").

nova, Ignatius Loyola, Vincent de Paul, Margaret-Mary Alacoque, and Louis-Marie Grignion de Montfort. The list could easily be extended by including numerous other saints, such as Ildefonsus of Toledo or Prosper of Aquitaine, who were venerated as doctors in local church calendars before the 19th-century standardization of the liturgy.[7] And third, there is the question of whether several centuries are needed to determine whether the impact of a candidate's "doctrine" will be deep and lasting; Ols mentions the case of Alphonsus Liguori, declared a doctor only 84 years after his death, at a time when his influence on moral theology was at its peak but who is now rarely consulted in theological discussions of moral issues.[8] Bearing all this in mind, the "relator" nonetheless says in closing that the material provided in the *Positio* should allow the theological consultors to reach a careful and mature decision regarding the suitability of Thérèse for the doctorate.

The "Présentation du rapporteur" is followed by the *Supplex libellus,* the formal petition for bestowing the doctorate on Thérèse, written at the behest of the superiors of the Congregation for the Causes of Saints,[9] and signed by the bishop and auxiliary of Bayeux-Lisieux (Pierre Pican and Guy Gaucher respectively) as well as the General and Postulator General of the Discalced Carmelites (Camilo Maccise and Simeón de la Sagrada Familia respectively). Dated 8 March 1997, the *Supplex libellus* is thus chronologically the first of the official documents included

---

[7] Ibid., vii-viii. This list of candidates currently "in process" seems to suggest what others have noted, namely, a certain desire to use the title as a way of duly acknowledging various countries, orders, rites, interest groups and so on. Gregory Narek, for example, is an important saint and mystical theologian in the Armenian Church, but virtually unknown in the Latin West.

[8] Ols notes that even recent papal documents on moral questions, such as *Veritatis Splendor,* rely more on Thomas Aquinas than Alphonsus Liguori. See ibid., viii.

[9] One presumes that the Congregation for the Causes of Saints was "acting on higher orders" in asking for this document. That is, the pope had presumably indicated that he wanted this cause to move forward, at least through the letter of 10 December 1996 from the Secretary of State requesting an update on the status of the process; see *Positio,* iv.

in the *Positio*, though it appears in second place. After reviewing the history of efforts toward Thérèse's doctorate,[10] this document enumerates some of the principal facets of her "eminent" doctrine, including her emphasis on the Fatherhood of God and Merciful Love, her recognition of the radical poverty of creatures, her approach to Christ as the revelation of God's love, her stress on the virtues of confidence and abandonment, her sense of the church, her approach to Mary (foreshadowing the Mariology of Vatican II), and her reinterpretation of eschatological realities.[11] These particular areas of her "doctrine" will be singled out repeatedly in the *Informatio* and the "vota" which follow. The authors also note her reliance on dependable doctrinal sources such as John of the Cross, *The Imitation of Christ*, and most importantly, Scripture itself; her enormous influence even beyond the bounds of Roman Catholicism, so pervasive that it is sometimes taken for granted; and her extensive use in magisterial documents, such as the *Catechism of the Catholic Church*. All of these points are spelled out in greater detail in the *Informatio* which follows, for which the *Supplex libellus* serves as a kind of preview. Perhaps most interesting, however, is that the authors recommend Thérèse for doctoral honors especially as a *woman*, a *contemplative*, and a *young person* and encourage the pope to declare Thérèse a doctor at the upcoming World Youth Day in Paris, a suggestion they presumably would not have made if they had reason to suspect it would be unwelcome.[12] As it happens, on 24 August 1997 at the World Youth Day Pope John Paul II did in fact announce his *intention* to bestow the title on Thérèse, and in his Apostolic Letter for Thérèse's doctorate, *Divini Amoris Scientia*, he stresses precisely

---

[10] *Supplex libellus*, in *Positio*, 2-4.

[11] Ibid., 5-8.

[12] Ibid., 13-14.

her importance as a doctor who is also a "woman," a "contemplative," and a "young person."[13]

The *Informatio*

By far the largest portion of the *Positio*, however, is the four-part *Informatio super dubio: An concedendus sit titulus Doctoris Ecclesiae Universalis S. Teresiae a Iesu Infante et Sacro Vultu, Moniale professae Ordinis Carmelitarum Discalceatorum* (hereafter *Informatio*).[14] As already noted, this document of 13 chapters and several appendices was produced on an extremely tight deadline by the committee of Thérèsian experts enumerated in the previous chapter of this book.

Part I of the *Informatio: The Data ("Le Donne")*

Part I of the *Informatio*, entitled "Le Donne," comprises six chapters of basic information on Thérèse's life, writings, and posthumous career.[15] Chapter 1 briefly outlines the history of Thérèse's move toward beatification and canonization, showing the unprecedented rapidity of her cause's progress through the complicated stages of the modern canonization process, and thereby clearly (though perhaps unnecessarily) demonstrating that the church has already acknowledged her extraordinary holiness of life, one

---

13 John Paul II, "Divini Amoris Scientia: Apostolic Letter." *Origins* 27 (20 November 1997): 395, no. 5. Hereafter this document will be cited by its Latin title and numbered section.

14 This formal title, in Latin, appears on page 15 of the *Positio*.

15 At the time the *Informatio* was being compiled, Joseph Baudry, O.C.D., the committee member who was writing the section on Thérèse's influence, contacted me for information on her impact in the United States and Canada. I also obtained a preliminary outline of the *Informatio*, indicating the authors of the various sections. From this outline it seems, for example, that the first chapter of the *Informatio* was written by Simeón de la Sagrada Familia (Fernandez), O.C.D., the second, third and fourth by Guy Gaucher, and the sixth by Jean Sleiman, O.C.D.

of the three requirements for the doctorate. Chapter 2 recalls the early efforts by Gustave Desbusquois and others to promote the doctorate of Thérèse—with a long extract from Desbusquois's presentation to the 1932 Thérèsian Congress[16]—and reviews the steps taken after 1970 to revive the cause. Chapter 3 offers a 30-page biography of Thérèse, from birth to death. Chapter 4 gives a brief description of her personality, stressing especially her intelligence, which is fairly characterized as "concrete," "aesthetic," "conceptual" (in the sense that, though not highly educated, she grasped ideas easily), "intuitive," and "devoted to truth," with the advantage of an "excellent memory"[17]; also mentioned are her youthful hypersensitivity, her joy and energy, her great capacity to love and be loved, and her wisdom. Chapter 5 provides a 21-page chronology listing the main events in Thérèse's short life and posthumous career; also included is a diagram of her family tree. Chapter 6, the longest chapter of Part I traces the vicissitudes of Thérèse's writings, from their composition, through their various early publications in versions heavily edited by Mother Agnès, down to the current critical editions of Thérèse's *Oeuvres complètes* (i.e., the eight-volume NEC and the one-volume "Totum").[18] This chapter frankly acknowledges some of the difficulties scholars have faced in trying to establish Thérèse's original wording, particularly in relation to the so-called "Last Conversations," where the only autographs are those of Thérèse's auditors, often written and rewritten years after the reported deathbed sayings. Nonetheless, while some textual details remain

---

[16] *Informatio*, in *Positio*, 48-50.

[17] Ibid., 89-90.

[18] The chapter ends with a list of 46 French language editions of *Histoire d'une Âme* and 55 translations, a number which has no doubt increased since the publication of the *Positio*. See *Informatio*, in *Positio*, 175-176. (Note that this list counts "American" as a different language than "English," and "Spanish" as a different language than "Latin American Spanish.")

in dispute, this chapter indicates that Thérèse's corpus of written works is now sufficiently well established to allow a confident judgment on her doctrinal eminence.[19]

Part II of the Informatio: St. Thérèse's Doctrine

The second section of the Informatio, entitled "La doctrine de Sainte Thérèse de l'Enfant Jésus," comprises three chapters on the content and sources of Thérèse's teaching, and thus moves closer to the heart of the question placed before the theological consultors. Chapter 7, presumably written by Conrad De Meester, provides a general overview ("aperçu général") of the Saint's doctrine, touching on both its "method" and content. De Meester notes, for example, that Thérèse's approach is not academic and technical but "existential" and personal. Her insights were gained moment by moment, through reflection on the Scriptures and attention to her own experience. As she puts it:

> But it is especially the Gospels that sustain me during my hours of prayer, for in them I find what is necessary for my poor little soul. I am constantly discovering new lights, hidden and mysterious meanings.
>
> I understand and I know from experience that: "The kingdom of God is within you." Jesus has no need of books or teachers to instruct souls; He, the Doctor of doctors, teaches without the noise of words. Never have I heard Him speak, but I feel that He is within me at each mo-

---

[19] In other words, it would have been premature to try to evaluate Thérèse's "eminence of doctrine" without a clear idea of which texts, and therefore which teachings, were actually hers. Otherwise it would be difficult to tell whether the "doctrine" in question came from Thérèse herself or from her redactors. With the "Nouvelle édition du centenaire," however, one can argue that we now have a more reliable edition of Thérèse's writings than we have for the works of many other "doctors of the universal church."

ment; He is guiding and inspiring me with what I must say and do. (Ms A 83v)[20]

At the same time, Thérèse repeatedly manifests an awareness of being called in some way to teach others, including her own sisters, the novices entrusted to her guidance, her missionary "brothers," and even those innumerable "little souls" for whom her account of the graces she had received would "do much good."

De Meester goes on to enumerate Thérèse's "doctrinal" contributions, including her insights regarding Christ and the Trinity, God's merciful love, the Church and the sacraments, Mary, the universal call to holiness through loving fidelity in "little things," and her "little way of confidence and love," which retrieves the New Testament understanding of what it means to be "poor in spirit" and to become "like a little child." Though brief, this chapter identifies many of the theological themes subsequently taken up in the votes of the theological consultors.

Chapter 8, entitled "The Theology of Thérèse of Lisieux" ("La théologie de Thérèse de Lisieux"), is one of the longest and most important chapters in the *Informatio*, but also (in this writer's opinion) one of the more problematic. Here the authorship is clear, since the bulk of the chapter is actually condensed—and typically quoted verbatim—from François-Marie Léthel's *L'amour de Jésus: La christologie de sainte Thérèse de l'Enfant-Jésus* (Paris: Desclée, 1997),[21] a book which in turn incorporates various texts

---

[20] *Story of a Soul: The Autobigraphy of Saint Thérèse of Lisieux*, trans. John Clarke, 3d ed. (Washington, DC: ICS Publications, 1996), 179. Note that the words "the Doctor of doctors" were inadvertently omitted in the ICS Publications edition.

[21] Thus pages 209-213 of the *Informatio* correspond with pages 17-22 of *L'amour de Jésus*, 214-216 with 53-56, 216-219 with 57-61, 219-223 with 67-74, 223-237 with 79-97, 238-239 with 29-30, 240-243 with 148-150, 243-251 with 125-144, 253-264 with 173-190, 264-279 with 211-250, 288-300 with 99-118, 305-308 with 74-78, and so on. As indicated earlier, Léthel is a professor of theology and a member of the pontifical faculty of the Teresianum in Rome.

Léthel has written over the past dozen years.[22] Given the time constraints within which the committee was working, this "recycling" is certainly understandable, but it means that the most extensive treatment of Thérèse's "doctrine" in the official documentation was originally written with other audiences and purposes in mind. Thus, as in the book from which this material was taken, Thérèse's whole message is here presented entirely from a Christological perspective. This is certainly a legitimate approach, especially given the prominence of Jesus in Thérèse's spirituality (she invokes his name more than 1600 times in her writings), but Léthel does not mention that other approaches are possible and have indeed shed light on aspects of Thérèse's thought that he tends to overlook.[23]

Léthel examines Thérèse's approach to Christ as member of the Trinity, creator, and savior, and her personal identification with the mysteries of his infancy and passion (as already evidenced in her religious subtitles "of the Child Jesus and the Holy Face"), noting how she seamlessly "joins crèche and cross." He does a masterful job of analyzing and interrelating Thérèse's many im-

---

[22] Compare pages 17 to 22 of Léthel's book *L'amour de Jésus*, for example, with the opening paragraphs of chapter 8 of the *Informatio*, and with his almost identically worded "L'amour de Jésus" in *Thérèse de l'Enfant-Jésus: Docteur de l'amour*, ed. Centre Notre-Dame de Vie (Venasque: Éditions du Carmel, 1990), 113 ff. Or compare his treatment of the "flesh" of Christ in *L'amour de Jésus*, 119-123, with the section on the same theme in *Théologie de l'amour de Jésus: Écrits sur la théologie des saints* (Venasque: Éditions du Carmel, 1996), 171-172, and its verbatim repetition on pages 239-240 of chapter 8 in the *Informatio*. In fact, many of the major subject headings in chapter 8 of the *Informatio*, and even much of the phraseology, is already found in Léthel's doctoral dissertation, *Connaître l'amour du Christ qui surpasse toute connaissance: La théologie des saints* (Venasque: Éditions du Carmel, 1989). Indeed, it seems fair to say that Léthel's publications over the last 12 years, though numerous, have tended to cover similar ground in similar terms, amplifying and refining his basic approach.

[23] Carmelite theologian Christopher O'Donnell, for example, uses ecclesiology, and particularly Thérèse's understanding of the communion of saints, as the organizing principle for his presentation and analysis of Thérèse's contribution. See Christopher O'Donnell, *Love in the Heart of the Church: The Mission of Thérèse of Lisieux* (Dublin: Veritas, 1997). Others begin with her doctrine of the "little way."

ages and symbols (e.g., fire and water, flower and lyre, blood and dew). He shows how the seemingly trite verses of her poems and plays often convey a very precise and profound theological (and Christological) content. A close and careful reader, Léthel is attentive to even the tiniest nuances of the saint's texts, drawing out their Mariological, sacramental, "theologal," and missiological implications.[24] Yet, at times, he seems somewhat too eager to find meaning everywhere and to immediately transmute Thérèse's limitations into virtues, as if she were incapable of an idle word or a banal sentiment. He argues, for example, that Thérèse's poor literary style should be regarded not as a failing but as a "manifestation of spiritual poverty, of Thérèse's evangelical poverty," and thus precisely the appropriate vehicle for her message of evangelical "littleness."[25] But surely even Thérèse herself recognized that her literary defects were not necessarily an asset in effectively communicating with potential readers; otherwise she would not have asked Mother Agnès to edit her works. One need not canonize her every grammatical and orthographic mistake.

More problematically, Léthel insists on interpreting Thérèse through the categories of what he calls the "theology of the saints," a particular methodological approach he has developed in a series of books and monographs over a number of years, starting with his doctoral dissertation, *Connaître l'amour du Christ qui surpasse toute connaissance*, which opens with his often-repeated programmatic claim: "All the saints are theologians, only the saints are theologians. Such is the most fundamental principle of this

---

[24] See *Informatio*, in *Positio*, 279-311. "Theologal" is the term used often in the *Positio* for what pertains to the three theological virtues of faith, hope, and love, which figure more centrally in Carmelite spiritual theology than the gifts and fruits of the Holy Spirit.

[25] *Informatio*, in *Positio*, 213. Léthel compares Thérèse in this respect with the New Testament writers, whose sometimes poor Greek literary style was the appropriate vehicle for the "good news" of salvation.

study."[26] Taking his cue from 1 John 4:7 ("Everyone who loves is born of God and knows God"), Léthel has often stated, in so many words, that "since theology is nothing other than this knowledge of God, one can say that everyone who loves is a theologian.... But love, charity, which is inseparably love of God and of neighbor, is the very essence of Christian sanctity," and thus the saints who have loved the most are *ipso facto* the greatest theologians. This allows him to place figures such as Joan of Arc, Charles Péguy, and Thérèse of Lisieux—and, later, Francis and Clare, Teresa of Avila and Catherine of Siena, Cardinal de Bérulle and Louis-Marie Grignion de Montfort, Gemma Galgani and Dina Bélanger —alongside such traditionally recognized theological giants as Augustine, Irenaeus, Anselm, and Aquinas, in developing a highly schematic theological framework.[27] Among his major foundational claims, repeated in chapter 8 of the *Informatio*, is that "in relation to the masculine heart of Jesus which is forever the heart of a Son and Spouse, the feminine heart is in a privileged position to receive and respond (*correspondre*) to that Love with all the love of a mother for her Son and of a [female] spouse ("épouse") for her [male] Spouse ("Époux")."[28] This is what he calls the "privilege of the feminine," though some men, "such as Francis of Assisi and John of the Cross," were also able to express "these two great harmonics, maternal and spousal, of communion with Jesus."[29] From this perspective, Léthel is able to link the saints as "theologians of the love of Christ" with Mary as Vir-

---

[26] Léthel, *Connaître l'amour du Christ* , 3. For a critique of Léthel's "theology of the saints," see Domenico Sorrentino, "Sulla 'Teologia dei santi' di Léthel," *Asprenas* 41 (1994): 389-404.

[27] See, for example, the numerous charts and diagrams in *Connaître l'amour du Christ* and *Théologie de l'amour de Jésus*, outlining the complex interrelationship he sees between various theological principles and themes.

[28] See chapter 8 of the *Informatio*, in the *Positio*, 214.

[29] Ibid.

gin-Mother and the one who knew and loved Christ most perfectly, and with the church as "virgin-spouse" and "feminine
personification of humanity."[30] To this schema he likewise adds
two other "essential chords (*cordes*)"[31] of the human heart, namely,
filial love and fraternal love. Just as Jesus came as Son of the heavenly Father and brother to all in need, so human beings, transformed in his likeness, share a filial love toward God and a sis-
terly and brotherly love toward each other.[32] Much of chapter 8
of the *Informatio*, then, becomes an effort to show how Thérèse,
in responding to the love of Christ, exhibited these fundamental
"four chords" (of *spousal*, *maternal*, *filial*, and *fraternal* love) and
articulated them in her writings.[33] Indeed, for Léthel this is tantamount to showing that she is truly an outstanding "theologian"
in his sense.

Léthel's intriguing theological program, of which we have
described only a small part, deserves a full-scale evaluation in its
own right. Here, however, we must limit ourselves to a few observations. First, while making good use of certain scriptural insights and the church's dogmatic tradition, Léthel also invokes a
number of fundamental claims that seem arguable at best. Thus,
his list of "four essential chords" of the human heart seems to
absolutize certain culturally and historically conditioned kinship
relations, while deemphasizing other relationships with an equal
biblical pedigree, e.g., teacher/learner, master/servant, member of
the household, and most especially, friend, as in "I no longer call

---

[30] Ibid.

[31] Note that the word *corde* in French can mean both a musical chord or note and also a
string on a musical instrument such as a lyre, one of Thérèse's favorite symbols. I have
translated it differently according to the context.

[32] Ibid., 232.

[33] Ibid., 293-300.

you servants but friends" (cf. John 15:12-15).[34] Again, his ideas of what constitute the authentically "masculine" and the "feminine" are largely asserted rather than defended, without any reference to contemporary psychology, social theory, or feminist critiques. Many on this side of the Atlantic would surely wonder, for example, if his stress on the feminine "sacerdotal" dimension of Thérèse's self-sacrificing love is in part simply an effort to rationalize women's exclusion from the ordained priesthood and from various positions of authority within the church. In fact, Léthel makes little attempt to respond to any "hermeneutics of suspicion" except to insist flatly that saints such as Thérèse, Clare, and Catherine of Siena are *beyond* all suspicion, "precisely because their hearts have been purified and because their 'strings' (*cordes*) have been 'retuned' (*réaccordées*)."[35] But surely holiness alone is no guarantee of the adequacy of one's understanding of gender roles or other social issues, nor does it prevent saints from assimilating to some degree the limitations of their own cultural and historical context.

A second observation follows closely on the first, namely, that Léthel's theological method, while creatively drawing upon the contributions of saints often neglected by mainstream theology, nevertheless seems somehow insular, static and *a priori*, without an adequate foundation in the concrete historical process.[36]

---

[34] If, for example, cultures are possible (or actually exist) where individuals may have multiple spouses, or where marriage is regarded more as a contractual agreement between two families or tribes than as a love relationship between two individuals, or where children adopt a filial attitude toward *many* paternal and maternal figures of the tribe rather than to a single mother and father, can Léthel reasonably absolutize his arguably late modern European conception of filial, spousal, and maternal relationships as "essential" to the human person?

[35] Note again that the word *cordes* in French can be translated to refer both to the "strings" of a musical instrument (as here) or musical "chords" (as above).

[36] For example, he seems to want to demonstrate the perpetual *physical* virginity of Jesus and Mary on the basis of a particular view of virginity's *theological* significance; see *Informatio* in the *Positio*, 295. We are not here denying Mary's "virginitas in partu," but simply questioning the way in which Léthel tries to establish empirical facts from his distinctive theological principles.

No doubt he would respond that his approach is thoroughly *incarnational* and thus historically grounded, inasmuch as it focuses on God's entry into our concrete human situation, assuming our very flesh and blood and sharing in our particular lived experiences in the person of Jesus. Still, Léthel does not seriously engage other current theological methods and positions and seems strangely out of step with most contemporary authors in singling out a few key saints, including Thérèse, and treating them (along with Jesus himself) almost as timeless contemporaries, in abstraction from the larger historical and cultural settings out of which they came (and which may have played as strong a role as their personal relationship with God in shaping some of their convictions). This even leads him at times to an apparent circularity. He seems, for example, to want to use the personal convictions of Thérèse and other saints as a kind of "mystical proof" of such traditional doctrines as that Jesus enjoyed the full beatific vision from the first moment of his conception, and even during his passion (i.e., because these theologian-saints were convinced that he did), while at the same time appearing to concede that this was something the saints of earlier eras simply *took for granted* in order to make sense of their conviction that Christ had lived, suffered, and died specifically *for them.* Here again, the fact that at a particular moment in history certain saints profited from the unquestioning acceptance of the Christological assumptions of their time scarcely proves that no other Christological viewpoints are valid or spiritually fruitful today.[37]

Third, though Léthel gives an admirable exposition of Thérèse's profound love of Christ, not all of it appears equally appropriate to the question at hand. To spend so much time, as he

---

[37] See *Informatio,* in the *Positio,* 256. My point is that there may be other ways today of grounding the crucial claim that every moment of Jesus' earthly life and death was somehow intended "for us," individually and personally as well as collectively.

does, underscoring the similarities between Thérèse and certain other saints such as Joan of Arc, Clare, and Louis-Marie Grignion de Montfort, seems relevant only if one already views the latter as "theologians" and thus accepts Léthel's equation of sanctity with authentic Christian "theology"; many of the theological consultors clearly do not, as we shall see. In fact, from Léthel's premises one might try to argue that *any* great saint, being thus a great "theologian," is thereby qualified to be named a "doctor of the church," a consequence most of those involved in the process want to avoid as a dangerous "devaluation" of the title.

In short, although Léthel's "theology of the saints" offers a helpful framework for organizing the presentation of Thérèse's "doctrine," wedding the two so closely together in the *Informatio* poses the risk of confusing a judgment on Thérèse's "doctrinal eminence" with a judgment on Léthel's particular methodology, a methodology which has yet to receive wide discussion or acceptance within the larger theological community. As a matter of fact, some of the consultors make a point of mentioning that their positive assessment of Thérèse's doctorate should not necessarily be interpreted as a wholesale endorsement of Léthel's views.

Chapter 9, the final chapter of Part II of the *Informatio* examines Thérèse's literary sources.[38] Of course, Thérèse was not an academician carefully footnoting her references, and what she learned through reading she tended to make distinctively her own. Therefore it is not easy to trace all her literary influences. Nevertheless, after listing over 50 works to which she was exposed (to some degree or another), this chapter discusses the ones that clearly left the greatest mark, including the catechism of her childhood, *The Imitation of Christ*, Abbè Arminjon's *Fin du monde*

---

[38] Information I received indicates that Jean Sleiman is also the author of this chapter.

présent et mystères de la vie future, Dom Guéranger's *The Liturgical Year*, several works by and about St. Teresa of Avila, the *Spiritual Canticle* and *Living Flame of Love* of St. John of the Cross, and various liturgical texts (e.g., those of the Breviary).

But as this chapter notes, more important for Thérèse than all the rest was the Bible itself. We have already noted her affirmation in *Story of a Soul* that "it is especially the *Gospels* that sustain me.... I am constantly discovering in them new lights, hidden and mysterious meanings" (Ms A 83v).[39] And to Père Roulland, her missionary "brother," she writes:

> At times, when I am reading certain spiritual trea-
> tises in which perfection is shown through a thousand
> obstacles, surrounded by a crowd of illusions, my poor
> little mind quickly tires; I close the learned book that is
> breaking my head and drying up my heart, and I take up
> Holy Scripture. Then all seems luminous to me; a single
> word uncovers for my soul infinite horizons, perfection
> seems simple to me, I see it is sufficient to recognize one's
> nothingness and to abandon oneself as a child into God's
> arms. Leaving to great souls, to great minds the beauti-
> ful books I cannot understand, much less put into prac-
> tice, I rejoice at being little since children alone and
> those who resemble them will be admitted to the heav-
> enly banquet. (LT 226)[40]

In fact, *Story of a Soul* begins with a meditation on two biblical texts (on Mark 3:13 and Romans 9:15-16), and is replete with biblical references; virtually every important new insight or new

---

[39] *Story of a Soul*, 179. It is clear from the context that Thérèse is not speaking here of extraordinary "private revelations" or of occult messages divined from the texts, but rather of a deeper personal penetration into what has already been given to the church in God's word.

[40] Quoted from Thérèse, *General Correspondence*, trans. John Clarke, 2 vols. (Washington, DC: ICS Publications, 1982-1988), 2: 1093-1094.

stage in her adult life—including the discoveries of her "little way" and of her vocation to be "love in the heart of the church," as well as her profound reflections on the "Suffering Servant" and the meaning of fraternal charity—arises out of prayerful reflection on her own experience in the light of the words of Scripture. In an era when the reading of Scripture was not strongly encouraged among the Catholic faithful, she even wished she could "have studied Hebrew and Greek to be able to read the word of God in the same human language in which God deigned to express it."[41] This chapter of the *Informatio*, then, is evidently meant to show that Thérèse amply fulfilled one of the six requirements specified by the CDF for a positive judgment on "doctrinal eminence," namely, that the candidate's doctrine be drawn "from the pure sources of the Word of God, Tradition, and the Magisterium of the Church."[42]

Part III of the Informatio: *Thérèse's Influence and Relevance*

As its title suggests, the three chapters of the third major section of the *Informatio*, "Le rayonnement et l'actualité de Sainte Thérèse de l'Enfant-Jésus et de la Sainte-Face," describe the influence and contemporary relevance of Thérèse and her message. Chapter 10 deals with the recognition given to Thérèse's doctrine by the church's magisterium, through papal decrees, interventions at the Second Vatican Council, various synodal statements, liturgical texts (of both the Latin and Eastern rites), the *Catechism of the Catholic Church*, and so on. We have already noted that virtually all the popes since Pius X have demonstrated a profound appreciation for Thérèse's message and proposed her to the faithful

---

[41] Thérèse, *Her Last Conversations*, trans. John Clarke (Washington, DC: ICS Publications, 1977), 132 (4 August 1897, no. 5).

[42] As noted in the preceding chapter, the one-page document in Italian from the CDF is entitled "Norme di procedure e criteri dottrinali per il giudizio circa la 'eminens doctrina' dei santi proposti come 'Dottori della Chiesa'," and has not yet been formally published.

as a reliable guide; their numerous references to her are again sum-marized here.[43]

Chapter 11, the longest in the *Informatio*, presents a host of persons and institutions that have been strongly influenced by Thérèse's example and teaching.[44] The categories are overlapping, and the lists are by no means exhaustive. Mentioned as devotees of Thérèse recognized by the church for their holiness of life are three then-canonized saints (Raphael Kalinowski, Maximilian Kolbe, Teresa of the Andes), several "blesseds" (including Titus Brandsma, Elizabeth of the Trinity, and both Faustina Kowalska and Edith Stein, who have since been canonized), and more than a dozen "venerables" and "servants of God" (including some who have since been beatified).[45] Also noted are tributes to Thérèse from 20 cardinals and bishops (e.g., Yves Congar, Jean Daniélou, Jean-Marie Lustiger, Carlo M. Martini, Joseph Ratzinger, Christoph Schönborn), 20 major spiritual authors or spiritual figures (e.g., Dom Marmion, Dorothy Day, Mother Teresa), 23 theologians (e.g., Réginald Garrigou-Lagrange, Hans Urs von Balthasar, Louis Bouyer, René Laurentin), 6 philosophers (e.g., Henri Bergson, Maurice Blondel, Jacques Maritain, Jean Guitton), 21 writers (e.g., Paul Claudel, François Mauriac, Georges Bernanos, Thomas Merton), 5 political figures, and numerous artists from various fields (e.g., Édith Piaf, John Tavener, Michael Lonsdale, Henri Ghéon).[46] This chapter also mentions some 1600 churches and chapels (including 8 basilicas and 10 cathedrals)

---

[43] The only exception is John Paul I, who did not live long enough to speak of Thérèse in his capacity as pope. However, he writes of her appreciatively in *Illustrissimi*, published while he was still Patriarch of Venice; see Albino Luciani, *Illustrissimi: Letters from Pope John Paul I*, trans. William Weaver (Boston: Little, Brown and Co., 1978), 146-152.

[44] Since Joseph Baudry, O.C.D., sent out appeals for information to include in this chap-ter, he was clearly involved in its composition.

[45] See *Informatio* in the *Positio*, 387-406.

[46] Ibid., 406-484.

dedicated to the saint,[47] as well as scores of journals, reviews, organizations, congresses, spiritual centers, internet sites, radio and television programs, videos and CDs, all aimed at promoting the message of St. Thérèse.[48] But still more impressive is the list of more than 70 religious congregations, secular institutes, and new ecclesial movements that look to Thérèse of Lisieux as their special patron or explicitly incorporate her "doctrine," in one way or another, as part of their charism.[49] This chapter ends with the itinerary of Thérèse's relics in 1994-1996 (which generated a popular response virtually unprecedented in modern Europe), and a brief description of devotion to the saint and her message among the Orthodox, the Anglicans, and even Muslims and those of other faiths.[50] The data here leave little doubt about the vast influence of Thérèse not only as a holy woman but also as a teacher and guide.

Chapter 12 discusses Thérèse's relevance for today's church and world ("Actualité de la doctrine de Sainte Thérèse de Lisieux pour l'église et le monde d'aujourd'hui"). The likely author here is the current General of the Discalced Carmelites—Camilo Maccise, O.C.D., of the Mexican province—since the text emphasizes some of his favorite themes (e.g., the "new evangelization") and refers, as he often does, to the pope's statements to the Latin American Church.[51] Once again Thérèse's importance as

---

[47] Ibid., 530-531.

[48] Ibid., 484-496, 519-528.

[49] Ibid., 496-519.

[50] Ibid, 543-554. As the *Informatio* points out, some Orthodox authors rank her among the church's greatest saints, comparing her favorably with the saints of the East. Devotion to Thérèse is also particularly strong among Muslim women of Cairo, Egypt, where there is a shrine in the saint's honor.

[51] Alert readers will notice, for example, similarities between this chapter and Camilo Maccise, "Influence de sainte Thérèse sur la vie spirituelle du monde moderne," in *Une sainte pour le troisième millénaire: Actes du colloque internationale pour le centenaire de la mort de sainte Thérèse de l'Enfant-Jésus de la Saint-Face, Lisieux 30 septembre-4 octobre 1996* (Venasque: Éditions du Carmel, 1997), 59-80. Compare also Camilo Maccise, "Attualità e universalità della dottrina di Teresa di Liseux," in *La Scienza dell' Amore: Teresa di Lisieux*, ed. Guido Mazzotta (Rome: Urbaniana University Press, 1999), 61-84.

a *woman*, a *young person*, and a *contemplative* are stressed.[52] Quoting *Vita Consecrata*, this chapter argues that Thérèse brings a much needed complement of feminine intelligence to theological reflection, and encourages, in the words of John Paul II, "a culture of equality between men and women."[53] Thérèse is also praised for speaking with the enthusiasm of youth, and for showing young people of today how to channel their idealism into a total self-gift, in the midst of the ordinary circumstances of life. She is said to offer a timely understanding of the consecrated life, rooted in spiritual realism about the gradual (and often dark and painful) process of growth in fraternal charity and community living. Her insight into the apostolic fruitfulness of the contemplative life continues to be extremely influential and important.

> She invites us to pass from consideration of a judging God to consideration of a paternal-maternal God, from mistrust to simple and loving confidence which abandons itself to Him, from seeking perfection to seeking communion with God, from complication to simplicity, from laws which enslave to the concrete and effective law of love which liberates, from immaturity to maturity, from exterior asceticism to evangelical abnegation, from merits to "empty hands," from purely spiritual considerations to the Word of God, from complicated prayer to simple contemplative regard, from an inaccessible Mary to a Mary very near [to us], such as the Gospels describe.[54]

---

[52] Recall that Camilo Maccise was also one of the authors of the *Supplex libellus*, where these same three aspects were singled out; see *Positio*, 13.

[53] Ibid., 558. The source of the papal quotation is not given, though the context suggests it is from *Vita Consecrata*.

[54] Ibid., 569-570.

Thérèse turns Christian spirituality back to fundamental gospel principles, according to this chapter, while at the same time providing an important voice in the ongoing dialogue with other churches and religions, as well as with the world of unbelief, as shown by the remarkable way her story and message has crossed traditional religious, national, and cultural boundaries. Her influence shows no signs of diminishing. For all these reasons, says the author, her "doctrine" remains highly relevant.

Part IV of the Informatio: *Conclusion*

Pulling together the threads from the previous 12 chapters and the *Supplex libellus,* then, the 13th and concluding chapter of the *Informatio* succinctly summarizes the case for a positive judgment on Thérèse's "eminence of doctrine." The presumed author, Jesús Castellano Cervera, O.C.D.,[55] first briefly reviews the long evolution of the title "doctor of the church" and its requirements, noting, as we have seen, how the criteria have gradually broadened to include not only those who have had a major impact on theology in general, but also some who have made an important contribution to a *specific field* of Christian life and mores.[56] He then argues that Thérèse adequately meets each of the six fundamental, and obviously overlapping, "norms and criteria" for evaluating doctrinal eminence, formulated by the CDF and approved by John Paul II on 10 November 1996.[57] First, Thérèse amply displays a particular "charism of wisdom, the fruit of the Holy

---

[55] Jesús Castellano Cervera, O.C.D., is president and professor of the Teresianum in Rome, as well as a consultor for the Congregation for the Doctrine of the Faith. This concluding chapter of the *Informatio* closely follows what he has written elsewhere on the question of "doctrinal eminence" and Thérèse's doctorate.

[56] See *Informatio* in the *Positio,* 589.

[57] These are the "Procedural Norms and Doctrinal Criteria for the Judgment Concerning the 'Eminence of Doctrine' of Saints Proposed as 'Doctors of the Church'" (*Norme di procedura e criteri dottrinali per il giudizio circa la "eminens doctrina" dei santi proposti come "Dottori della Chiesa"*), mentioned briefly in the previous chapter of this work.

Spirit"[58]; indeed, her writings clearly reveal her conviction that she had received—not from books but from the One who "reveals his secrets to the lowly"—a profound insight into God's merciful love and a teaching to communicate to others, one which has been enthusiastically embraced by countless believers since her death. Second, Thérèse arguably "excels" (*eminet*) by the "quality of her writing, the height and profundity of her doctrine, the mature sapiential synthesis achieved, and effective positive influence exercised."[59] Though not a professional author or systematic theologian, her texts reveal in simple language a deeply synthetic and practical grasp of Christian doctrine, and her "lived theology," which has "produced innumerable fruits of sanctity and apostolate," is rooted in the "fundamental mysteries of our faith, from the Trinity to the Eucharist, from creation to the last things, from love for Christ to the discovery of her vocation at the heart of the church."[60] The third requirement is that doctors be "authentic masters and witnesses of Catholic doctrine and Christian life" whose writings shed particular light "on the confession and defense of the Catholic faith, on the preaching of the Gospel, on the understanding of worship and the spiritual life, or on a specific domain of Catholic doctrine"; Castellano recalls Thérèse's doctrinal contribution to a renewed scripturally based understand-

---

[58] See *Informatio* in the *Positio*, 589-593. The first criterion, in Italian, reads: "I giudizio circa l'eminente dottrina si configura come un *discernimento ecclesiale circa l'esistenza di un particolare carisma di sapienza* per il bene della Chiesa, conferito dallo Spirito Santo ai Santi proposti come candidati al titolo di Dottore, comprovato e suffragato dall'influsso benefico che i loro scritti e la loro dottrina hanno esercitato nel Popolo di Dio (Cfr. *Lumen gentium* n. 12)." Italics are in the original text.

[59] The second criterion, in Italian, reads: "A questo scopo si deve dimostrare che l'insegnamento dei Santi, candidati al titolo di Dottore, non solo è pienamente conforme con la fede e la vita cristiana, *ma eccelle ('eminet') per la qualità degli scritti, per la altezza e la profondità della dottrina, per la matura sintesi sapienziale raggiunta, per l'effetivo l'influsso positivo esercitato,* in maniera che essi possano essere riconisciuti come testimoni qualificati della vivente tradizione della Chiesa (Cfr. *Dei Verbum* n. 8)." Italics are in the original text.

[60] See *Informatio* in the *Positio*, 594-595.

110

ing of Mary, the church, the "last things," and—most importantly—God as Father and Merciful Love, the radical poverty of
creatures, Christ as the revelation of God's merciful love, and the
centrality of confidence and abandonment in the spiritual life.[61]

The fourth condition is that a candidate's doctrine should
be drawn "from the pure sources of the word of God, Tradition,
and the Magisterium of the church,"[62] a requirement amply
fulfilled by Thérèse, who nourished herself on the catechism, *The
Imitation of Christ,* and the writings of Teresa and John of the
Cross, but whose primary source was the Scriptures. Moreover, it
can scarcely be denied that, in the words of the fifth criterion,
Thérèse's works enjoy a "wide diffusion, positive reception, and
particular beneficial influence among the people of God"
confirmed by magisterial use,[63] since her *Story of a Soul* is one of
the best-known and most influential Catholic texts of modern
times, frequently cited by the popes and the *Catechism of the Catholic Church.* And even though only a century has elapsed since her
death, there is every reason to expect that Thérèse's doctrine will

---

[61] Ibid., 596-597. The third criterion, in Italian, reads: "Occorre quindi che i futuri Dottori della Chiesa siano autentici *maestri e testimoni della dottrina cattolica e della vita cristiana,* e che i loro scritti apportino particolari luci nella confessione e difesa della fede cattolica, nella predicazione del Vangelo, nella comprensione del culto e della vita spirituale, o in un campo specifico della dottrina cattolica." Italics are in the original text.

[62] The fourth criterion, in Italian, reads: Ció sarà piú evidente se si illustrerà che la loro dottrina è attinta *alle pure sorgenti della Parola di Dio, della Tradizione e del magistero della Chiesa, e ne constiuisce un incisivo approfondimento sapienziale,* frutto dello Spirito Santo, il quale fa progredire la comprensione delle realtà e della parole trasmesse, sia con la predicazione della verità revelata, sia mediante la riflessione teologica, sia attraverso lo studio e la contemplazione, sia anche per messo di una profonda esperienza delle stesse realtà soprannaturali (Cfr. *Dei Verbum* n. 8)." Italics are in the original text.

[63] The fifth criterion, in Italian, reads: "E' inoltre conveniente comprovare che gli scritti dei candidati al titolo di Dottore hanno avuta *un'ampia diffusione, una "recezione" positiva e un particolare influsso benefico nel Populo di Dio,* confermato eventualmente dall'uso che della loro dottrina ha fatto il Magistero della Chiesa e dalla particolare attenzione revolta ad essi da parte della teologia cattolica nello studio e illustrazione dei misteri della fede e della vita cristiana. Tale influsso deve avere un *carattere di universalità* in modo che possa interessare tutta la Chiesa." Italics are in the original text.

continue to display the "durability" and "relevance"[64] required by the sixth criterion; if anything, with the appearance of critical editions of her writings and more careful presentations of her thought, her influence among the young, among missionaries, among contemplatives, among Catholics in general and people of other denominations and faiths, only seems to be growing. Castellano thus concludes that Thérèse fulfills the criteria for "eminence of doctrine," and he repeats the claim of the *Supplex libellus*, namely, that bestowing the title upon her would have special significance in recognizing as a doctor someone who was at once a *woman*, a *contemplative*, and a *young person*.[65]

Postulatory Letters and Bibliography

Appended to the *Informatio* is a select bibliography of over 1600 works on Thérèse and her message, along with a collection of letters from 43 episcopal conferences, 6 cardinals, 11 bishops, 6 priests, 23 religious congregations and their members, and 12 lay groups and individuals, all formally petitioning the doctorate for St. Thérèse. Clearly, none of these lists is meant to be exhaustive. Other episcopal requests are known to have been made.[66] And the bibliography notes that, as of the first months of 1997, an average of five or more editions of Thérèse's writings were being

---

[64] The sixth criterion, in Italian, reads: "L'esame della dottrina del candidato deve portare a concludere che essa è eminente in quanto possiede *un messaggio sicuro e durevole*, è capace di contribuire a confermare e approfondire il deposito della fede, illuminando anche nuove prospettive di dottrina e di vita. In questo modo si potrà meglio illustrare *la particolare incidenza ed attualità della eminente dottrina* del candidato a Dottore, come persona a cui si riconosce un particolare carisma dottrinale, dono dello Spirito Santo alla sua Chiesa, il quale la guida verso tutta intera la verità e a tale scopo la provvede in ogni tempo di doni gerarchici e carismatici (Cfr. *Lumen Gentium* n. 4)." Italics are in the original text.

[65] See *Informatio* in the *Positio*, 603.

[66] See Castellano, "El doctorado de Santa Teresa del Niño Jesús," 84-85.

published each year, along with 60 to 70 articles and books about her.[67] These appendices are evidently intended as further evidence of the wide diffusion of Thérèse's message, and the enthusiastic reception it has received among both the hierarchy and the ordinary faithful.[68]

The Votes of the Theological Experts

The committee assigned to draw up the *Informatio* completed the bulk of its work during a week-long meeting in Venasque, France, from April 2 to 8, 1997.[69] Meanwhile, as part of the same canonical process, the two dicasteries involved sought opinions on Thérèse's candidacy from seven theological experts: five chosen by the Congregation for the Doctrine of the Faith, and two chosen by the Congregation for the Causes of Saints. Their responses, from pages 825 to 920, comprise the last major section of the large red bound volume of the *Positio*.

These experts were evidently given a copy of the "Procedural Norms and Doctrinal Criteria" to use as a guide, but because of pressing deadlines did not have an opportunity to read the massive *Informatio*; in fact, only one of them even refers to it.[70]

---

[67] See *Informatio* in the *Positio*, 668.

[68] At the end of the printed version of the *Positio* is an "iconographic appendix" compiled by the Carmel of Lisieux, with 16 pages of images, most of them representing Thérèse in a teaching pose, often holding a book, with her hand upraised. They are meant to illustrate the popular acknowledgment of Thérèse as teacher. It is not clear at what point this appendix appeared among the materials for the cause. Possibly it was submitted with the *Informatio*.

[69] See *Positio*, iv, and Castellano, "El doctorado de Santa Teresa del Niño Jesús," 84-85.

[70] Only the first CDF theologian mentions the *Positio*, simply noting that it "probably" includes "more than I would be able to say on the subject" of Thérèse's doctrinal eminence. On the other hand, the vote of the second CDF theologian is dated "9 April 1997" (that is, only one day after the committee finished work on its 800-page *Informatio*) and that of the third CDF theologian is dated even earlier, namely, "21 March 1997," so obviously neither of them had a copy of the *Informatio* committee's work in hand.

As a result, these experts develop their responses to the "dubium" regarding Thérèse's candidacy more or less independently, while often repeating the same points made in the *Informatio* or in the other "vota."

These seven opinions, unfortunately, are not signed, but in most cases the authorship can be ascertained from other evidence. For example, without naming them, Jesús Castellano has elsewhere helpfully described the five CDF experts, in order, as an "archbishop from Central Europe," a "religious woman (*religiosa*) attached to a Pontifical University of Rome," and three others belonging to "a Spirituality Institute of a Roman University"; he also indicates that the two experts for the Congregation for the Causes of Saints are "theologians attached to two academic European academic centers, one Swiss and the other Spanish."[71] Likewise, in the subsequent round of voting by the much larger body of "consultors" for each congregation, several consultors refer back to the original experts by name in discussing their opinions.

*Vote of the First Theologian for the Congregation
for the Doctrine of the Faith*

Piecing together the available clues, then, one can confidently identify the CDF's "first theologian" as Christoph Cardinal Schönborn, O.P., the archbishop of Vienna and director of François-Marie Léthel's dissertation at Fribourg. Here he modestly describes himself as a non-expert on Thérèse and an "elderly professor of theology and pastor." His interest, he says, is simply in whether "the greatest saint of modern times" has "an eminent *doctrinal* contribution, the *sine qua non* in order to be proclaimed a 'doctor of the church'," for even if one agrees with

---

[71] Castellano, "El doctorado de Santa Teresa del Niño Jesús," 85.

Léthel that "all saints are theologians," not all saints are *doctors*.[72]

Schönborn limits himself to a consideration of the first two and the last of the six "criteria" for doctrinal eminence.[73] In relation to the first criterion, he cites several passages from her writings indicating that Thérèse was well aware of having received "a doctrine, and a mission to transmit it universally."[74] Moreover, her "charism of wisdom" has "changed the climate" of the church, away from the vestiges of Jansenism still prevalent at the end of the 19th century, and back to the "Mystery of a God who is Love."[75]

Regarding the second criterion, requiring a "mature sapiential synthesis" expressed in writings notable for the "height and profundity of their doctrine," Schönborn enumerates some of the great themes around which her message is structured: the three decisive existential experiences of her "Christmas grace," her response to an image of Christ on the cross, and the conversion of Pranzini; her "theocentrism" toward a God of Merciful Love; her Christocentrism in a Trinitarian context; her insights into both the poverty and the infinite desires of creatures; her "little way," which focuses on living in faith, hope, and love, and retrieves the ancient understanding of "divinization"; her "ecclesiology of mercy," which calls the church both to humility and mission; and her recognition of a "universal call to holiness" which paved the way for the teaching of Vatican II.[76] In all of these ar-

---

[72] *Positio,* 825-826. Note, however, that Schönborn's comments on Thérèse often echo those of Léthel.

[73] For the fourth criterion, regarding sources, Schönborn is content simply to quote the canonization homily of Pius XI, where the latter speaks of Thérèse's reliance on the *Imitation,* John of the Cross, Teresa of Avila, and the Scriptures; see ibid., 842.

[74] Ibid., 828.

[75] Ibid., 829.

[76] Ibid., 830-841. This list, in fact, offers the most decisive evidence identifying Schönborn as the first CDF "expert," since the ninth "votum" of the later CDF consultors repeats this list and ascribes it to "the vote of His Excellency Mons. Schönborn." See *Positio* supplement, 32.

eas, he suggests, Thérèse has made important contributions with doctrinal implications.

Finally, with respect to the sixth criterion, requiring a "durable" and "relevant" doctrine, Schönborn notes that "Thérèse is universal," and that her message has a universal appeal. Countless people have found in her a sure spiritual guide. Schönborn favors her doctorate because, he says, he is convinced that Thérèse is a "gift of Merciful Love to our times, drawing us after her toward true happiness and true life."[77]

Vote of the Second Theologian for the Congregation for the Doctrine of the Faith

Sr. Françoise Thérèse Lamoureux, O.P., whom the later consultors likewise refer to by name,[78] is the second CDF theologian, that is, author of the second "votum." Vice-rector of the Angelicum, she certainly fits Castellano's description as a "religious woman (religiosa) attached to a Pontifical University of Rome." She is responsible for several recent articles on the saint of Lisieux.[79] Here she situates "Thérèse's particular charism of wisdom for the good of the church," as required by the first criterion for doctrinal eminence, "in her 'little way,' culminating in her 'Act of Oblation to Merciful Love'." Thus she describes "how Thérèse discovered her little way, its nature, and the motives which urge

---

[77] See Positio, 845. Here Schönborn is alluding to Thérèse's reflections, toward the end of Manuscript C, on the verse from the Song of Songs, "Draw me, we shall run" (Song 1:3). Thérèse observes that those captivated by God cannot help but draw others in their train (Ms C 34r-36v). The words "Merciful Love" are often capitalized in the Theresian literature when used as a name of God.

[78] See Positio supplement, 33.

[79] See Françoise Thérèse Lamoureaux, "L'antigiansenismo di Teresa di Lisieux," Rivista di scienze dell'educazione 34 (1996): 257-264; "Teresa di Lisieux e l'amore del prossimo," Rivista di vita spirituale 50 (1996): 493-510.

us to make her doctrine our own," namely, that it is "sure" and "easy" (*facile*), in the same sense that the Lord's yoke is "easy."[80] Lamoureux's presentation is fairly conventional and straightforward. She recalls how Thérèse discovered the "little way" by herself, in texts of the Old Testament included in Céline's copybook. She also demonstrates its complete accord with the gospel theme of "spiritual childhood" as presented, for example, in Matthew 18:3 ("Unless you turn and become like children, you will never enter the kingdom of heaven"), a passage which, surprisingly, Thérèse never directly quotes. Lamoureaux discusses the role of confidence and abandonment in Thérèse's understanding of the "little way," noting that this "abandonment" is not quietism but an "achieved repose," the "delicious fruit" of an active, self-sacrificing love.[81] Perhaps most useful in this "votum" is Lamoureux's comparison of Thérèse and Aquinas, where she mentions that both approach the death of Christ primarily in terms of love rather than justice. Lamoureux concludes by insisting that "Thérèse of Lisieux has become Thérèse of the whole world" because her "spiritual and theological doctrine has nourished and nourishes millions of people," from popes to the humblest believers: young and old, religious and lay, those from every culture and social class.[82] In effect, she is arguing that, besides possessing a "notable charism of wisdom," Thérèse also fulfills the requirements of having a wide impact and relevance.

---

[80] See *Positio*, 848, 869-872.

[81] Here she is alluding to PN 52, i.e., Thérèse's poem, "Abandonment Is the Sweet Fruit of Love," found in *The Poetry of Saint Thérèse of Lisieux*, trans. Donald Kinney (Washington, DC: ICS Publications, 1996), 206-208, 317-319. Its title in French is "L'abandon est le fruit délicieux de L'amour."

[82] Ibid., 872-873. She quotes Cardinal Poupard's strong recommendation, at the 1990 Synod on Priestly Formation, that Thérèse's message be given an important place in the training of future clergy.

*Vote of the Third Theologian for the Congregation
for the Doctrine of the Faith*

Charles A. Bernard, S.J., the well-known spiritual theologian who until recently taught at the Gregorianum, is the third theological expert consulted by the CDF.[83] After a brief cover letter affirming that Thérèse fulfilled, one by one, criteria for doctrinal eminence, he devotes the bulk of his "votum" to a consideration of the modern character of Thérèse's message. Her young, fresh, spontaneous, and straightforward personality seem strikingly contemporary, and she anticipated 20th-century developments, for example, in her appreciation of John of the Cross, who was not widely read in her time.[84] She appeals to people of today because of her focus on the essentials rather than the extraordinary, her understanding of the importance of desire, and her generous turn toward others in the midst of her own spiritual darkness.[85] Her love of Scripture, her realism about the world, her liberty of spirit and warm familiarity with God, the expansion of her heart within the confines of the cloister to the dimensions of the whole world, her compassion for sinners and unbelievers, all strike a responsive chord. Thérèse's message, says Bernard, should not be exiled to the past; she is a "word of God to our world,"[86] and a worthy candidate for the doctorate.

---

[83] Bernard has subsequently published his "votum" under his own name; see Charles André Bernard, "Actualité et modernité de Thérèse de Lisieux," *Didaskalia* 27 (1997): 3-21. Moreover, as a former professor at the Gregorianum, he fits Castellano's description, and the later consultors also mention him by name. Thus the authorship of this third "votum" seems clearly established. Bernard also has written on Thérèse, in "L'amour sauveur dans la vie de sainte Thérèse de Lisieux: essai sur son itinéraire spirituel," *Revue d'ascétique et mystique* 32 (1956): 297-328, 420-449, for example, and more recently in chapter 9 of *Le Dieu des mystiques, tome II: La conformation au Christ* (Paris: Éditions du Cerf, 1988), 625-715. The latter chapter is entitled: "Mystique de Jésus: Sainte Thérèse de Lisieux ou de l'Enfant-Jésus et de la Sainte-Face."

[84] See *Positio*, 877-879.

[85] Ibid., 879-884.

[86] Ibid., 888.

Vote of the Fourth Theologian for the Congregation for the Doctrine of the Faith

The fourth theologian consulted by the CDF is Mihály Szentmártoni, S.J., who teaches courses in religious psychology in the Institute of Spirituality at the Gregorianum.[87] He is the only one of the seven initially consulted experts to oppose the bestowal of the doctorate on Thérèse, though he gives no more than the briefest explanation of his reasons (his "votum" comes to little more than a single page).[88] Szentmártoni concedes that there is a "universal consensus on the legitimacy of the 'little way'… as a charism of wisdom for the good of the church," and acknowledges that her doctrine "has a character of excellence in its evangelical wisdom and psychological profundity." He realizes that her doctrine is drawn from the pure sources of Scripture and Tradition, and that it has been positively received by popes, bishops, theologians, and the ordinary faithful. Nevertheless, he considers it "inopportune" to declare Thérèse a doctor for three reasons: first, because she lacks a "doctrinal corpus" in the sense of a "structured and systematic teaching"; second, because of the "psychological difficulty" in recognizing a young woman of 24 as a "master and doctor"; and third, because naming another doctor from the Carmelite family (who already claim John of the Cross and Teresa of Avila) would seem to unduly favor Carmelite spirituality over others. Regrettably, he devotes no more than a few sentences to each of these objections, which are quickly dismissed by the later consultors, as we shall see. Some, for example, argue that Thérèse's youth actually makes her a *more* desirable candidate in the con-

---

[87] This authorship is one of the easiest to confirm, since many of the later consultors explicitly say that they strongly *disagree* with the specific reasons given in the "votum" by "Szentmártoni" for denying Thérèse the doctorate. See *Positio* supplement, 17, 32, 35, 39.

[88] See *Positio*, 891-892.

temporary context, to inspire the young and to underscore that God's wisdom is revealed not merely to professional scholars and those of advanced years but even "to the merest children" (cf. Matthew 11:25). In any case, Szentmártoni passes up an excellent opportunity to explore further the crucial question of whether and in what sense a systematic body of theological teaching should be required of a "doctor of the church."

Vote of the Fifth Theologian for the Congregation for the Doctrine of the Faith

The favorable "votum" of the fifth expert chosen by the CDF is the shortest of all.[89] The author maintains that Thérèse's "charism of wisdom for the good of the church" is beyond doubt, and that her simplicity is not a "simplicity of impoverishment" but a concentrated in-depth richness; her writings represent "an incisive deepening of the pure and authentic Gospel" and have exercised an enormous positive influence on the church. In itself, her discovery of her "personal vocation" to be "love in the heart of the church" is replete with spiritual and doctrinal implications. The lack of a "doctrinal corpus," he says, need not be an insurmountable obstacle.

Vote of the First Theologian for the Congregation for the Causes of Saints

The Congregation for the Causes of Saints likewise sought preliminary opinions from two theological experts of their own. The first is Servais Pinckaers, O.P., a professor of moral theology

---

[89] Ibid., 893-894. The author identifies himself as a Jesuit who has spent time in India and has written a booklet entitled *La vocazione personale*. Since Castellano has already identified him as belonging to the same Institute as the previous two experts, those who know more biographical details about the Gregorianum faculty could no doubt identify him by name. His contribution is so brief, however, that it is not discussed by the consultors.

at the University of Fribourg in Switzerland.[90] Pinckaers opens with yet another overview of the history of the title. He recalls Aquinas's position that the pivotal charism of doctor includes "a certain plenitude of knowledge of divine things, the capacity for well-argued speech that will render the teaching efficacious, and finally, the gift of eloquence."[91] He also observes that:

> In perusing the list of Doctors proclaimed since the Council of Trent, we note an evolution. The title is officially recognized at liturgical and juridical levels. Its connection with sanctity is strictly maintained, but it is progressively separated from the role of a Doctor or theologian, to be associated just as often with preachers such as Anthony of Padua and Lawrence of Brindisi, and with spiritual figures like John of the Cross and Teresa of Avila. Observable, too, is a dropping off of the demand for important written works. Finally we note, in the bestowing of the title, a care to respect a certain balance among theological trends and religious families in the Church. This can be clearly seen in the nominations made by Pius XI: Peter Canisius, John of the Cross, Robert Bellarmine, and Albert the Great.[92]

Nevertheless, says Pinckaers, whatever other changes may have occurred, "the teaching of the Gospel is the prime matter of the charism of doctor... exercised by word and writing, but also by lived experience and the example of holiness."[93]

---

[90] Again, this identification can be made with confidence not only because Pinckaers fits Castellano's description, but more importantly because his "votum," only slightly revised, has already been published under his own name. See Servais Pinckaers, "Thérèse of the Child Jesus, Doctor of the Church," *Josephinum Journal of Theology* 5 (Winter/Spring 1998): 26-40.

[91] *Positio*, 899 and Pinckaers, "Thérèse of the Child Jesus," 28.

[92] *Positio*, 900 and Pinckaers, "Thérèse of the Child Jesus," 29.

[93] Ibid. I have quoted from the latter but slightly adapted the wording to conform better to the original French of the *Positio*.

In Thérèse's case, Pinckaers foresees the objection that she never held an official teaching office in the church, that her writings are "rather slight in comparison with the work of recognized Doctors," and that "awarding the Doctorate to Thérèse of Lisieux" might "contribute to a devaluation of the title."[94] In response, he notes that those declared doctors in modern times have been largely drawn not from among the practitioners of "scientific theology" but from the field of "spiritual theology," from authors of "works of spirituality based on some experience whose conditions and progress they describe." "Theology," Pinckaers says, "is, in effect, a work of wisdom," wherein we can distinguish two levels: (1) "the wisdom of the Spirit, which gives understanding of the mystery of Christ and the experience of charity," and which is "the first element in theology"; and (2) "the elaboration of this wisdom through theological reflection and a discerning use of available philosophical and cultural contributions, and the application of various methods and techniques of thought and expression."[95] Thérèse fails to qualify as a theologian on the second (technical) level, claims Pinckaers, but she nonetheless deserves recognition on the first level, as one who has imbibed deeply of the divine wisdom from which "scientific theology" springs. He briefly discusses three areas in which Thérèse offers an intensification and deepening of the message of the Gospel: (1) in her emphasis on the primacy of love, the very source of all theology, and her profound reflections on Jesus' command to "love one another as I have loved you"; (2) in her "little way," which can help to guard theologians against excessive rationalism; and (3) in her courageous confrontation, during her trial of faith, with the nihilism and atheism that has so deeply marked the modern era.[96] Moreover, Pinckaers says, the lowliness of her literary style and the homey-

---

[94] *Positio*, 900-901 and Pinckaers, "Thérèse of the Child Jesus," 30.
[95] *Positio*, 902 and Pinckaers, "Thérèse of the Child Jesus," 32.
[96] *Positio*, 903-908 and Pinckaers, "Thérèse of the Child Jesus," 32-38.

ness of her examples mirror what we find in teaching of the New Testament itself. As for her timeliness, Pinckaers suggests that she may be the "doctor" ideally suited to our times, offering the perfect counterpoint to "the dryness of an excessively rational theology and exegesis" and to "a society that no longer wants to hear about God."[97]

One may argue with several of Pinckaers's points. The distinction between "theologians" and "spiritual writers" may be less sharp than his analysis suggests. He seems to underestimate Thérèse and her texts in claiming that she was simply "not capable" of giving "a theological interpretation" to her spiritual experience as described in *Story of Soul,* or that "she proceeded by way of intuition and imagery rather than by reasoning" and "narrated rather than argued." On the contrary, as we will argue in the next chapter, a more careful reading of her works reveals countless instances of "thinking through" religious problems through an authentic, if often informal, pattern of sound ratiocination. Nonetheless, Pinckaers makes a good case for including, among the doctors, certain saints like Thérèse whose teachings have illuminated the church despite their lack of scholarly credentials.

Vote of the Second Theologian for the Congregation for the Causes of Saints

The final "votum" from the theological experts is from a Spanish theologian, possibly José Luis Illanes.[98] His judgment on

---

97 *Positio,* 909 and Pinckaers, "Thérèse of the Child Jesus," 39-40.

98 A "Mons. Illanes" is mentioned only once in the documents, by a consultor who praises his "votum" without describing it; see *Positio* supplement, 46. Since Castellano has already indicated that the second expert for the Congregation for the Causes of Saints is a "theologian connected with an academic center in Spain," this may well be José Luis Illanes, a priest of Opus Dei, member of the faculty of theology at the University of Navarre, and visiting professor at the Pontifical Atheneum of Santa Croce, who has published and taught widely in the field of fundamental theology and spirituality.

Thérèse's candidacy is favorable, and he notes that doctrinal eminence needs to be considered not in the abstract but in the context of the ongoing life and needs of the church.[99] In the first section this author argues that although Thérèse was not a professional theologian, she is a theologian in the "primordial sense" of one who has deeply penetrated Scripture "with the heart and mind," and who has dealt with the "principal mysteries of our faith." He recalls that, in a still Jansenistic era when spirituality was often identified with the extraordinary, and a sharp distinction was drawn between the ascetical and the mystical, Thérèse taught that true Christian perfection consisted in loving union with God. Her writings speak to us of the importance of spontaneous prayer, of continuous and profound contemplation of God, of generous and voluntary self-mortification in the ordinary events of daily life, of the liturgy and sacraments as nourishment for love, and of love for God overflowing into love of neighbor.[100] The author recalls Thérèse's Christological and Marian insights, as well as her profound penetration into the mysteries of grace and God's "prevenient" mercy. In short, he argues for the "eminence, universality, and relevance of her doctrine."

In part two of his "votum," this author concludes from the evolution of the title "doctor" that the church recognizes the ongoing need to explain the faith in contemporary terms, not just according to ancient methods and formulae. And although the title should not be given lightly or hastily, neither should the delay be so long that it seems as if vital Christian thought belongs only to the past. Declaring Thérèse a "doctor of the church," this author says, would help heal the division between theology and spirituality. And he notes, finally, that most modern "doctors" are precisely spiritual authors.[101]

---

[99] *Positio*, 910.

[100] Ibid., 914.

[101] Ibid., 918-920.

CDF Consultation and Votation of 5 May 1997

The solicited opinions of the seven theological experts, together with the rest of the material in the *Positio*, were forwarded next to the two dicasteries involved and distributed to their official consultors, in preparation for a vote in each congregation.[102] The consultors apparently also received copies of the six criteria formulated by the CDF for evaluating doctrinal eminence, as well as a set of Thérèse's writings in the NEC version.[103]

On Monday, May 5, 1997, the "consulta" of the Congregation for the Doctrine of the Faith met in ordinary session to discuss and vote on Thérèse's candidacy for the title "doctor of the church." Present were the secretary for the Congregation (Tarcisio Bertone), the undersecretary (Jozef Zlatnansky), and 20 consultors: Cardinal Giovanni Battista Re, Archbishop Jorge María Mejía, Bishop Stanislaw Rylko, Bishop Pierre Duprey, George Marie Martin Cottier, O.P., Albert Vanhoy, S.J., Prosper Grech, O.S.A., Jesús Castellano Cervera, O.C.D., Réal Tremblay, C.SS.R., Karl I. Becker, S.J., Rev. Fernando Ocáriz, Gilles Pelland, S.J., Rev. Antonio Miralles, Mons. Marcello Bordoni, Mons. Rino Rischella, Rev. Angel Rodríguez Luño, Mons. Romano Penna, Angelo Amato, S.D.B., Luis Ladaria, S.J., and Donato Valentini, S.D.B.[104] Some members and consultors from the Congregation for the Causes of Saints were also present, but without a vote.[105] The CDF consultors gave their responses to the question proposed

---

[102] The format and order in which this material was presented to the consultors is not entirely clear. In the supplementary gray volume, some of the consultors refer back to these original materials by page numbers that do not correspond to the numbering in the published version of the *Positio*.

[103] See Castellano, "El doctorado de Santa Teresa del Niño Jesús," 86.

[104] The consultors are listed by last name in the *Positio* supplement, 3. Their full names appear in the *Annuario Pontificio* for 1997. Nine other official consultors were apparently absent, including, unfortunately, Umberto Betti, O.F.M., whose important studies on the title "doctor of the church" were discussed in the first chapter of this work.

[105] See Castellano, "El doctorado de Santa Teresa del Niño Jesús," 86 and *Positio*, v.

in the *Positio*, and then formally voted on the following proposition:

> Whether it can be demonstrated that the teaching of St. Thérèse of Lisieux, candidate for the title of "Doctor of the Church," is not only in full conformity with faith and Christian life, *but also excels ('eminet') through the quality of the writings, the sublimity and profundity of its doctrine, the mature sapiential synthesis attained, and the effective positive influence exercised*, in such a way that it can be recognized as a special witness of the living tradition of the Church (cf. *Dei Verbum*, n. 8)?[106]

Thus they were asked, in effect, to vote specifically on the *second* of the six criteria for judging doctrinal eminence.[107] As the published results indicate, there were nineteen votes in favor, two in favor "iuxta modum," i.e., with reservations (wondering whether the criteria used are too broad), and one opposed, on the grounds that Thérèse's eminence is in *life* rather than *doctrine*, and that bestowing the doctorate upon her would further diminish the title without adding to her influence.[108]

---

[106] See *Positio* supplement, 3: "Si puó dimostrare che l'insegnamento di S. Teresa di Lisieux, candidata al titolo di 'Dottore della Chiesa', non solo è pienamente conforme con la fede e la vita cristiana, *ma eccelle ('eminet') per la qualità degli scritti, per la sublimità e la profundità della dottrina, per la matura sintesi sapienziale raggiunta, per l'effettivo influso positivo esercitato*, in maniera che essa possa essere riconosciuta come testimone qualificata della vivente tradizione della Chiesa (cfr. *Dei Verbum*, n. 8)?" The question of the *Positio* is formulated more briefly: "Si può dimostrare che l'insegnamento di Santa Teresa del Bambino Gesù 'eccelle' ('eminet') per la qualità degli scritti per la sublimità e la profundità della dottrina, per la matura sintesi sapienziale raggiunta e per l'effettivo influso positivo esercitato?" (Ibid.).

[107] Recall that the second of the six criteria is worded almost identically: "A questo scopo si deve dimostrare che l'insegnamento dei Santi, candidati al titolo di 'Dottore della Chiesa', non solo è pienamente conforme con la fede e la vita cristiana, *ma eccelle ('eminet') per la qualità degli scritti, per la sublimità e la profundità della dottrina, per la matura sintesi sapienziale raggiunta, per l'effettivo influso positivo esercitato*, in maniera che essa possa essere riconosciuta come testimone qualificata della vivente tradizione della Chiesa (cfr. *Dei Verbum*, n. 8)?"

[108] *Positio* supplement, 3.

The main reasons given by the majority for bestowing the title are neatly summarized in the brief introduction to the printed text of the "vota." Regarding the *quality of her writings*, consultors favoring the doctorate argue that: (1) they are "sufficient in number"; (2) they fit the fundamental definition of theology as "faith seeking understanding (*fides quaerens intellectum*) through attention to Scripture and to other spiritual texts which can be regarded as *loci theologici*"; and (3) the writings excel by "their immediacy and explanatory capacity, which renders them rather attractive and engaging for the reader." The principal areas of *sublimity and profundity of doctrine* in Thérèse's writings, according to the majority, are: (1) the "deep understanding," despite limited access to Scripture, "of the mystery of the triune God, the Incarnation, the work of redemption, the presence of the Spirit in our soul, the greatness of the church as a community of faith and salvation"; (2) the "central place" given to "revelation which ascribes everything to the Trinitarian love of God"; (3) the "little way" which "reaches the heart of the Christian message, the Gospel of Mercy, configuring it in a profound way, underscoring the grace of divine filiation, of the perception of God as Father, of the offering as a victim of holocaust to the merciful love of God"; (4) the clear reflection of the Gospel "particularly in her pages on love and on abandoning oneself into the hands of God"; (5) the "importance" given to "love in the mystery of the church"; (6) her teaching "about the justice of God, which goes beyond the punitive sense and interprets it in the light of love"; (7) her "decision to rely only on love"; (8) her "underscoring of filial freedom"; (9) the "positive understanding of weakness and poverty along the way of love"; (10) her "struggle against falsehood"; and (11) her "love of Scripture."[109] Those favoring Thérèse's doctorate likewise find a *mature sapiential synthesis achieved* in the fol-

---

[109] Ibid., 4-5.

lowing respects: (1) The "little way" provides "a vision in which reason and faith, existence and word, advice and persuasion... are brought together in a unitary method for journeying to God"; (2) Thérèse offers "a sapiential reflection which, in conformity with the Gospel, shows the road to take to reach the heart of Christian faith"; (3) this is a "sapiential deepening especially of certain central truths of the faith, through a living out of life and through intuitions reached through contemplation (a *theologia cordis*)"; (4) "a series of central points of the Christian mystery appear in a new light in her doctrine: the God of Mercy (*Dio Misericordia*), Christocentrism, the paradox of the creature's poverty and infinite desires"; (5) she gives a "valid illustration of the connection between scientific theology and spiritual theology, scholarship (*scienza*) and wisdom, scholarship (*scienza*) and life"; (6) hers is "a spontaneous synthesis, more lived out than reflected, and therefore more interesting"; (7) "She has a gift of explaining in an exemplary way her spiritual experience and to render it universal."[110] Finally, regarding the *effective positive influence exercised* by her doctrine, those in the majority say that: (1) there has been "a universal reaction to her spirituality"; (2) her teaching has "exercised a great influence even on the level of the ecclesiastical magisterium"; (3) "It shows a persuasive force among the young and those no longer young"; (4) "The high level of spirituality attained by someone so young makes her writings all the more attractive"; (5) her doctrine offers a "valid basis for ecumenism and interreligious dialogue"; and (6) giving her the title "would allow a larger number of the faithful to follow with greater security the way indicated in her writings."[111]

This concise synthesis of the positive votes obviates the need to review each one in great detail (especially since so many points

---

[110] Ibid., 5.
[111] Ibid.

are repeated). Here we will limit ourselves to a summary of some additional points mentioned by the consultors. (It should be noted that two of the votes from the CDF consultation were not submitted in writing, and so are not included among the published "vota").

Votes 1 to 4

The first "votum" asserts that Thérèse's doctrine is "not the fruit of theological reflection, and does not pertain to speculative theology but to a sapiential deepening," and that hers is a true "theology of the heart"; he agrees with Schönborn that although Thérèse did not systematize her thought one can find in it a certain "sapiential synthesis."[112] The author of the second "votum," though favorable to Thérèse's doctorate, wonders why certain other figures might not also be judged suitable candidates on similar grounds, such as Ignatius Loyola, Paul of the Cross, Edith Stein, Gertrude the Great, Mechtild of Magdeburg, John Vianney (for his pastoral "magisterium") and Thomas More. "Votum 3" endorses the "excellent documentation" provided to the consultors, especially Schönborn's presentation on Thérèse's doctrinal eminence, and recalls von Balthasar's statements on Thérèse's ecumenical importance. The author of the fourth "votum" argues that it is actually a smaller subset of Thérèse's writings that truly deserve recognition as "excellent" for purposes of her doctoral candidacy: namely, Manuscripts B and C of her autobiographical writings, her "Offering to Merciful Love," certain letters of her final years (especially those to missionaries), and her last conversations. In these he finds the major theological insights already enumerated, on charity, mission, the nature of the church, and so on. He believes it is not too soon to declare Thérèse a doctor,

---

[112] Ibid., 6.

since Alphonsus Liguori was so honored even more rapidly after his death.[113]

Votes 5 to 9

The fifth consultor whose opinion is here recorded votes affirmatively because of the number of petitions from bishops' conferences, though he expresses concern about an "escalation" of doctorates and wonders why Ignatius Loyola should not also be considered. The author of the sixth "votum" agrees with "Mons. Schönborn, P. Bernard" and "F.M. Lamoureux," and feels that Szentmártoni's objection (about the lack of a doctrinal corpus) is answered by the theological synthesis presented in the *Positio* itself; this consultor attaches great importance to the use made of Thérèse in the magisterial teaching of the popes, especially since this was done without an eventual doctorate explicitly in mind. The long seventh "votum" draws heavily on Hans Urs von Balthasar, claiming that Thérèse's propositions are not new but that she illumines them in a new way, presenting not so much a system as an "elemental vision" and a "way," relevant to the "new evangelization" and to the current climate of moral relativism; this author suggests that Elizabeth of the Trinity would likewise be a suitable candidate for the doctorate alongside Thérèse, especially given von Balthasar's appreciation of the "theological mission" of both. The author of the eighth "votum" aligns himself strongly with Charles Bernard's "votum," which, he says, he couldn't have put better. "Votum 9" reviews the six criteria again, noting that the "excellent quality" of Thérèse's writings lies in their content rather than their style, and that she offers a "sapiential deepening" precisely in the sense understood by Thomas Aquinas in his analysis of the gift of wisdom (see *Summa Theologiae* II-II, q. 45).

---

[113] Votes 1 to 4 of the CDF consultors are found in the *Positio* supplement, 6-16.

The author of this "votum" discusses the contributions of the seven theological experts and enumerates again those Christian mysteries upon which Thérèse "sheds a new light"; he likewise places considerable weight on the use made of Thérèse by the popes and the *Catechism of the Catholic Church*.[114]

Votes 10 to 16

The author of the tenth "votum" supports Thérèse's doctorate especially because of the number of theologians who favor it and the many bishops' conferences who have requested it; he feels that Szentmártoni's objections are well answered by Bernard's contribution. The consultor behind the eleventh published vote identifies himself as a disciple of von Balthasar interested in reconnecting theology with spirituality, and notes that the CDF criteria require a charism not of *science* but of *wisdom*, which Thérèse certainly possessed; he notes that most of Szentmártoni's objections are to the *opportuneness* of declaring Thérèse a doctor at this time, and thus do not really touch upon her objective qualifications. The author of the twelfth vote, on the other hand, declares that Szentmártoni's first point, about Thérèse's lack of a doctrinal corpus, should be taken more seriously; he emphasizes that not all saints are doctors, and believes that some of those voting have confused excellent holiness with doctrinal eminence, perhaps because of a certain "infatuation" with Thérèse. Nevertheless, he votes in favor of the proclamation because of the bishops' requests and because of the good it will do in the church. "Votum 13" is positive, largely because of Thérèse's affinity with the Pauline understanding of divine justice from the perspective of love. The consultor whose opinion appears in fourteenth place votes favorably "in all respects," and is particularly impressed with

---

[114] Votes 5 to 9 of the CDF consultors are found in the *Positio* supplement, 16-35.

Thérèse's "Offering to Merciful Love." It is the sixteenth published "votum" that speaks of the "sufficient number" of Thérèse's writings, her "attention to Scripture and to other spiritual writings that can be considered *loci theologici*," her influence on "the young and those no longer young," and other points mentioned in the earlier synopsis.[115]

Votes 17 to 19

The author of the seventeenth "votum" casts the only solidly negative vote among the CDF consultors. He grants that Thérèse fulfills many of the criteria, but not the all-important second one (the one, recall, upon which the consultors were asked to focus), because of her lack of a "doctrinal corpus." Thérèse, he says, is not a "doctor of the church" comparable to Aquinas or Basil, and to call her such would reduce the significance of the title while detracting from the very "littleness" that makes her so appealing to many. Thus, although it might seem prophetic to declare her a doctor and thereby exalt spirituality, he considers it "inopportune" to do so.

"Votum 18" observes that the criteria for eminence of doctrine have been differently applied down through history. Responding to Szentmártoni's objections, this consultor maintains that Thérèse's youth and the danger of showing Carmelite spirituality undue favoritism are not relevant to the question of doctrinal eminence. Moreover, since many of those already declared doctors also lack a "systematic and structured" doctrinal corpus, its absence in Thérèse seems hardly a decisive impediment. This author notes that the significance of the appeals from episcopal conferences needs further analysis, to determine in each case what

---

[115] Votes 10 to 16 are found in the *Positio* supplement, 35-44.

proportion and number of bishops voted in favor of the request.[116] He believes that Thérèse's eminence of doctrine is no less than that of Anthony of Padua, Lawrence of Brindisi, and Catherine of Siena, and that, in terms of how the significance of the title has evolved over the last three centuries, she is qualified. Nevertheless, he expresses the wish for further study of the title before bestowing it upon Thérèse.

The author of the nineteenth and final printed "votum" from the CDF consultors agrees that the significance of the doctoral title has changed, especially with recent declarations. He believes it will change again if the title is bestowed on Thérèse, for what she offers is primarily an "eminence of life," a constant reminder by the testimony of her inimitable life of the fundamental gospel value of "spiritual childhood." Though he does not oppose granting Thérèse the title, he wonders if the intention is simply to placate women for their exclusion from the ordained priesthood by giving them a new "doctoressa."[117]

The Special Congress ("Congresso Peculiare") of the Congregation for the Causes of Saints on 29 May 1997

After the May 5 CDF meeting, a "dossier" of its results was forwarded to the cardinals and bishops who belonged to either of the two dicasteries involved and who were living in Rome, giving them at least a little time to read the material and prepare for

---

[116] Thus, he suggests, a relatively spontaneous request supported by all the bishops of a conference after careful consideration carries more weight than a request which narrowly passed by a simple majority, or was merely presented in the name of the conference by its leadership. One might add to this various recent discussions about the theological and ecclesiological significance of bishops' conferences within the church's hierarchy and magisterium.

[117] Votes 17 to 19 are found in the *Positio* supplement, 44-50.

the next phase, in accordance with the special procedure which the pope had approved in this case.[118] Roughly three weeks later, at 5 P.M. on May 29, 1997, a select group of theological consultors for the Congregation for the Causes of Saints "gathered to discuss the granting of the title 'Doctor Ecclesiae' to Saint Thérèse of the Child Jesus and the Holy Face."[119] This meeting occurred in the presence of key officials from the Congregation for the Causes of Saints: the Pro-Prefect (Archbishop Alberto Bovone), the Secretary (Archbishop Edward Novak), and the Undersecretary (Mons. Michele Di Ruberto); also attending was Adriano Garuti, O.F.M., an official from the CDF. The General Promoter of the Faith, Mons. Sandro Corradini, presided over the meeting but did not vote; he was simply substituting for the previously chosen presider, Mons. Antonio Petti, who was unable to attend for health reasons.[120]

Though the 1997 *Annuario Pontificio* lists 70 "consultori" to the Congregation for the Causes of Saints, only a dozen theological consultors were authorized to give their opinion at this "special congress," including the two "theological experts" for the Congregation for the Causes of Saints who had been asked earlier for their opinions, and whose "vota" (in reverse order) are reintroduced here. Besides these two—whom we have tentatively identified above as Servais Pinckaers, O.P., and José Luis Illanes, and who in fact are not listed among the Congregation's regular "consultori"—we do not know who the other voting consultors were or how they were chosen. What we do know is that the majority were still in favor of Thérèse's doctorate but that the results were somewhat more divided than at the May 5 CDF meeting. Even after some discussion, we are told, opinions re-

---

[118] See *Positio*, v.
[119] See *Positio* supplement, 51.
[120] Ibid.

mained unchanged and no consensus was reached; in the end there were 7 affirmative votes, 2 affirmative with reservations, and 3 opposed.[121] The supplement to the *Positio* (i.e., the gray volume) once again gives a useful summary of the outcome, this time vote by vote, which we will here follow and amplify.

Votes 1 to 4

The first and second "vota" we have already considered, since they are same "vota" submitted by the "theological experts" of whom the Congregation for the Causes of Saints had requested an earlier opinion. The author of the third "vota" is impressed by the steadily increasing number of requests for Thérèse's doctorate from the hierarchy and the faithful, and recalls that efforts to have Thérèse declared a doctor are not a recent fad, but go back as far as the 1920's, before any other women had received this honor. He notes Thérèse's consciousness of having a "doctrine" and a "mission," and the contribution she made in foreshadowing such themes as the "universal call to holiness" and the "new evangelization," founded on God's limitless love for all. He believes that the declaration would be especially opportune on the eve of the Great Jubilee Year 2000, and a great consolation for sinners, the young, those who feel lost, and so on. To the objection that granting Thérèse the doctorate might devalue the title, he responds that in addition to eminent doctrine a candidate must have a real influence on the universal church, something Thérèse manifests in abundance; unlike many other declared doctors, he notes, she is celebrated throughout the whole church with at least an obligatory memorial.

The fourth "votum" is positive especially because of the vast number of appeals received from episcopal conferences, cardinals,

---

[121] Ibid., 51-53.

bishops, priests, religious, and laity, appeals which themselves give testimony to the efficacy of her doctrine. He accepts the arguments of the *Informatio* and the theological experts that Thérèse adequately fulfills the requirement for doctrinal eminence. Granted, her approach is not scholastic or systematic, but is all the more appealing as a result.[122]

Votes 5 to 7

The fifth "votum" is essentially a detailed survey of the *Positio*. The author makes various comments and criticisms—he disagrees, for example, with Léthel's alignment of Thérèse with Anselm on the relationship between divine mercy and justice—but on the whole he maintains that the *Positio* provides an adequate basis for an affirmative judgment on Thérèse's "eminence of doctrine" and suitability for the doctorate. He is particularly impressed with the wide diffusion of her writings, the wealth of studies and congresses devoted to her doctrine, and the large number of religious communities that follow her spirit, all demonstrating the enormous impact of her doctrine on the church.

The sixth "votum" is from someone who says that he is also involved in the doctoral cause for Bernardine of Siena. He reviews the history of Thérèse's case and the contents of the *Positio* (which he deems adequate despite the haste with which it was written), concluding that the "essential content" of Thérèse's doctrine is "concentrated in the theme of *divine paternity* ... and our *adoptive filiation*," that is, in God's limitless merciful love for us and our complete abandonment in trust to him. Citing the constant use made of Thérèse's teaching by the popes and the *Catechism of the Catholic Church*, he concludes that Thérèse's doctrine is of "eminent" value not only because of its content and originality but

---

[122] Votes 1 to 4 of the "special congress" are both summarized and transcribed in the *Positio* supplement, 50-51, 54-93.

also because of its universality and relevance today, within the church and well beyond.

The author of the seventh "votum" sees Thérèse as a great spiritual master who expresses theological insights in an existential manner. He, too, attaches importance to the fact that the popes of this century have so often proposed her teaching to the faithful. Casting an affirmative vote, he notes that the influence of Thérèse's message has only continued to grow, and has great ecumenical appeal. She is an exemplary interpreter of the Gospels.[123]

Votes 8 and 9

These two votes are positive "iuxta modum," that is, with certain reservations. The eighth consultor calls his a "voto sofferto." Though he does not question Thérèse's holiness or influence, and recognizes the enthusiasm with which others have supported her doctorate, he is uncomfortable with giving her the title because she lacks a true "doctrinal corpus." Admittedly, she has an "experimental dogmatic," but to call this a "doctrine," he says, would be a dangerous enlargement of the concept and would reduce the value of the title. He does not want to vote against Thérèse but would prefer some other title designating her an "eminent spiritual guide."

The ninth consultor believes that the material provided is incomplete, and that the consultors' votes from the May 5 meeting did not delve deeply enough into certain aspects of the question. He willingly grants that Thérèse's youth is not in itself an obstacle, that she had a "sapiential" gift, that her teaching is orthodox, accessible to all, and of great value to the church. However, if the title "doctor of the church" requires a developed doc-

---

[123] Votes 5 to 7 of the "special congress" are both summarized and transcribed in the *Positio* supplement, 50-51, 93-135.

trinal corpus in the areas of dogmatic, moral, or spiritual theology, Thérèse would seem less qualified than other figures who have not yet received this recognition, "such as Irenaeus, Gregory of Nyssa, and Maximus the Confessor." If, on the other hand, the decisive consideration is the degree of influence exercised, then certainly she qualifies. Given the unclarity about the criteria, this consultor votes "placet iuxta modum."

Votes 10 to 12

In some ways the three strongly negative votes seem almost to offer a refreshing change for the reader, coming as they do after hundreds of pages of text almost entirely supportive of Thérèse's doctorate. The author of the tenth "votum" acknowledges Thérèse's contribution to the church as one who overcame the vestiges of Jansenism, as teacher of the "little way," as patroness of the missions and as a figure with ecumenical appeal. Nevertheless, she lacks "a doctrinal corpus, in the sense of a systematic and structured teaching," says this consultor, and cannot be compared with doctors of the Patristic period or even with the "giants" of Carmelite spirituality, John of the Cross and Teresa of Avila. He believes she should remain "little," and not be named a doctor.

The most extensive critique of Thérèse's doctoral cause is found in the eleventh "votum." Its author believes that the process is being unnecessarily rushed forward.[124] He, too, insists that Thérèse lacks a true "doctrinal corpus," and he critiques Léthel's attempts to piece one together. Though he praises Léthel for his efforts, this author maintains that Thérèse is "Christocentric"

---

[124] The dates of the final stages in the process, which he lists at the beginning of his "votum," do suggest that the consultors were given very little time to digest the massive amounts of background material or to reflect in depth on the issues involved; see *Positio* supplement, 142.

rather than "Christological," that her experience is "theologal" (that is, a living out of the "theological" virtues) rather than "theological," that she is the "greatest saint," not the "greatest doctor," of modern times. For all her merits, he finds in Thérèse no real theological contribution, and no critical deepening of doctrine. She is not a "magistra in sacra pagina" and has no "lectio" in the sense traditionally required. If Thérèse were to be declared a doctor, why not also Elizabeth of the Trinity, he asks, or even Dina Bélanger (1897-1932), who is in some ways even more original and deserving? This author also believes it is too soon to assess Thérèse's impact, and that the church should wait until at least 200 years after her death. Meanwhile, he proposes that the whole matter should be remanded to the decision of the pope, who by *motu proprio* could simply declare Thérèse a doctor and thereby settle the matter definitively, if he chooses to do so. But given this consultor's negative opinion on Thérèse's qualifications, one suspects that he believes such a move would effectively table the process of Thérèse's doctorate indefinitely.

The author of the twelfth and final "votum" sees Thérèse as a model of holiness and spirituality, but not a "model of doctrine," even though her example and certain of her insights have inspired what might be called an "agapic theology." He mentions Edith Stein as a possibly better candidate. The "little way," he says, is not the way of doctors.

The Final Steps

In the end, despite the few objections, a large majority of votes from the various official gatherings strongly favored bestowing the doctorate on Thérèse. If one adds together the "vota" of the consultors from the two congregations, they total 26 in favor, an additional 4 in favor "iuxta modum," that is, with reservations, and only 4 against. Add to this the opinions of the theological experts, who were six to one in favor of bestowing the title on Thérèse, and the proportion of positive votes becomes even more striking.[125]

Little wonder, then, that when more than 30 cardinals and bishops who belonged to the two congregations met in plenary session on June 17, 1997, they voted unanimously in favor of Thérèse's doctorate and greeted the outcome with spontaneous applause.[126] Two days later, Cardinal Joseph Ratzinger (Prefect of the CDF) and Archbishop Alberto Bovone (Pro-Prefect of the Congregation for the Causes of Saints) presented the results to the pope, who, as we know, would later announce, at World Youth Day in Paris, the forthcoming declaration of Thérèse as "doctor of the universal church."[127] And many of the phrases, themes, and arguments we have discussed, from the *Positio* and other documents of the process, would later find their way into the pope's homily for the declaration of Thérèse's doctorate on October 19, 1997, and into the Apostolic Letter, *Divini Amoris Scientia*, written for the occasion.

Reflections

It is easy to lose one's way amidst all of the "vota," documents, and criteria involved in Thérèse's doctoral cause. The sheer volume of materials is daunting, with a great deal of perhaps unavoidable repetition, given the nature of the process. It would seem redundant at this point to try to summarize further

---

[125] Recall, however, that there is an overlap between the votes of the consultors and those of the experts. The two experts for the Congregation for the Causes of Saints also served as consultors casting votes in the "special congress."

[126] See Castellano, "El doctorado de Santa Teresa del Niño Jesús," 87.

[127] Ibid., 87-88. See also *Divini Amoris Scientia*, no. 12.

what is already a summary. But in the final pages of this chapter, perhaps a few observations are in order.

First, through all of the pages of the *Positio* and the votations, it becomes evident that Thérèse's cause poses certain unique challenges, and underscores the continuing ambiguity surrounding the application of the three traditional prerequisites of outstanding holiness, doctrinal eminence, and a formal declaration by pope or council. If the candidate under consideration in this case had been Gregory of Nyssa or Maximus the Confessor, for example, many of the same questions would simply not arise. Their "eminence of doctrine" seems beyond dispute. Thérèse is one of those rare instances, I would suggest, of a saint who is universally identified with a particular *message*, communicated through her *writings*, deeply studied by *theologians*, and strongly endorsed by the church's *magisterium*, yet without possessing anything approaching a *doctrinal corpus*. It is difficult to think of another saint in whom this paradoxical combination of features is so powerfully present.[128] No one questions her extraordinary sanctity, the exemplarity of her life, her devotion to Scripture, her influence on the modern church, the interest she has elicited from scholars, and so on. But whether this is sufficient for a favorable judgment on "eminence of doctrine" still remains somewhat unclear. Even the various attempts in recent years to refine the notion of doctrinal eminence have helped only to a degree. The six "criteri dottrinali," for example, are largely overlapping, and further spell out doctrinal eminence in terms of "the existence of a particular charism of wisdom for the good of the church," a "mature sapiential synthe-

---

[128] Thus Joan of Arc, for example, is admired for her life but not particularly for her teachings. Francis of Assisi has influenced the church more by example than by his writings, and no one (pace Léthel) is seriously proposing him as a "doctor of the church." Ignatius of Loyola is known in part for the *Spiritual Exercises*, but (as far as I know) his texts have not been cited as often as those of Thérèse by magisterial documents of this century. In other words, among the saints who lack a doctrinal corpus, few exhibit the combination of other features mentioned here as strongly as Thérèse.

sis," a "wide diffusion, positive reception, and particular beneficial influence among the people of God," and so on, yet without further indication of how these latter qualities are to be determined. And so in one sense they simply move the argument one step backward; whether one believes a candidate like Thérèse offers a "mature sapiential synthesis," for example, will likely depend on whether one believes she evinces "doctrinal eminence," and vice versa.

Second, it is certainly possible to interpret the doctorate of Thérèse as opening the doors to a flood of other candidates. Indeed, some consultors express just such a concern, while others argue that if Thérèse is granted the title, there is no longer any reason to exclude Ignatius of Loyola, Edith Stein, Veronica Giuliani, Elizabeth of the Trinity, Dina Bélanger and a host of other favorites. If one regards the multiplication of doctors as an undesirable outcome, it could perhaps be offset by requiring an influence in the church comparable to Thérèse's, something of which few saints can boast. Or it may be time to consider, as one consultor suggests, a new official ecclesiastical title, such as "spiritual teacher," for those who have enriched the spirituality of the church by their message and example (though one could equally argue that this would exacerbate rather than help to heal the problematic split between theology and spirituality).

Third, it is worth noting that although the process begins (in the *Supplex libellus*) and ends (in John Paul II's Apostolic Letter *Divini Amoris Scientia*) by emphasizing Thérèse's importance as a doctor who is also a *young person*, a *woman*, and a *contemplative*, relatively little is made of these points in the *Positio* or the "vota." There is some limited discussion of the energy and freshness Thérèse brings to the doctoral ranks as a young person, and whether this enhances or detracts from her credibility as a doctor of the church. And Léthel speaks of the "privilege of the feminine" and of Thérèse's distinctively feminine approach to the mysteries of the faith. Yet none of the experts or consultors seriously explores whether and in what way Thérèse's status as a woman might affect her role as a doctor. In fact, the author of the eleventh "votum" from the consultors for the Congregation for the Causes of Saints, who opposes Thérèse's doctorate, is at pains to insist that although women were not chosen as doctors until recently, the traditional criteria are not gender-specific in themselves. No one argues, in other words, that women candidates should be held to different or lower standards of doctrinal eminence. That the question is not even seriously raised may show a blindness to "gender-issues" on the part of the congregations and their experts and consultors. On the other hand, it may simply show how far we have come in less than 30 years, that the bestowal of the doctorate on a woman is no longer considered remarkable.

But in the fourth place, it is also worth noting that, with the exception of the theological expert Sr. Françoise Lamoureux, none of the identifiable participants in the process were women or laymen. This is not to impugn the qualifications or competence of those who participated, nor is it to suggest that there was any deliberate attempt to exclude non-clerical input. It is more likely the result of the fact that the Discalced Carmelites available to quickly compile the *Informatio,* and the official consultors of the two dicasteries in 1997, were all clergy. Still, for a candidate who is praised throughout the process for her appeal to all believers and for her anticipation of Vatican II's teaching on the "universal call to holiness," the lack of formal input from other women and laymen seems unfortunate. Though it presumably would not have changed the outcome, it might have enriched the process considerably.

Fifth, one can observe different *kinds* of arguments used to support or oppose granting Thérèse the doctorate. Some are of a more *formal* nature, citing her use by the church's magisterium.

Some focus on the objective theological *content* (or lack thereof) in her writings, that is, the particular themes she explores and develops. And some are based on the broad *reception* her message has received, and the extensive influence it has attained. Granted, all of these arguments are foreseen in the criteria, but they have different premises and structures.

Lastly, however, there does seem to be fairly general agreement on those particular areas in which Thérèse arguably made a significant contribution. Again and again the consultors refer to her "little way," her emphasis on God as Merciful Love, her grasp of the radical poverty of human beings paradoxically combined with their infinite desires, her approach to the themes of mission and vocation, her Marian insights, and so on. In each case, the same key passages from Thérèse's writings are cited and analyzed repeatedly. If the consultors and experts do not all agree on whether Thérèse should be named a doctor, at least they generally agree on where to look for the evidence. In the following chapter, beginning with their leads, we will consider in more detail the significance of the fact that Thérèse is now numbered among the 33 "doctors of the universal church," and what Thérèse's doctorate might mean especially for contemporary theology.

Chapter Four

THE DECLARATION OF THÉRÈSE AS DOCTOR OF THE UNIVERSAL CHURCH AND ITS POTENTIAL THEOLOGICAL SIGNIFICANCE

hen all is said and done, virtually the only assured result of declaring someone a "doctor of the church" is on the level of cult; he or she is thereafter celebrated liturgically as a "doctor." One might argue that over time this exerts a certain influence on the worshipping community, including its theologians. Celebrants are more likely, perhaps, to preach on the message of the saint in question, and the faithful are, perhaps, more inclined to take the saint seriously as a teacher.

Beyond that, however, there are no guarantees that the doctoral declaration itself will have any particular intended effect, nor specifically that the saint in question will exert a noticeably greater influence on the church's theology and praxis. Granting the doctorate to Lawrence of Brindisi in 1959, for example, did not noticeably enhance interest in his doctrine among professional theologians, nor did it inspire the ordinary faithful to start avidly reading his works. Recent scholarly writings on Teresa of Avila and Catherine of Siena generally owe more to the rise of women's studies and the current popularity of spiritual classics than to their being declared doctors.

We are still too close chronologically to the bestowal of the doctoral title on Thérèse to know with any certainty what its ultimate impact will be. Nonetheless, this chapter will consider some of the potential theological implications of Thérèse's doctorate, both those intended and those perhaps unforeseen. We will first examine the official papal statements directly connected with her declaration as "doctor of the universal church," to see how Pope John Paul II proposed that this action be understood. Then we will examine how this declaration has so far been "received" within the church and offer some suggestions on the role that she and other saints and doctors may play in the ongoing development of theology.

Papal Statements on Thérèse's Doctorate

As we have seen, the declaration of Thérèse as "doctor of the universal church" on October 19, 1997, did not occur in a vacuum, but in the midst of various celebrations and statements intended to explain the significance of this event for the people of God. Of these, the Apostolic Letter *Divini Amoris Scientia*,[1] written for the occasion and published on the same day as Thérèse's doctoral declaration, bears the most magisterial weight. But there are other sources to consider as well, including the homily that Pope John Paul II delivered at the doctoral Mass, several papal allocutions from the same time period and even the structure and content of the ceremonies themselves. We will briefly discuss each of these in turn.[2]

---

[1] See John Paul II, "Divini Amoris Scientia: Apostolic Letter." *Origins* 27 (20 November 1997): 390-396. Like the documents of Vatican II, *Divini Amoris Scientia* is organized into numbered sections. Hereafter this text will be cited by its Latin title and numbered section.

[2] The proclamation of Thérèse's doctorate was marked by a number of other official and semi-official acts and documents by individual bishops, heads of religious congregations,

Divini Amoris Scientia

The opening lines of Pope John Paul II's Apostolic Letter *Divini Amoris Scientia* are worth quoting in full, since they set the tone for the entire document:

> The knowledge of divine love, which the Father of mercies pours out through Jesus Christ in the Holy Spirit, is a gift granted to the little and the humble so that they may know and proclaim the secrets of the kingdom, hidden from the learned and the wise; for this reason Jesus rejoiced in the Holy Spirit, praising the Father who graciously willed it so (cf. Lk 10:21-22; Mt 11:26).
>
> Mother church also rejoices in noting that throughout history the Lord has continued to reveal himself to the little and the humble, enabling his chosen ones through the Spirit who "searches everything, even the depths of God" (1 Cor 2:10), to speak of the gifts bestowed on us by God... in words not taught by human wisdom but taught by the Spirit, interpreting spiritual truths in spiritual language (1 Cor 2:12, 13). In this way the Holy Spirit guides the church into the whole truth, endowing her with various gifts, adorning her with his fruits, rejuvenating her with the power of the Gospel and enabling her to discern the signs of the times in order to respond ever more fully to the will of God (cf. *Lumen gentium*, 4, 12; *Gaudium et spes*, 4).
>
> Shining brightly among the little ones to whom the

---

and so on. The Superiors General of the Carmelites and Discalced Carmelites, for example, released a joint letter in which they hailed Thérèse as, among other things, a model for the "New Evangelization"; see *A Doctor for the Third Millennium: Letter from the OCD and O.Carm. General Superiors on the occasion of the Doctorate of Saint Thérèse of Lisieux* (Rome: Casa Generalizia OCD, 1997). However, since such materials were usually directed toward a particular audience rather than to the church in general, we will not consider them here. In any case, such materials are too abundant to deal with them adequately in this context.

secrets of the kingdom were revealed in a most special way is Thérèse of the Child Jesus and the Holy Face....[3]

Here at the outset, Pope John Paul II clearly frames the doctorate of St. Thérèse by situating her not among "the learned and the wise" but among "the little and humble" to whom God reveals his mysteries. There is no attempt to equate her with other doctors like Augustine and Aquinas in terms of academic competence or scholarly achievement. Rather, Thérèse is said to offer a "special charism of Gospel wisdom," received in prayer from the "divine teacher" and "then expressed with particular originality in her writings." Her "science" is "the luminous expression of her knowledge of the mystery of the kingdom and of her personal experience of grace," rather than a systematically developed body of doctrine. She is among the instruments used by the Holy Spirit to help the church "discern the signs of the times" and grow "into the whole truth." The language in these opening lines is already clearly different from what one would expect were the candidate a prominent patristic author or great medieval theologian.

Then, in the second numbered section, John Paul II goes on to recall that the "reception" of Thérèse in this century was "quick, universal and constant," not only with regard to "the example of her life" but also with regard to "Gospel teaching." She

---

[3] John Paul II, *Divini Amoris Scientia,* no. 1. Perhaps unfortunately, the printed version in *Origins* translates the Latin title (and first words of the text) as "*knowledge* of divine love," rather than "*science* of divine love," as it is consistently translated in most other editions, including the one which appeared in the weekly English language edition of *L'Osservatore Romano.* The *Origins* text also diverges from the latter version in adjusting the spelling and punctuation to U.S. standards. The phrase "science of divine love" is an allusion, of course, to a famous passage at the beginning of Manuscript B, where Thérèse writes to her sister Marie, "The science of Love (*la science d'Amour*), ah, yes, this word resounds sweetly in the ear of my soul, and I desire only this science" (Ms B 1r). See *Story of a Soul: The Autobiography of St. Thérèse of Lisieux,* trans. John Clarke, 3d ed. (Washington, DC: ICS Publications, 1996), 188-189.

moved through the canonization process with unprecedented speed, and in 1927 she was declared co-patron of the missions, at the request of "many missionary bishops." In addition:

> Many institutes of consecrated life and ecclesial movements ... chose her as their patron and teacher, taking their inspiration from her spiritual doctrine. Her message, often summarized in the so called "little way," which is nothing other than the Gospel way of holiness for all, was studied by theologians and experts in spirituality. Cathedrals, basilicas, shrines and churches throughout the world were built and dedicated to the Lord under the patronage of the saint of Lisieux. The Catholic Church venerates her in the various Eastern and Western rites.[4]

Here we notice echoes particularly of the data provided in the eighth chapter of the *Informatio* (on Thérèse's influence) and an implicit claim that she fulfills the fifth of the CDF "Norms and Criteria," which requires a "wide diffusion, positive 'reception,' and particular beneficial influence among the people of God."

The third numbered section mentions that Thérèse has been proposed to the faithful by the popes of this century not simply as a worthy example of holiness but as "a teacher of the spiritual life with a doctrine both spiritual and profound, which she drew from the Gospel sources under the guidance of the divine Teacher" and then passed on to her brothers and sisters especially through the three "autobiographical" manuscripts that comprise *Story of a Soul*. It is worth noting that here again John Paul II refers to Thérèse not as a "master of sacred doctrine" but as "one of the great masters of the spiritual life in our time."

The fourth numbered section recalls the numerous petitions for Thérèse's doctorate received from episcopal conferences as well

---

4   John Paul II, *Divini Amoris Scientia*, no. 2.

as other groups and individuals, along with an increasing number of "study conferences" and publications devoted to her teaching, all of which, according to the pope, inspired him "carefully to study whether the saint of Lisieux had the prerequisites for being awarded the title." Here one is reminded of the great weight given to these requests from episcopal conferences by many of the theological consultors in Thérèse's doctoral process.[5]

Sections 5 and 6 review Thérèse's life and writings. The pope states that "her principal work remains the account of her life in three autobiogaphical manuscripts... first published with the soon-to-be-famous title of *Histoire d'une Âme*." He singles out for special mention therein her discovery of the call to be "love in the heart of the church" as bride of Christ and mother of souls, as well as the "beautiful" and "moving" pages devoted to her trial of faith, the unity between love of God and love of neighbor, and her missionary vocation. The pontiff goes on to mention her other writings, including the 266 surviving letters (wherein she develops "a teaching that is actually a profound exercise in the spiritual direction of souls") and her 54 poems (especially "Pourquoi je t'aime, O Marie!" which represents "an original synthesis of the Virgin Mary's journey according to the Gospel").[6]

In section 7, however, we finally come to the heart of the question of Thérèse's qualifications for the doctorate. "From careful study of the writings of St Thérèse of the Child Jesus," says the pope, "and from the resonance they have had in the church, salient aspects can be noted of her 'eminent doctrine,' which is the fundamental element for conferring the title of doctor of the church." The crucial importance of the previously discussed one-

---

[5] See the discussion of the consultors' "vota" in the previous chapter.
[6] Again, the pope here closely follows the views expressed in the *Informatio* regarding which of Thérèse's texts are most important, and why.

page document identifying six "norms and criteria"[7] for judging doctrinal eminence, given to the theological consultors to guide their "vota," now becomes clearer. From this point on in *Divini Amoris Scientia*, without ever explicitly referring to the earlier document (which in any case has never been formally published), Pope John Paul takes up each of the six "criteria" in turn—and often in the same words, with the same phrases italicized—to show that Thérèse manifests the requisite "eminence of doctrine."

Thus, with respect to the first requirement of *un particolare carisma di sapienza*, the pope writes that "we find a special charism of wisdom" in Thérèse, who "without any particular theological training but illumined by the light of the Gospel, feels she is being taught by the divine Teacher." He recalls the canonization homily in which Pius XI had declared that the "Spirit of truth" had given her such a "knowledge of things above... that she shows everyone else the sure way of salvation."[8]

Next, the pope virtually repeats the original wording of the second criterion in claiming that Thérèse's teaching "not only conforms to Scripture and the Catholic faith, but excels (*eminet*) for the depth and wise synthesis it achieved." He goes on to say that "her doctrine is at once a confession of the Church's faith, an experience of the Christian mystery and a way to holiness," that "Thérèse offers a mature synthesis of Christian spirituality," and that "she combines theology and the spiritual life." What she

---

[7] The text of this one-page document, entitled "Norme di procedura e criteri dottrinali per il giudizio circa la 'eminens doctrina' dei santi proposti come 'Dottori della Chiesa'," was quoted in full and discussed in the preceding chapter. Since the document has not yet been published, the six "doctrinal criteria" it specifies will simply be cited here by their numbers. In the original text of the "Norme di procedura e criteri dottrinali," key phrases are italicized, and often these italics are carried over into most editions of *Divini Amoris Scientia* itself. Unfortunately, these italics have been largely omitted in the *Origins* translation.

[8] Though the word "feels" is used twice in this section, the clear implication is that Thérèse does not merely *feel* herself to be "instructed" from above, but that what she feels is in fact the case, and has been confirmed by the church's judgment.

"synthesizes" or brings into "harmonious unity," according to John Paul II, are the "dogmas of the Christian faith" understood both as "a doctrine of truth" and an "experience of life." In other words, she lived integrally what she believed and reproduced in her own life the Gospel truths she received; her life and her message are one.[9] The pope concedes that "in the writings of Thérèse of Lisieux we do not find perhaps, as in other doctors, a scholarly presentation of the things of God," but he insists that "we can rightly recognize in the saint of Lisieux the charism of a doctor of the church, because of the gift of the Holy Spirit she received for living and expressing her experience of faith, and because of her particular understanding of the mystery of Christ." The pope thus confirms that a "scholarly presentation" is not strictly necessary in candidates for the doctorate.

Moving on, the third requirement of candidates for the doctorate according to the "Norme di procedura" is that they be *authentic masters and witnesses of Catholic doctrine and Christian life*" whose writings shed particular light "on the confession and defense of the Catholic faith, on the preaching of the Gospel, on the understanding of worship and the spiritual life, or on a specific domain of Catholic doctrine." In numbered section 8 of *Divini Amoris Scientia*, Pope John Paul makes the corresponding claim that "with her distinctive doctrine and unmistakable style, Thérèse appears as an authentic teacher of faith and the Christian life," offering a teaching "in providential harmony with the church's most authentic tradition, both for its confession of the Catholic faith and for its promotion of the most genuine spiritual life." Here it is perhaps worth noticing that the pope has slightly altered the wording of the "Norme" in characterizing Thérèse as an "authentic teacher of faith" rather than an "authen-

---

[9] The pope here repeats from the "Norme di procedura" the same reference to *Dei Verbum*, no. 8.

tic master of Catholic doctrine." His words could also be interpreted, at first reading, as suggesting that Thérèse's main contribution as a doctor is simply "the promotion of the spiritual life."
As if to insure that this phrase not be understood too narrowly, however, Pope John Paul immediately goes on to say that Thérèse "has made the Gospel shine appealingly in our time; she had the mission of making the church, the mystical body of Christ, known and loved; she helped to heal souls of the rigors and fears of Jansenism." While admitting once again that she "does not have a true and proper doctrinal corpus," he nevertheless maintains that "a particular radiance of doctrine shines forth from her writings which, as if by a charism of the Holy Spirit, grasp the very heart of the message of revelation in a fresh and original vision, presenting a teaching of eminent quality." If she is indeed a "master of the spiritual life," hers is a spirituality inseparable from the fundamental divine self-revelation which Catholic doctrine articulates and theologians explore.

> The core of her message is actually the mystery itself of God-Love, of the triune God infinitely perfect in himself. If genuine Christian spiritual experience should conform to the revealed truths in which God communicates himself and the mystery of his will (cf. *Dei Verbum*, 2), it must be said that Thérèse experienced divine revelation, going so far as to contemplate the fundamental truths of our faith united in the mystery of Trinitarian life. At the summit, as the source and goal, is the merciful love of the three divine Persons, as she expresses it, especially in her "Act of Oblation to Merciful Love." At the root, on the subject's part, is the experience of being the Father's adoptive children in Jesus; this is the most authentic meaning of spiritual childhood, that is, the experience of divine filiation, under the movement of the Holy Spirit. At the root again, and standing before us, is

our neighbor, others for whose salvation we must collaborate with and in Jesus, with the same merciful love as his.[10]

Thus the "spirituality" of Thérèse is not self-enclosed and separated off from the concerns of systematic theology but has the broadest possible scope. "Through spiritual childhood one experiences that everything comes from God, returns to him and abides in him for the salvation of all, in a mystery of merciful love," says the pope. "Such is the doctrinal message taught and lived by this saint." John Paul II ends this number by underscoring Thérèse's remarkable penetration into "the mysteries of [Christ's] infancy, the words of his Gospel, the passion of the suffering servant engraved on his holy face, in the splendor of his glorious life, in his Eucharistic presence," the "particular light" Thérèse received "on the reality of Christ's mystical body, on the variety of its charisms, gifts of the Holy Spirit, on the eminent power of love," and Thérèse's "wise delving into the mystery and journey of the Virgin Mary, achieving results very close to the doctrine of the Second Vatican Council in Chapter 8 of the constitution *Lumen Gentium* and to what I myself taught in the Encyclical letter *Redemptoris Mater*." In this sense, the pope seems to be saying, Thérèse is a "master and witness" not only of "Christian living" but of "Catholic doctrine," as it is appropriated in her life of committed discipleship.

The ninth numbered section of *Divini Amoris Scientia* picks up on the fourth criterion of the "Norme," namely, that a candidate's doctrine be drawn "from the pure sources of the word of God, Tradition, and the Magisterium of the church." The pope here notes that "the primary source of [Thérèse's] spiritual experience and her teaching is the Word of God in the Old and New

---

[10] John Paul II, *Divini Amoris Scientia*, no. 8.

Testaments." He also mentions, among her most important secondary sources, the catechism, *The Imitation of Christ*, and the works of St. John of the Cross and St. Teresa of Avila (two Carmelite saints and doctors with whom she is described again as a "master of the spiritual life").

The fifth requirement of the "Norme"—that the candidate's works enjoy a "wide diffusion, positive reception, and particular beneficial influence among the people of God," with a *"character of universality,"* and confirmed by magisterial use—is addressed in the tenth numbered section of the Apostolic Letter. The pontiff simply declares that the "universality of Thérèse's doctrine" and the "broad reception of her message" have already been amply documented "in the studies made in view of conferring on her the title of 'doctor of the church,'" that is, in the *Positio*. Nonetheless, he recalls the frequent references to Thérèse by the popes of modern times (including himself) and the *Catechism of the Catholic Church*. He considers it "particularly important" that "the church's magisterium has not only recognized Thérèse's holiness, but has also highlighted the wisdom of her doctrine." Indeed, "Thérèse possesses an exceptional universality," reaching beyond all boundaries and influencing not only recently recognized saints and blesseds but also the church's pastors, "experts in theology and spirituality," clergy, religious, new ecclesial communities, and "men and women of every condition and every continent."

Regarding the sixth "Norme" requirement, that the candidate offer a "secure" and "durable" doctrine manifesting a "particular impact" and "relevance," the pope insists in numbered sections 11 and 12 that the reasons he has already outlined "are clear evidence of how timely is the saint of Lisieux's doctrine and of the particular impact her message has had." Furthermore, he says, Thérèse's qualities as a *woman*, a *contemplative*, and a *young person* "contribute to making her designation as a teacher for the church of our time even more significant." She speaks "with that practicality and deep resonance of life and wisdom which belongs to the feminine genius,"[11] she "offers a witness and theological illustration of the beauty of the contemplative life" which "possesses a mysterious fruitfulness for spreading the Gospel," and her youthfulness makes her "particularly effective in illumining the paths of young people." "Thérèse is a teacher for our time, which thirsts for living and essential words, for heroic and credible acts of witness," according to the pope; "for this reason she is also loved and accepted by brothers and sisters of other Christian communities and even by non-Christians." The Apostolic Letter then concludes by recalling the final steps in the process leading up to Thérèse's doctorate and repeating the formula of the solemn declaration bestowing the title upon her.

There is much in *Divini Amoris Scientia* deserving of further elaboration and study. For our purposes, however, it may be sufficient to point out a certain "dialectic" (or even ambiguity) that seems to run through the text. On the one hand there is an acknowledgment that Thérèse is in certain respects an unusual candidate for doctoral honors, since she lacks a "doctrinal corpus" and a "scholarly presentation of the things of God." She is most often described in the text not as a theologian or *magistra in sacra pagina* but as a "master of the spiritual life" and a "teacher of spiritual doctrine." The pope seems to be implicitly conceding that her function as a "doctor of the church" is somehow different from that of the great patristic authors and medieval authorities. Yet at the same time, he insists on "the continuity which links the doctors of the church to each other: in every historical context they remain witnesses to the unchanging Gospel and, with the light and strength that come from the Holy Spirit, they become its messengers, returning to proclaim it in its purity to

---

[11] Unfortunately, the pope does not elaborate here on what he means by "feminine genius," and how it is manifested in Thérèse's case.

their contemporaries" (no. 11). If Thérèse's contribution is said to be primarily in the area of "spiritual doctrine," it is, for all that, no less truly *doctrinal*, in the pope's view. She is, according to him, a "master of the spiritual life" not merely as one who offers the edifying example of a holy life or outlines stages in a spiritual itinerary but, more importantly, as one who shares with us the riches of her deep penetration and insight into the central mysteries of the faith, particularly in their existential impact.

The Homily During the Mass Proclaiming Thérèse a
Doctor of the Church

In his homily[12] for the Mass held in St. Peter's Square on October 19, 1997, at which he formally bestowed the title "doctor of the universal church" on the Saint of Lisieux, Pope John Paul II briefly returns to the now familiar theme of Thérèse's importance as a *woman*, a *young person*, and a *contemplative* (no. 2), though without much further elaboration. But since the occasion had been chosen to coincide with World Mission Sunday, John Paul II devotes considerably more attention to the "missionary" aspect of her life and message, and the way she exemplified and underscored the calling of all the faithful to "mission" by their very baptism.

> Thérèse Martin, a Discalced Carmelite of Lisieux, ardently desired to be a missionary. She was one, to the point that she could be proclaimed patroness of the missions. Jesus himself showed her how she could live this vocation: By fully practising the commandment of love,

---

[12] The official English language translation of this homily, like that of the Apostolic Letter, has been published in various places. Here, as before, I will quote from the text as printed in *Origins*; see John Paul II, "St. Thérèse of Lisieux Proclaimed a Doctor of the Church: Homily," *Origins* 27 (6 November 1997): 349, 351-352. Like *Divini Amoris Scientia*, it will be cited here according to its numbered sections.

she would be immersed in the very heart of the church's mission, supporting those who proclaim the Gospel with the mysterious power of prayer and communion. Thus she achieved what Vatican Council II emphasized in teaching that the church is missionary by nature (cf. *Ad Gentes*, no. 2). Not only those who choose the missionary life but all the baptized are in some way sent *ad gentes*.

Further on, he recalls the "high point" of Thérèse's spiritual doctrine in her discovery that she could fulfill her seemingly impossible desires to become an apostle and martyr through her vocation to be "love in the heart of the church" (no. 4). Toward the end of the homily the pontiff mentions Thérèse's "intense personal commitment supporting the apostolic work of Father Maurice Bellière and Father Adolphe Roulland," her two missionary brothers, and her "one ideal... to love [Jesus] and to make him loved,"[13] not by accomplishing extraordinary deeds but by faithfully following the "little way" (no. 6).

Regarding the specific question of her doctorate, however, the homily manifests a "dialectic" similar to what we found in *Divini Amoris Scientia*. The pope acknowledges that "something surprising is happening" in granting to this woman who "was unable to attend a university or engage in systematic study" and who "died young" such an "outstanding recognition which raises her in the esteem of the entire Christian community far beyond any academic title" (no. 3). And yet, he insists, "her ardent spiritual journey shows such maturity, and the insights of faith expressed in her writings are so vast and profound that they deserve a place among the great spiritual masters" (no. 4).

---

[13] The homily text refers here to Thérèse's letter of 24 February 1897 to Abbé Bellière (LT 220 in the critical edition of her correspondence). See Saint Thérèse of Lisieux, *General Correspondence*, trans. John Clarke, 2 vols. (Washington, DC: ICS Publications, 1982, 1988), 2: 1059.

Indeed, when the magisterium proclaims someone a doctor of the church, it intends to point out to all the faithful, particularly to those who perform in the church the fundamental service of preaching or who undertake the delicate task of theological teaching and research, that the doctrine professed and proclaimed by a certain person can be a reference point, not only because it conforms to revealed truth but also because it sheds new light on the mysteries of the faith, a deeper understanding of Christ's mystery. The council reminded us that, with the help of the Holy Spirit, understanding of the *depositum fidei* continually grows in the Church, and not only does the richly contemplative study to which theologians are called, not only does the magisterium of pastors, endowed with the "sure charism of truth," contribute to this growth process, but also that "profound understanding of spiritual things" which is given through experience, with the wealth and diversity of gifts, to all those who let themselves be docilely led by God's Spirit (cf. *Dei Verbum*, no. 8).... It is for this reason that the spiritual experience of the saints has a special value for deepening our knowledge of the divine mysteries, which remain ever greater than our thoughts, and not by chance does the Church choose only saints to be distinguished with the title of "doctor."[14]

Thus, on the one hand, the pope places Thérèse among the "great spiritual masters" rather than the "great theologians" and speaks of her primarily as an "eminent model and guide on the path of Christians" and a "teacher of life for the whole church," terms that could perhaps be applied to many saints who lack a specifically doctrinal mission. He even explicates the contribu-

---

[14] John Paul II, "St. Thérèse of Lisieux Proclaimed a Doctor of the Church: Homily," no. 3.

tion of saints like Thérèse in terms of their "spiritual experience." But on the other hand, as the context makes clear, what holds "special value" in this case are not the saints' unusual subjective experiences *as such* but the deeper insight that occurs when holy persons assimilate the central mysteries of the faith not merely intellectually but with their whole being, with all their graced capacities. "It is precisely this convergence of doctrine and concrete experience, of truth and life," says the pope, "which shines with particular brightness in this saint," Thérèse of Lisieux (no. 5). As a doctor of the church, he suggests, Thérèse's teaching can now serve preachers and theologians "as a reference point... because it sheds new light on the mysteries of faith, a deeper understanding of Christ's mystery." Unfortunately, the pope fails to elaborate on precisely how Thérèse might fulfill this important function.

The Doctoral Mass and Related Papal Statements

The eucharistic liturgy within which Thérèse was formally declared a doctor of the church was itself memorable and in some respects unprecedented.[15] A large wooden reliquary of Thérèse's remains, brought from Lisieux, led the entrance procession and was placed in front of the altar, near the pope's chair, on the gospel side, where it was prominently displayed throughout the Mass. The processional hymn consisted of verses from Psalm 66 alter-

---

[15] The description of the Mass is taken from the program booklet printed for the occasion and from several articles. See especially *Cappella Papale Presieduta dal Santo Padre Giovanni Paulo II per la Proclamazione a "Dottore della Chiesa" di Santa Teresa di Gesù Bambino e del Santo Volto* (Vatican City: Tipografia Vaticana, 1997); Jesús Castellano Cervera, "El Doctorado de Santa Teresa del Niño Jesús," *Revista de Espiritualidad* 226-227 (1998): 91-97; and Redemptus Maria Valabek, "St. Thérèse of Lisieux, Doctor of the Church," *Carmelite Digest* 37 (1997):49-63. The official program (hereafter *Proclamazione*) begins with a biographical profile of Thérèse in four languages (Italian, French, English, and Spanish), and lists the unusual features of the ritual on pages 23 to 25.

nating with stanzas from Thérèse's "Canticle to the Holy Face."[16] In his introduction to the penitential rite, Pope John Paul declared that "today we bless the Father of mercies, because he has revealed his secrets to the little and humble," and added that "today the light of the Gospel shines on the face of the young Carmelite, Thérèse of Lisieux, who with her eminent doctrine teaches the church the divine science of love." Following the *Kyrie*, the Pro-Prefect of the Congregation for the Causes of Saints and the Postulator General of the Discalced Carmelites approached the pope and read a summary of *Divini Amoris Scientia*, presenting the reasons for granting Thérèse the title of doctor, which the pontiff then proceeded to do in these words:

> Fulfilling the wishes of many brothers in the episcopate and of a great number of the faithful throughout the world, after consulting the Congregation for the Causes of Saints and hearing the opinion of the Congregation for the Doctrine of the Faith regarding her eminent doctrine, with certain knowledge and after lengthy reflection, with the fullness of our apostolic authority we declare Saint Thérèse of the Child Jesus and the Holy Face, virgin, to be a doctor of the universal church. In the name of the Father, and of the Son and of the Holy Spirit.[17]

The official proclamation was followed by a triple "Amen" sung by the assembly. Then, as the crowd in St. Peter's Square applauded and cheered, various religious from around the world, dressed in native garb, threw flower petals upon the reliquary and

---

[16] In the ICS Publications translation, this poem (PN 20) is known as "My Heaven on Earth." See *The Poetry of Saint Thérèse of Lisieux*, trans. Donald Kinney (Washington, DC: ICS Publications, 1996), 109-110, 272-273.

[17] See *Divini Amoris Scientia*, no. 12; and *Proclamazione*, 37.

large standing crucifix, recalling one of Thérèse's favorite devotional practices as well as her promise to send "a shower of roses" after her death.[18] Meanwhile, the schola sang verses from Thérèse's poem, "Jeter des fleurs" with an antiphon from Sirach 39:13-14. After the *Gloria* and the opening prayer, the Liturgy of the Word followed, with biblical texts chosen "to underscore Thérèse's wisdom and her work on behalf of the missions."[19] Read in French, the text of the first reading, from Isaiah 60:1-6 ("Arise, shine; for your light has come, and the glory of the Lord has risen upon you..."), was quoted by Thérèse herself in one of her letters to her "missionary brother," Adolphe Roulland.[20] The second reading, in English, from Ephesians 3:2-12 ("the mystery of Christ... now revealed by the Spirit to the holy apostles and prophets"), was chosen "to illuminate the teaching and missionary task (*il compito magisteriale e missionario*) of Thérèse of Lisieux."[21] The Gospel, from Matthew 11:25-30 ("what you have hidden from the learned and the clever you have revealed to merest children"), already cited in the opening rites of the Mass,

---

[18] "Every night during June of 1896, Thérèse and the five young sisters in the novitiate would meet after Compline—about eight o'clock—at the granite cross in the courtyard [of the Lisieux Carmel]. They would gather the petals shed beneath the twenty or so rose bushes there and throw them at the Crucifix"; see the introduction to PN 34, "Strewing Flowers," ("Jeter des fleurs") in *The Poetry of St. Thérèse of Lisieux,* trans. Donald Kinney, 158. This gesture recalls Thérèse's delight in scattering petals as a child during eucharistic processions (Ms A 17r), as well as her famous reflections in Manuscript B on her own small sacrifices as so many "flowers strewn before Your throne," "worthless petals" given in love, to be gathered up by the church and made "infinitely valuable" by the touch of the "divine hands," and then scattered upon the "Church Militant" and "Church Suffering" (Ms B 4v). See *Story of a Soul,* trans. John Clarke, 41, 196-197. Compare also PN 51, "An Unpetalled Rose," in *The Poetry of St. Thérèse of Lisieux,* 201-204, and the brief commentary on in it James Wiseman, "The Spirituality of St. Thérèse as Seen in Her Poetry," *Communio* 24 (Fall 1997): 535-536. On her promise to send a "shower of roses" after her death, see Thérèse of Lisieux, *Her Last Conversations,* trans. John Clarke (Washington, DC: ICS Publications, 1977), 62.

[19] See *Proclamazione,* 24.

[20] See *Proclamazione,* 24. The letter in question to P. Roulland is LT 193; see *General Correspondence,* trans. John Clarke, 2: 978.

[21] See *Proclamazione,* 24.

was proclaimed in Latin and Old Slavonic, recalling Thérèse's influence in both the Western and Eastern Churches. Then students from the Pontifical Russian College in Rome (the Russicum) honored their patroness by singing a *Troparion* and *Kondakion* composed in 1930 by the Russian poet Wenceslao Ivanov for the office of the Saint (Pius XI had named Thérèse the patroness of the Russicum in 1929).[22]

After the homily (discussed above) and the Creed, the General Intercessions followed, in Spanish, Swahili, Tagalog (from the Philippines), Portuguese, Polish, and Chinese. The petition in Portuguese, for example, was "for the teachers and students of Rome's universities and for all students of theology, so that, like St. Thérèse of Lisieux, in the school of Christ, Doctor of doctors, they might discern the secrets hidden in the living Word of God and might with a sapiential theology (*teologia sapiencial*) enlighten the paths for men and women of our time, especially for the poor and for those who are seeking the light of truth, even in the midst of the darkness of doubt."[23] The Chinese prayer was that "by the teaching of St. Thérèse, youthful and mature teacher of the spiritual life, we be able to advance on her little way which is the sure and universal path of Gospel holiness."[24]

During the Offertory Procession, as the gifts were brought up by representatives of the faithful from different lands, the choir sang verses from another famous poem of Thérèse, "Jesus, My Beloved, Remember" (PN 24), with an antiphon from Luke 1:54. The Preface was taken from the Discalced Carmelite proper for

---

[22] See Jesús Castellano Cervera, "El Doctorado de Santa Teresa del Niño Jesús," 95.

[23] See *Proclamazione*, 63. My translation here is based on Valabek, "St. Thérèse of Lisieux, Doctor of the Church," 63. I have, however, corrected his mistranslation of "sapiencial" as "supernatural."

[24] *Proclamazione*, 64. The Italian parallel version given in the official program uses the words "maestra di vita spirituale" of Thérèse. Again, I have slightly amended Valabek's translation in "St. Thérèse of Lisieux, Doctor of the Church," 60.

the feast of St. Thérèse. Later, after a communion hymn based on biblical texts in accord with Thérèse's teaching (Mt 11:28, Ps 130, Ps 115), the cantor intoned Thérèse's last poem, "You Who Know My Extreme Littleness," written for communion 11 weeks before her death. Then a long excerpt was read, in French, from Manuscript B, namely, the famous passage where Thérèse speaks of feeling within herself "the vocation of the warrior, the priest, the apostle, the doctor, and the martyr," and of finding her desires fulfilled in her vocation "to be love in the heart of my mother, the church."[25]

Because the ceremonies ran long, the pope then delivered his regular Sunday Angelus address from his place, before the final blessing of the Mass.[26] He mentioned Thérèse's role as patroness of the missions, and her "spirit of filial abandonment to Our Lady," before going on to greet various groups of pilgrims. Since this liturgy also served as the official opening Mass for the beginning of the academic year at the pontifical schools of Rome, the pope gave the faculty and students of these institutions a special welcome, and observed that "the 'lesson' that little Thérèse offers the Christian people is particularly significant for you: indeed, all who are called to contemplate and transmit the truths of the faith must cultivate that deep intimacy with God which belongs to the 'little' and the 'humble.' Treasure this teaching!" To the French groups he spoke of Thérèse as "a model of spiritual life and apostolic courage"; he encouraged the Spanish pilgrims to adopt "the sim-

---

[25] Whatever the significance of the editing, this reading from Manuscript B after Communion omitted the paragraph that begins "I feel in me the vocation of the PRIEST" (Ms B 2v 40ff.), though it preserved the word "priest" in Thérèse's collective naming, a few lines earlier, of the vocations she feels: "the vocation of the WARRIOR, THE PRIEST, THE APOSTLE, THE DOCTOR, THE MARTYR." See *Story of a Soul*, 192.

[26] The text of this address is found in John Paul II, "St Thérèse Lived Filial Abandonment to Mary (Sunday Angelus: 19 October)." *L'Osservatore Romano*, English language edition, 22 October 1997, 1, 4.

plicity and trust that the new doctor of the Church taught us in her spiritual way." After the final blessing, the relics of St. Thérèse were carried back into St. Peter's, for continued veneration. Meanwhile the faithful, including many cardinals and bishops, swarmed toward the altar to take away roses as souvenirs.

The following day, in a special audience with pilgrims who had come for the doctoral ceremonies, John Paul once again warmly greeted all the participating groups,[27] and commented:

> You have wished to come and learn from her who embodies for us the "little way," the royal way of Love. St. Thérèse of the Child Jesus and the Holy Face belongs to that group of saints whom the Church recognizes as teachers of the spiritual life. She teaches as a doctor, for although her writings were not of the same nature as those of theologians, for each of us they are a powerful help in understanding the faith and the Christian life.[28]

Here for a final time we encounter the same "dialectic" seen before: Thérèse "teaches as a doctor," and her writings "are a powerful help in understanding the faith," but she is primarily presented as among the "teachers of the spiritual life," whose message needs to be lived more than intellectually analyzed. The pope tells the pilgrims in closing: "Dear brothers and sisters, dear friends, it is up to you daily to live this doctrine which is now publicly offered to the whole Church."[29] In the case of many other "doctors of the universal church," such an exhortation might only

---

[27] The text of the pope's words to the pilgrims at the papal audience on 20 October 1997 are found in John Paul II, "Thérèse: Model of a Life Offered to God," *L'Osservatore Romano*, English language edition, 29 October 1997, 2. Like *Divini Amoris Scientia* and the papal homily for the doctoral declaration, it will be cited hereafter by its numbered sections.

[28] Ibid., no. 1.

[29] Ibid., no. 5.

have confused his audience. What would it mean, for example, to be told to "live the doctrine" of Peter Chrysologus or Bede the Venerable? In Thérèse's case, however, the sense is clear: to "live her doctrine" is to follow her "little way."

Implications of the Doctoral Ceremonies and Pronouncements

Even before she was given the title of doctor, Thérèse was perhaps already more widely known and loved than any of the previous recipients. Though she herself is acclaimed for her "simplicity," the faithful relate to Thérèse in myriad ways and for a complex variety of reasons. She is, for them, at once a teacher, a model, an intercessor, a friend, and much more besides. The official ceremonies and papal texts for Thérèse's doctorate attempt to acknowledge and incorporate all of these perspectives, even those not immediately relevant to the question of her doctoral status. This may in part explain the many different nuances and themes, which make it more difficult to specify precisely what the Magisterium intended by bestowing doctoral honors on Thérèse.

The papal Mass for the doctorate was itself notable for involving representatives from the many nations and religious communities Thérèse has touched (both in the Eastern and Western Churches, and especially in mission lands), and for the way in which the ceremonies were tailored specifically to Thérèse herself, reflecting her own warmth and spontaneity. During a pontificate sometimes characterized as preoccupied with adherence to traditional liturgical rubrics, the introduction of new ritual gestures—such as the strewing of flower petals, or the meditative reading of the Saint's text after communion—seemed especially striking. Striking also was the response of the assembly, which (from this participant's observations) reacted more enthusiastically to the appearance of the reliquary at the head of the entrance procession, and to the ceremonial strewing of the petals, than to the actual doctoral proclamation itself. What seemed to matter most to the assembled worshippers was not simply the witnessing of new honors bestowed on a figure of the past, but their remarkable sense of proximity to the living presence of the honoree herself.

The choice of World Mission Sunday for the ceremonies was obviously significant, providing John Paul II with the opportunity to relate Thérèse's doctorate to the themes of mission and evangelization, special concerns of his pontificate. Thérèse's status as co-patron of the universal missions was alluded to numerous times in the ceremonies and documentation. In one sense this might seem to have little direct bearing on her qualifications for the doctorate; after all, no one has yet suggested that being the *other* co-patron of the missions qualifies St. Francis Xavier for similar doctoral honors. Yet, unlike Francis Xavier, Thérèse's selection as co-patron was not based on years of labor in the missionary field but on the fundamentally evangelical orientation of her *life* and the *message* conveyed through her written reflections upon it. In other words, it was her lifelong interest in spreading the Gospel, her conviction of the apostolic value of a life dedicated to prayer for the sake of the church and the confidence of so many missionaries in her ongoing intercession, that led to a growing chorus of requests, especially from missionary bishops, that this young nun who never left the Carmelite cloister receive the title of patron of the missions. Recall also that at the Second Vatican Council a number of the Council Fathers wanted her name and example invoked in the "Decree on the Church's Missionary Activity," *Ad Gentes Divinitus*, to help illustrate and clarify its message. What they recognized was that Thérèse's *lived* (and reflected upon) personal zeal for the missions also included an important *teaching*, concerning the apostolic fruitfulness of the contemplative life in the church, and the fact that "all the baptized are in some way sent *ad gentes.*"[30] This is merely one instance of a pattern we find repeated over and over again: in Thérèse, life and doctrine are inextricably interwoven. Often what appears at first to be simply an edifying example from the life of a saintly young nun, similar to what can be gleaned from the biographies of countless holy persons, can be seen from another perspective as an important message for the church, with theological and doctrinal implications, when interpreted through the inspired self-reflection Thérèse shares in her writings. At the "school of Thérèse," Pope John Paul seems to say, devotees learn not only to admire her own zeal for the missions but also to appreciate more deeply the missionary dimension of their own baptismal vocation.

Besides mission, the papal ceremonies and documents identify or allude to other important components of Thérèse's teaching. As we have already seen, the pope specifically mentions a number of the more notable elements dealt with in Thérèse's writings: "the mysteries of [Christ's] infancy, the passion of the suffering servant engraved on his holy face,... his Eucharistic presence," her "particular light on the reality of Christ's mystical body," her "wise delving into the mystery and journey of the Virgin Mary," and so on.[31] These are the same themes singled out for special attention in the *Positio,* as areas in which Thérèse made the most significant contributions.

John Paul II seems a bit less clear, at first glance, on what constitutes the "core" or "high point" of Thérèse's message, since he identifies it variously as "the mystery itself of God-Love,"[32] or "the so called 'little way',"[33] or the central truth "that God is our

---

[30] John Paul II, "St. Thérèse of Lisieux Proclaimed a Doctor of the Church: Homily," no. 2.

[31] John Paul II, *Divini Amoris Scientia,* no. 8.

[32] Ibid.

[33] Ibid., no. 3.

Father and we are his children,"[34] or Thérèse's "moving discovery of her special vocation in the church."[35] Yet in reality, for the pope as for the *Positio*, all of these expressions are interrelated, and are simply so many ways of describing her central insight: namely, the gradual recognition of her own radical weakness as creature and her accompanying "rediscovery" (through constant reflection on Scripture and her own experience) of a God who is all Merciful Love, who calls her to reciprocate that love "infinitely" by surrendering with the confidence and "abandonment" of a child to the activity of God's love within her, in the smallest details of her life—returning love for love, becoming incorporated through God's transforming love into the mystical body of Christ and letting God love his creation through her. Or rather, without denying that Thérèse's "core" insight can be described and analyzed formally in this way, what is most instructive for the faithful is to see how she *lived* out these insights concretely. A summary list of Thérèsian "principles" without reference to their existential roots in her particular practice and self-reflection would leave us with only an emaciated understanding of her "doctrinal" contribution. That seems to be the pope's point in emphasizing that "it is precisely this convergence of doctrine and concrete experience, of truth and life, of teaching and practice which shines with particular brightness in this saint." In this respect, Thérèse would seem to fit very well with the contemporary insistence on a doctrinal and spiritual "teaching" thoroughly grounded in a *practice*.

Interestingly, John Paul II did not take the occasion of Thérèse's doctorate to explore at any length the general history and significance of the title "doctor of the universal church" (as one might have expected given the fact that this is the first and

---

[34] Ibid., no. 10.
[35] John Paul II, "St. Thérèse of Lisieux Proclaimed a Doctor of the Church: Homily," no. 4.

only time so far that he has bestowed the title). Throughout the papal ceremonies and documents related to the declaration, the continuing validity of the three traditional requirements—outstanding holiness, eminent doctrine, and declaration by a pope or council—seems to be taken for granted. The pope notes, for example, that "not by chance does the church choose only saints to be distinguished with the title,"[36] and describes "eminent doctrine" as "the fundamental element for conferring the title of doctor of the church."[37] Thus, in the case of an already canonized candidate like Thérèse, whose outstanding holiness can be assumed, the question of her qualifications for the doctorate comes down to whether or not she manifests the necessary "doctrinal eminence." And in *Divini Amoris Scientia*, Pope John Paul II seems to suggest that the answer to this question can be determined by whether or not Thérèse satisfies the six requirements outlined in the "Norme di procedura e criteri dottrinali" (though he never cites this unpublished document by name). At the very least, these requirements clearly provide him with the framework for identifying the "salient aspects" of Thérèse's doctrinal eminence.

As we have already seen, however, these six "criteria" are themselves somewhat vague, overlapping, and in need of further refinement; the text from which they are taken reads like an interim document. Undoubtedly, since "doctrinal eminence" is a kind of omnibus term for a certain constellation of qualities, the six criteria are useful in helping to disentangle some of the different threads involved. They help to remind us that the "eminence of doctrine" found in a saint's writings cannot be judged in the abstract, without reference to its past impact on the church, its possible future usefulness, and so on. Still, the criteria do not specify precisely, for example, how the "existence of a particular

---

[36] Ibid., no. 3.
[37] *Divini Amoris Scientia*, no. 7.

charism of wisdom" (criterion 1) is to be determined, or the eminent "quality of writing and height and profundity of doctrine" (criterion 2). How many writings are necessary in a candidate for the title? How close a dependence on Scripture and Tradition is required (criterion 4)? How explicitly and directly must the themes in the candidate's writings be related to doctrinal issues (cf. criteria 3 and 5)? How often, and in what contexts, must the candidate's doctrine have been used in Magisterial teaching (criterion 5)? How long does it take to decide that a candidate's message is "secure and durable" (criterion 6)? Perhaps, given that "doctrinal eminence" is ultimately bestowed by the Holy Spirit, scientific precision in determining its presence should not be expected. Still, one can understand how different consultors (and different members of the faithful) could arrive at different conclusions in Thérèse's case using the same six criteria, and thus at different judgments regarding her qualifications for the doctorate. Even the pope himself to some extent modifies the wording of the "Norme di procedura e criteri dottrinali" in his Apostolic Letter, to better fit Thérèse's case (calling her, as we noted, an "authentic teacher of faith" rather than, in the words of criterion 3, a "master… of Catholic doctrine").

In any case, John Paul II foresees and attempts to forestall the objection that Thérèse does not merit the title because she is not comparable, in terms of the scope of her writings and her doctrinal contributions, to the "great doctors" such as Augustine and Ambrose, or Basil and Gregory Nazianzen. While stressing her continuity with previously recognized doctors as a "witness to and messenger of the unchanging Gospel,"[38] he frankly admits that she "does not have a true and proper doctrinal corpus"[39] and that "her writings were not of the same nature as those of theolo-

---

[38] Ibid., no. 12.
[39] Ibid., no. 8.

gians."[40] Rather, in the documents related to Thérèse's doctorate, the pope most often describes her as a "teacher" or "master" of the spiritual life, with a "spiritual doctrine." Perhaps he is recalling the observation of certain theological consultors that many of the modern doctors (for example, Francis de Sales, John of the Cross, Teresa of Avila) could be similarly characterized. In any case, for John Paul II the fact that a candidate's contribution lies principally in the area of "spirituality" does not automatically disqualify him or her for the title, or in any way lessen the importance of the message. On the contrary, one of the principal reasons recommending Thérèse's declaration, according to the pope, is that her "spiritual teaching" is so firmly anchored in fundamental Christian doctrine, arising out of it and shedding light back upon it (rather than being rooted, say, in private revelations or subjective religious experiences). Thus in the official documents the terms "spiritual life" and "spiritual teaching" are understood in the most comprehensive sense, not as a separate realm of religious psychology apart from systematic theology and doctrine. Indeed, the pope may feel that Thérèse is an *ideal* "doctor" for our times, as contemporary theologians and others struggle to overcome the long-standing divide between theology and spirituality.

In declaring Thérèse a "doctor of the universal church," then, Pope John Paul has carefully framed what he believes the implications of this declaration to be. On the one hand, in his homily for the doctoral Mass the pope makes the striking assertion that "when the magisterium proclaims someone a doctor of the church, it intends to point out to all the faithful, particularly those who perform in the church the fundamental service of preaching or who undertake the delicate task of theological teaching and research, that the doctrine proclaimed by a certain per-

---

[40] John Paul II, *L'Osservatore Romano*, English language edition, 29 October 1997, 2.

son can be a reference point, not only because it conforms to revealed truth, but also because it sheds new light on the mysteries of the faith, a deeper understanding of Christ's mystery."[41] On the other hand, the pope does not say that the doctrine thus proclaimed *must* be used by theologians as a "reference point," still less as the *only* "reference point." The doctoral declarations of Anthony of Padua and Lawrence of Brindisi in 1946 and 1959, for example, put no special ecclesiastical pressure on theologians to study and use their "doctrine," and both "doctors" apparently continue to be largely ignored in theological circles and even in magisterial statements (neither is cited in the *Catechism of the Catholic Church*). In the documents surrounding the present doctorate there is no suggestion that Thérèse should replace Augustine in courses and studies on the theology of grace, for example, or that *Story of a Soul* can be substituted for the *Summa Theologiae*. Still, according to John Paul II, she is henceforth an officially recognized teacher in the church, with a "doctrinal" mission authorized by the Magisterium. What are the prospects for this doctrinal mission and how has Thérèse's doctorate been "received" so far? Have questions raised about her qualifications been adequately answered? What sort of "reference point" might the doctrine of Thérèse provide and is she now likely to have more "theological" significance along the lines suggested by the pope and the authors involved in her doctoral process?

The "Reception" of Thérèse's Doctorate: Some Objections and Replies

Though it is too soon to gauge the long-term impact of declaring Thérèse a doctor of the universal church, it seems fair to

---

[41] John Paul II, "St. Thérèse of Lisieux Proclaimed a Doctor of the Church: Homily," no. 3.

say that initial responses have been generally positive, though perhaps not as enthusiastic as Pope John Paul II might have hoped.[42] The event was widely reported in the popular Catholic press, though not at great length; in the secular media the event seemed largely overshadowed by the death of Mother Teresa of Calcutta some weeks earlier. As one might have expected, various religious journals devoted special issues to Thérèse's doctorate, wherein professional theologians spoke favorably of her message; a number of symposia, lectures, and liturgical celebrations were organized to mark the occasion. Yet these special events and publications were often largely sponsored or promoted by Thérèse's own Carmelite family,[43] and typically summarized the current state of Thérèsian scholarship rather than breaking significant new ground. To date, few practicing theologians have made any fresh attempts, in light of the doctoral declaration, to incorporate Thérèse's contributions into their own work. In the final part of this chapter we will suggest some ways in which they might begin to do so.

Meanwhile, criticisms of the declaration have been relatively rare and typically echo the objections already raised (and sometimes answered) in the *Positio*. Often they seem to involve misapprehensions about Thérèse herself or the consequences of ranking her as a doctor, as I will now briefly indicate. There were some, for example, even among the Carmelites, who initially

---

[42] In its bibliography of materials published on Thérèse in 1997, the year of the doctorate, the Carmelite journal *Carmelus* lists roughly 500 items; see "Bibliographia Carmelitana Annualis 1997," *Carmelus* 45 (1998): 306-353. Though not all of the items listed refer explicitly to Thérèse's doctorate, many do.

[43] The fact that members of her own religious order have played a major role in promoting study of Thérèse's doctrine in no way casts doubt on the value of the doctrine itself, any more than Dominican efforts on behalf of St. Thomas make the significance of his doctrinal contribution more questionable. Here the suggestion is simply that, if Thérèse is to be effectively a doctor of the *universal* church, her doctrine should increasingly capture the interest of theologians outside the Carmelite family.

opposed bestowing the title on Thérèse not because they doubted the value of her message, but because they feared it would somehow betray the very "littleness" which she cultivated and which the faithful find so attractive in her. The concern was that placing her alongside the theological giants such as Aquinas and Augustine might seem to put her beyond the reach of ordinary believers; they might find "Doctor Thérèse" more intimidating. We may recall the opinion of certain consultors in the doctoral process who felt that the title would conflict with Thérèse's humility and simplicity, and that she should instead remain "little."[44] Perhaps the best response to this particular objection is simply to point out that these fears have not been realized. On the contrary, in the years following her doctoral declaration, devotees of St. Thérèse have turned out in ever increasing numbers for the worldwide pilgrimage of her relics and popular presentations of her life and message have continued to multiply. There is simply no evidence that the doctorate has made her any less appealing to the ordinary faithful.

A quite different objection comes from those who, without denying Thérèse's sanctity, consider her particular example and message outdated, and suspect an ideological agenda behind her declaration as a doctor. In an interesting exchange that appeared in *Sisters Today*, William C. Graham, author of the *National Catholic Reporter*'s "Bookshelf" column, argued in this vein at some length. While acknowledging Thérèse's orthodoxy and outstanding personal holiness, as well as the influence of her piety on "former generations of faithful Catholics," his principal objection seems to be that "hers is not an essentially contemporary spirituality" and that "her approach is not one that will be shared or

---

[44] See *Positio* supplement, 45, 142.

imitated by those waiting and working for an ecclesiogenesis."[45] In particular, he finds in Thérèse an outmoded approach to obedience, expressing itself, for example, in her desire to be allowed to fast, which might hint of "anorexia or bulimia, a personal and unhealthy response to a male-dominated Church and a prioress-dominated convent."[46] He questions the claim that "she would have much to bring to the ecumenical encounter" and suspects more darkly that her past canonization, and recent efforts to have her declared a doctor, are part of a "Roman strategy" to inculcate unquestioning docility among the faithful.[47]

John P. Russell subsequently published a reply to Graham, emphasizing, among other things, that Thérèse's spirituality is rooted in the Gospel itself, that Thérèse herself was no legalist but strong willed with a well-developed personality of her own, and that is was the great Catholic theologian Hans Urs von Balthasar who claimed that there are "innumerable points of contact between Thérèse and the [Protestant] Reformers."[48] Graham responded in turn by thanking Russell for the information he pro-

---

[45] William C. Graham, "Is There a Case Against Saint Thérèse as Doctor of the Church?" *Sisters Today* 67 (January 1995): 57.

[46] Ibid., 57.

[47] Ibid., 57-58.

[48] See John P. Russell, "St. Thérèse of Lisieux: Doctor of the Church?" *Sisters Today* 69 (1997): 7-12. This quotation from von Balthasar, which appears on page 10 of Russell's article, is quoted from *Thérèse of Lisieux: The Story of a Mission* (New York: Sheed and Ward, 1954), 209. In the most recent edition of the same work, *Two Sisters in the Spirit: Thérèse of Lisieux & Elizabeth of the Trinity* (San Francisco: Ignatius Press, 1992), the same passage appears on page 283. The "points of contact" mentioned by von Balthasar here include: "the rejection of Old Testament justification by works; the demolition of one's own ideal of perfection to leave room for God's perfection in man; the transcendent note in the act of faith, the center of which remains in God; the existential fulfillment of the act of faith, which means more than a mere intellectual assent to the content of faith and involves utter personal fidelity toward the personal truth of God; and, finally, disregard for one's own failings—even for that joy over them that says *felix culpa*." For a brief discussion of St. Thérèse and Luther on the theology of grace, see John Welch, "Saint Thérèse's Discovery of Merciful Love," in *Master of the Sacred Page: Essays and Articles in Honor of Roland E. Murphy, O.Carm., on the Occasion of His Eightieth Birthday*, ed. Keith J. Egan and Craig Morrison (Washington, DC: Carmelite Institute, 1997), 389-401.

vided, and again granting Thérèse's saintly qualities, but insisting that some of issues he raised had still not been addressed: "Are there concerns about anorexia or bulimia, a personal and unhealthy response to a male-dominated Church and a prioress-dominated convent? Was she a victim of Roman strategy in being so quickly elevated to saintly status? Were threats to Church authority dealt a blow by this elevation?"[49]

On one level, Graham's questions seem oddly misdirected, and suggest a lack of familiarity with the details of Thérèse's life and posthumous career. He appears to base much of his opinion of the Saint on certain isolated phrases attributed to Thérèse, without indicating their source or their context.[50] Why he fixes, for example, on the question of Thérèse's fasting remains unclear, unless it is because anorexia and bulimia have become popular motifs in feminist studies of medieval religious women. Actually, at the time she entered Carmel, Thérèse was not yet old enough to be bound by the full monastic fast; not surprisingly, she looked forward to being able to join the other sisters in this respect. But the issue of fasting or of preoccupation with food appears hardly at all in her writings. Similarly, the unprecedented rapidity with

---

[49] See William C. Graham, "My Response to Father Russell," *Sisters Today* 69 (1997): 13-14.

[50] For example, presumably in order to underscore that Thérèse persisted in a "childish" mentality of slavish obedience throughout her life, he cites her as saying that one of her "first memories" was of wanting to be a religious, and that "I haven't changed my resolution since then!" See Graham, "Is There a Case Against Saint Thérèse as Doctor of the Church?", 57. These citations come from Ms A4v; see *Story of a Soul*, 20. But this completely ignores the clear evolution in her understanding of what her religious vocation might entail, from the ardent desire to save souls through prayer that she received after her "Christmas conversion" at age 14, to the discovery of her "little way" and her vocation to be "love in the heart of my mother, the church." As for the statement he attributes to Thérèse that "everything is played out before we are twelve," I have been unable to find it anywhere in her writings, and it seems to flatly contradict what she says elsewhere (for example, about "growing up" at the time of her "Christmas conversion"). Graham likewise ignores Thérèse's comments on her difficult struggles at the beginning of her life in Carmel to overcome an immature dependence on the prioress, Marie de Gonzague.

which devotion to Thérèse spread at the beginning of the 20th century had little to do with any deliberate Roman scheming, and in fact seems to have caught church authorities by surprise; the Vatican had to suspend its own rules regarding the elapsed time required for a canonization in order to keep pace with popular sentiment. Her message of the "little way" accessible to all the faithful would seem to run directly *counter* to any attempt to maintain a spiritual "caste system" in which holiness is controlled by, and largely limited to, ecclesiastical authorities and their minions.

Yet despite the defects in his particular presentation, Graham does put his finger on a concern expressed in certain quarters about how Thérèse's doctorate, and her message, might be misused. In his recent book, *Understanding Christian Spirituality*, Michael Downey seems to rank the contemporary devotees of *Story of a Soul* among those practicing a backward-looking "seeking refuge" style of spirituality (rather than a "retrieving riches" spirituality).[51] In her article on "sacrifice" in the *New Dictionary of Christian Spirituality*, Mary Barbara Agnew exercises a certain "hermeneutics of suspicion" regarding Thérèse's sacrificial language, observing that feminist theologians "have recognized that the call to surrender and oblation has served to reinforce the patriarchal situation that limits women's expectations to passive, subordinate, and auxiliary roles." She goes on to say of Thérèse that "seemingly, she grounded her spirituality in this oppressive woman's role," although "recent scholarship tends to vindicate the powerful and healthy personality who chose a 'little way' to live out this oblation" to Merciful Love.[52] In short, the fear is that

---

[51] Michael Downey, *Understanding Christian Spirituality* (New York: Paulist, 1997), 55.

[52] Mary Barbara Agnew, "Sacrifice," in *The New Dictionary of Catholic Spirituality*, ed. Michael Downey (Collegeville, MN: Liturgical Press, Michael Glazier Book, 1993), 846. What "this oppressive woman's role" refers to here is not quite clear. Grammatically, it could refer back to Thérèse's inability "to seek priesthood because of her sex," or to the offering of herself as a "victim of Merciful Love." Whether the latter is truly oppressive when understood properly, however, is a question Agnew seems to entertain with her observation on "recent scholarship."

Thérèse's doctorate might be used as an occasion to promote an older sentimental and privatized piety, and an ideal of female passivity, that characterized some expressions of the church's spirituality in general, and some devotions to Thérèse in particular, before Vatican II. Such concerns are perhaps reinforced by occasional comments in the relevant papal documents about Thérèse as an example of the "female genius," or John Paul's remark to the visiting pilgrims that:

> In the difficulties which necessarily occur in daily life, she never demanded her rights, but was ever ready to yield to her sisters, even at great interior cost. This is an attitude which, in every era of the Church's life, must be imitated by the baptized of whatever age or state. Only the virtue of humility, which Thérèse insistently asked of Christ, makes true concern for others possible.[53]

Seen in perspective, however, what is perhaps most striking is that such remarks appear so seldom in the official documents, especially given that Thérèse is only the third female doctor of the church, and given the pope's repeated (though undeveloped) claim that Thérèse's status as a *woman* makes her doctorate especially timely. Neither the theological experts and consultors nor John Paul himself explore the implications of Thérèse being both a woman and a doctor, or use her directly to promote a particular social agenda regarding women's role in church and society. If anything, it is the critics of current Vatican policies, and those favoring a greater openness within the church to women's gifts and ministries, who have invoked her memory. Thus, in a series of widely-quoted articles, Joann Wolski Conn has attempted a feminist retrieval of Thérèse as a mature woman,

---

[53] John Paul II, "Thérèse: Model of a Life Offered to God," no. 4.

capable of "profound and mutual relationships," and "a resource for 'a discipleship of equals'."[54] Mary Collins compares Thérèse with Theresa Kane in presuming "to speak directly to popes to accomplish their purposes when these were at odds with the norms of ecclesiastical life," and in "openly [entertaining] the unthinkable possibility that women might be called by God to the Church's priestly ministry."[55] The Women's Ordination Conference has for many years regarded Thérèse as a special patron, particularly because of her powerful statement in *Story of a Soul* that "I feel in me the *vocation of* the PRIEST" (Ms B2v).[56] Indeed, her image is used on the paper "money" which the conference encourages the faithful to put in the collection baskets at Mass to show their support for the ordination of women. Other authors cite a famous passage in her description of her pilgrimage to Rome, in which she defends her sex with both humor and great feeling:

> I still cannot understand why women are so easily excommunicated in Italy, for every minute someone was saying: "Don't enter here! Don't enter there, you will be excommunicated!" Ah! poor women, how they are mis-

---

[54] Joann Wolski Conn, "A Feminist View of Thérèse," in *Carmelite Studies V: Experiencing St Thérèse Today*, ed. John Sullivan (Washington, DC: ICS Publications, 1990), 120, 139. See also Joann Wolski Conn, "Thérèse of Lisieux from a Feminist Perspective," *Spiritual Life* 28 (Winter 1982): 233-239.

[55] Mary Collins, "Daughters of the Church: The Four Theresas," in *Women—Invisible in Theology and Church*, ed. Elisabeth Schüssler Fiorenza and Mary Collins, *Concilium* 182 (Edinburgh: T.&T. Clark, 1985), 19. In a more recent article, Mary Bryden underscores similar aspects of Thérèse, and critiques *Divini Amoris Scientia* for so heavily emphasizing how the popes of this century have praised her message; she detects in this "a noticeable tendency... to draw Thérèse into a framework of hierarchy and patriarchy of which she was never a part," apparently failing to realize that the use made of Thérèse in magisterial teaching is directly relevant to the question of whether she qualifies not merely as a saint but also as a doctor of the church. See Mary Bryden, "Saints and Stereotypes: The Case of Thérèse of Lisieux," *Literature and Theology* 13 (March 1999): 4.

[56] See *Story of a Soul*, 192.

understood! And yet they love God in much larger numbers than men do and during the Passion of Our Lord, women had more courage than the apostles since they braved the insults of the soldiers and dared to dry the adorable Face of Jesus. It is undoubtedly because of this that He allows misunderstanding to be their lot on earth, since He chose it for Himself. In heaven, He will show that His thoughts are not men's thoughts, for then the *last will be first*. More than once during the trip I hadn't the patience to await heaven to be first. (Ms A 66v)[57]

It is worth recalling, as well, that Père Desbuquois and others promoting Thérèse's doctorate in the late 1920's and early 1930's believed, in part, that it would be one way for the church to both recognize and embrace the positive results of the women's movement. On the other hand, most experts believe that Pius XI resisted the idea not because he had any doubts about the value of Thérèse's doctrine but primarily because he was unwilling to consider the possibility of granting the title to a woman. It would be ironic, to say the least, if denying Thérèse the doctorate in 1932 and bestowing it on her in 1997 were both construed "suspiciously" as acts of ecclesiastical sexism. Granted, even one of the theological consultors in the process asked rhetorically if Thérèse were being proposed for the title simply to appease women for denying them the priesthood.[58] But if in fact that were the hidden agenda, Thérèse would seem an odd choice to advance it. On the contrary, some of those petitioning her doctorate feared that

---

[57] Ibid., 140. In fact, as Thérèse goes on to recount, she simply ignored the cloister regulations at Santa Maria della Vittoria in Rome in order to view the paintings in the inner cloister of the attached Discalced Carmelite monastery. The elderly friar she encountered made no fuss, seeing that she was a child. No doubt one reason she recalled this incident so vividly was that it seemed to illustrate her claim, in relation to the "little way," that everything will be forgiven to those who know how to remain as spiritual children.

[58] *Positio* supplement, 50.

her statements about having "the vocation of a priest" might be regarded by the Vatican as a liability and stand in the way of her chances. In short, there is simply no indication so far of a systematic effort at any level to utilize the doctorate of Thérèse to discredit Catholic feminism or endorse more traditional roles for women.

Nor has the Vatican tried to present Thérèse as the champion of a pre-Vatican II spirituality and devotionalism. If anything, though some old-style materials on Thérèse continue to appear, the majority of publications since the title was bestowed have focused less on the sentimental childhood anecdotes favored in the past and more on the mature Thérèse, who struggled with the same fears and questions as people today and found the secret to holiness in the circumstances of everyday life. If anything, the studies inspired by her doctorate tend to show how she moved *beyond* the limitations of the French Victorian spirituality in which she was reared. Once again, Thérèse would be an odd choice if the Vatican were simply attempting to turn the clock back, since she is increasingly regarded as an *innovator* in the realm of Catholic spirituality.

But in the end, perhaps the most substantive objection evoked by the declaration of Thérèse's doctorate is the same one already encountered several times in the canonical process, namely, that Thérèse's writings and teaching are simply not "substantive" enough to merit her the title "doctor of the church," unless the meaning of the title is so altered as to allow virtually any saint to qualify. Consider, for example, a brief exchange of letters on Thérèse's qualifications in the *National Catholic Reporter* at the time of the declaration. Reacting to a story on the doctorate, one correspondent wrote that:

> Without in any way wishing to detract from the
> holiness, courage and popular appeal of St. Thérèse of

Lisieux and her "little way," it is difficult to see how she meets the traditional criteria of the title *doctor*....

Her single writing consists of a personal journal published posthumously after heavy editing. As a cloistered nun who died at the age of 24, she never engaged in teaching or defense of the faith as typically understood of "doctors." To divorce eminent learning and accomplished teaching from this title seems to be a revisionist understanding of traditional usage. It also seems to be an indirect devaluation of the public role of theology and theologians in the life of the church.

...This great injustice [of the past exclusion of women from teaching offices in the church] is not remedied by an affirmative action type gesture that equivocates the accepted understanding of the title....

Of course, the justification that Thérèse teaches by the wisdom of her humble spirituality is unassailable, except to point out that by the same criterion no saint could be denied a doctorate.... Even the unparalleled influence of St. Ignatius' 'Exercises' did not earn him the title.

The church could not do without the sanctity and inspiration of a St. Thérèse. However, its teaching mission can only be accomplished by doctors with specifically different charisms from those of St. Thérèse. A "spiritual attitude" does not a doctor make.[59]

Several correspondents quickly came to Theresè's defense, noting that in fact "we have more writing from Thérèse than from some other doctors, for example, St. John of the Cross"; that "Thérèse did, of course, teach, and teach consciously" within her community and through her letters; that "the church declares a

---

[59] See the letter to the editor by John W. McGee, under the heading "Thérèse a doctor?" in *National Catholic Reporter* 34 (31 October 1997): 21.

doctor on the depth of the teaching and the effect of the teaching on the church," not merely on the basis of the quantity of writings or their degree of scholarship; and that McGee would do well "to study the *positio*" in order to understand the reasons for this declaration.[60] Ironically, however, McGee's objections (as we may recall) actually echo some of the very concerns posed by the minority among the theological consultors in the canonical process, who wondered if Thérèse's writings were of sufficient number and theological depth and worried that declaring Thérèse a doctor might devalue the title, change its meaning, or open the floodgates to a host of other "spiritual" candidates equally qualified.[61] Indeed, some of John Paul II's statements seem to have these objections in mind, as he tries to position Thérèse's doctorate carefully in relation to the traditional understanding of the title. Whether Thérèse's doctorate is the exception or whether she represents a new direction toward less stringent requirements in the choice of future candidates remains to be seen. In either case, defenders of Thérèse's doctorate could presumably argue, on

---

[60] These comments appear in letters to the editor by Molly Vacha and David Centner in *National Catholic Reporter* 34 (21 November 1997): 24 and *National Catholic Reporter* 34 (5 December 1997): 23. Bishop Ahern has popularized the claim that Thérèse's literary output exceeds that of John of the Cross. Thus he says that "most do not know that she has given us more prose than St. John of the Cross and three times more poetry, which is astonishing in view of the fact that he was a university professor who died at the age of 49 whereas Thérèse never went to high school and died at 24"; see Patrick V. Ahern, "Thérèse, Doctor of the Church," *Origins* 27 (4 September 1997): 193. Leaving aside the fact that John of the Cross was never a university professor, the fact that Thérèse's *Oeuvres complètes* are currently published in an eight-volume edition can be somewhat misleading; much of the material there consists of notes and introductions, along with the 1898 edition of *Histoire d'une Âme* and an enormous volume of what *others* reported concerning her final words and conversations. With their introductions, Thérèse's complete texts (including her autobiographical manuscripts, letters, poems, prayers, and plays, but excluding the *Last Conversations*) come to roughly 900 pages in the French single-volume "Totum," roughly comparable to the number of pages John's writings occupy in the single-volume editions of his works.

[61] As we saw, several of the consultors likewise asked, with McGee, "If Thérèse is a doctor, why not Ignatius of Loyola and many others?"

formal grounds alone, that Thérèse must indeed possess the requisite theological depth and "eminence of doctrine" because the church, through the pope, has now solemnly declared that she does. Still, a more satisfying answer to the objection that Thérèse lacks theological importance would be to indicate, if only briefly, her actual and possible significance for the theological enterprise in the ongoing study and development of church doctrine. This is what we will attempt to do in the remainder of the present chapter.

Thérèse's "Theological" Mission and Method

The declaration of Thérèse as "doctor of the universal church" has occurred at a critical juncture in the history of theology itself. The rigid and pervasive Catholic neoscholasticism of the early 20th century has given way to a pluralism of theological methodologies, including Transcendental Thomist, process, feminist, liberationist, and hermeneutical approaches, among others. Indeed, even the most philosophically trained of modern popes, John Paul II, seems in his numerous writings to draw as heavily on his training in phenomenology as on traditional Thomism.

Yet if there is one point on which these different approaches agree, it is on the pressing need to overcome the sharp division between theology and spirituality that began in the Western Church during the late medieval period and developed especially in the post-Tridentine era. In his early and influential essay "Theology and Sanctity," for example, Hans Urs von Balthasar recounts "the impoverishment brought about by the divorce between the two spheres," and calls for a renewed "theology of the saints," a "theology at prayer." As his article makes clear, what he envisions (and promoted throughout his life) is not so much a less intellectually exacting and more devotional theologizing, but rather one which is ever attentive, as the saints were, to the existential import of the divine self-revelation under study.[62] Feminist and liberation theologians of every sort are equally convinced that a Christian theology divorced from the *praxis* of Christian discipleship is all but inevitably alienating and oppressive.

But even if theology and spirituality need to be rejoined, and even if all the saints are "theologians" in the sense of living close to those central mysteries of the faith which professional theologians examine, presumably not all saints are "doctors of the universal church," as some participants in Thérèse's process wisely observe.[63] To maintain otherwise would be to reduce "doctor of the church" to a synonym for "saint" and destroy the value of the title as a way of distinguishing those holy men and women who have a special *doctrinal* mission within the community of faith. One may agree to an extent with Robert Ellsberg's claim that: "The lessons of the saints are not contained in a set of 'teachings.' It is the saint's life itself that is our text, that offers meanings and mysteries that are never fully exhausted, and that reverberates with possibility and challenge even across the distance of centuries."[64] Yet even if no saint's significance is entirely reducible to a body of "teachings," nevertheless there are some saints who seem to have been given a particular charism of explicitly presenting an articulated *teaching* for the good of the church, just

---

[62] See Hans Urs von Balthasar, "Theology and Sanctity," in *Word and Redemption: Essays in Theology 2* (New York: Herder & Herder, 1965), 65, 69, 84-85.

[63] See, for example, Schönborn's comments in the *Positio*, 826 or those of the twelfth CDF consultor in the *Positio* supplement, 39.

[64] Robert Ellsberg, "Saints for Today," *New Theology Review* 12 (May 1999): 22. The analysis of saints' lives in terms of their "textual" character, using the tools of literary and cultural studies as well as recent continental philosophy, is becoming increasingly common. See for example, Alex García-Rivera, *St. Martín de Porres: The "Little Stories" and the Semiotics of Culture* (Maryknoll, NY: Orbis Books, 1995); and Edith Wyschogrod, *Saints and Postmodernism: Revisioning Moral Philosophy* (Chicago: University of Chicago Press, 1990).

as there are others who have contributed especially by their unflagging care for the poor, the strength of their witness as martyrs, or their role in the foundation of a new religious family. Hans Urs von Balthasar places Thérèse among those saints, rare in modern times, who have been entrusted with "a primarily theological mission."[65]

> For the faithful, they are, above all, a new type of conformity to Christ inspired by the Holy Spirit and therefore a new illustration of how the gospel is to be lived. For theologians, on the other hand, they are rather a new interpretation of revelation; they bring out scarcely suspected treasure in the deposit of faith. Even when the saints have not been theologians, nor themselves very learned, their sheer existence proves to be a theological manifestation that contains most fruitful and opportune doctrine, the directions of the Holy Spirit addressed to the whole Church and not to be neglected by any of her members.[66]

What does it mean, for the church and for theology, that "contrary to all expectation... the simple, modest story of this little girl should eventually culminate, as it irrefutably does, in the enunciation of theological truths"?[67] And how, if at all, do systematic theologians make use of a saint whose "message" is so closely bound to the narrative of her own life?

Before examining Thérèse's possible contributions in particular theological areas, let us consider for a moment what might be learned from her overall approach to issues. If Thérèse is a "doctor," what can be said about her general "methodology" in acquir-

---

[65] Hans Urs von Balthasar, *Two Sisters in the Spirit: Thérèse of Lisieux and Elizabeth of the Trinity*, 28.

[66] Ibid., 25.

[67] Ibid., 29.

ing and communicating her "doctrine"? In what sense, if any, is she "theological"?

Clearly, Thérèse is not a professional theologian in the usual sense; even if she had the intellectual gifts required, she lacked the necessary training and opportunity. Authors such as Léthel may contend that she is a "theologian" in some broader sense, according to which *all* saints are "theologians."[68] Yet even the pope concedes that "her *writings* are not of the same nature as those of theologians."[69] First-time readers of *Story of a Soul*, for example, are sometimes put off by what can seem to be nothing more than a string of sentimental childhood stories and pious expressions. Ida F. Goerres, for example, observes:

>...How sweet all this is, how well meant, how finely observed, how pleasantly narrated—but how "little", here too. The story confines the heart instead of expanding it. What a narrow horizon and what a poverty of content. There is much talk of sorrows and crosses: the little novice is scolded; Papa cannot come to her Clothing.... There is talk of sacrifices and mortifications, and then come the examples: ...how Sister Thérèse in the laundry gently endured, for the love of God, her careless workmates splashing her with dirty water; how she practiced perfect poverty by not objecting when a pretty water jug was removed from her cell....
>
> Does not such self-observation, such weighing everything in the most delicate of balances, constitute a serious weakening of the genuine Christian concept of sacrifice?...
>
> The disillusioned reader henceforth abides by the

---

[68] Recall François-Marie Léthel's programmatic assertion, "All the saints are theologians, and only the saints are theologians," discussed above in chapter 3.

[69] John Paul II, "Thérèse: Model of a Life Offered to God," no. 1.

impression that the much-praised sanctity of the "little way" consists in fashioning an extraordinarily high opinion of oneself on the basis of insignificant achievements and that natural fulfillment of human obligations which every other ethic passes over silently out of good taste, if not out of humility or modesty.[70]

Certainly, Thérèse's habits of constant self-examination and of personalizing everything that impinges upon her, can strike some modern readers as neurotic or narcissistic. Even the weather and the stars in the sky are sometimes described as if they had been arranged specifically for her benefit![71] Certainly, Thérèse is a product of the French Catholic Victorian piety of the late 19th century, even if in many ways she transcended its limitations. Certainly, *Story of a Soul* bears the marks of the circumstances in which it was written, initially as a response to the request of her eldest sister, who wanted precisely the kind of sweet family anecdotes that Thérèse records in the early pages of Manuscript A, but who ended up omitting them as too intimate in the first published version of *Histoire d'une Âme*.

Nonetheless, countless readers, without the aid of sophisticated commentaries, have spontaneously recognized something deeper in the text. Thérèse's *Story of a Soul* is more than a pious memoir. As Thérèse herself says in the opening pages:

It is not, then, my life, properly so-called, that I am going to write; it is my *thoughts* on the graces God deigned

---

[70] Ida F. Goerres, *The Hidden Face: A Study of St. Thérèse of Lisieux* (New York: Pantheon, 1959), 8-11. In fact, however, Goerres goes on to reject this approach as a misreading of the "little way," and to praise Thérèse for overcoming the bourgeois values of her upbringing.

[71] Recall the well known passages where, as a child, she sees the first initial of her name written in the stars (Ms A 18r) or her gratitude to Jesus for providing snow on the day she received the habit (Ms A 72r); see *Story of a Soul*, 42-43, 154-155.

to grant me. I find myself at a period in my life when I can cast a glance on the past; my soul has been matured in the crucible of exterior and interior trials....

It is with great happiness, then, that I come to sing the mercies of the Lord with you, dear Mother [Agnès]....

It seems to me that if a little flower could speak, it would tell simply what God has done for it without trying to hide its blessings.... The flower about to tell her story rejoices at having to publish the totally gratuitous gifts of Jesus. She knows that nothing in herself was capable of attracting the divine glances, and His mercy alone brought about everything that is good in her. (Ms A 3r-v)[72]

No doubt from the pen of many 22-year-olds, the comment about now being able to make a mature assessment of one's life might sound naive and self-important, but the rest of her texts bear out Thérèse's claim. More significantly, Thérèse proposes to recount not her own accomplishments but God's work in her, or more specifically, her *thoughts* on these graces. As the reader quickly discovers, even as a child Thérèse was very far from living "the unexamined life." She was an intellectually precocious young girl, with clear memories, often religious in nature, going back to earliest childhood. She tells us that she "began to think seriously (*penser sérieusement*)" when she was "still very little" (Ms A 8v).[73] Later, at the age of 11, as she was preparing for first communion:

---

[72] Thérèse of Lisieux, *Story of a Soul*, 15. Manuscript B was composed in response to Marie's request that Thérèse "write to you *my dream* and '*my little* doctrine' as you call it"; see ibid., 189. At the beginning of Manuscript C, addressed to Mother Marie de Gonzague, Thérèse again speaks of their common "desire that I finish *singing* with you the *Mercies of the Lord*"; see ibid., 205. In all three manuscripts, then, Thérèse's primary goal was not simply to tell the story of her life but to recount the mercies of God and what she had learned from them.

[73] Ibid., 25.

> ...one of my teachers at the Abbey asked me what I did on my free afternoons when I was alone. I told her I went behind my bed in an empty space which was there, and that it was easy to close myself in with my bedcurtain and that *"I thought."* "But what do you think about?" she asked. "I think about God, about life, about ETERNITY ... I *think!"* The good religious laughed heartily at me, and later on she loved reminding me of the time when I *thought,* asking me if *I was still thinking.* (Ms A 33v)[74]

Thérèse interprets this "thinking" as rudimentary mental prayer, through which "God was already instructing me in secret,"[75] but in any case the obvious answer to her teacher's question was that, indeed, Thérèse continued throughout her life to "think," particularly about religious matters. At school she was so devoted to learning her catechism lessons that Abbé Domin, the instructor, dubbed her his "little doctor" (Ms A 37v),[76] though "she got indignant at the idea that little children who died without baptism might be deprived of heaven."[77] And as she grew older she continued to reflect ever more deeply upon her life and her faith.

Thus the common impression of Thérèse's writings and thought as "intuitive" and "spontaneous" can be misleading to the extent that the underlying conceptual (and, in their own way, logical) elements are thereby overlooked. It is worth recalling, for example, that *Story of a Soul* begins, not with the details of her birth, but with an expression of obedience to *Jesus* in taking up her task, a *prayer* before the statue of Mary, a consultation of *Scrip-*

---

74 Ibid., 74.
75 Ibid., 75.
76 Ibid., 81.
77 Gaucher, *Story of a Life* (San Francisco, CA: HarperSanFrancisco, 1987), 50. This is often cited as an example of her originality in religious matters and independence of thought, even as a child.

ture (Mark 3:13 and Romans 9:15-16), and a *question* with serious "theological" overtones—"I wondered for a long time why God has preferences, why all souls don't receive an equal amount of graces"—which leads her immediately to a profound reflection on God's providence, albeit a reflection couched in the floral imagery she so often favored.

> Jesus deigned to teach me this mystery. He set before me the book of nature…. I understood that if all flowers wanted to be roses, nature would lose her springtime beauty, and the fields would no longer be decked with little wild flowers.
>
> And so it is in the world of souls, Jesus's garden. He willed to create great souls comparable to lilies and roses, but He has created smaller ones…. Perfection consists in doing His will, in being what He wills us to be.
>
> I understood, too, that Our Lord's love is revealed as perfectly in the most simple soul who resists His grace in nothing as in the most excellent soul; in fact, since the nature of love is to humble oneself, if all souls resembled those of the holy Doctors who illumined the Church with the clarity of their teachings, it seems God would not descend so low when coming to their heart. But He created the child who knows only how to make his feeble cries heard; He has created the poor savage who has nothing but the natural law to guide him. It is to their hearts that God deigns to lower himself. These are the wild flowers whose simplicity attracts Him. When coming down in this way, God manifests His infinite grandeur…. [Everything] works out for the good of each soul. (Ms A 2v–3r)[78]

---

[78] Thérèse of Lisieux, *Story of a Soul*, 13-15.

Here Thérèse strikes a theme that will run throughout the "autobiographical manuscripts," one that would not be out of place (absent this particular imagery) among the great patristic authors and medieval theologians, namely, that the solution to our deepest "why?" questions somehow lies ultimately in the mystery of God's "kenotic" love for his manifold creation and the infinite divine desire to receive the creature's love in return. "God as Merciful Love" becomes the hermeneutical lens through which she will boldly and creatively reread all of the elements of Christian doctrine as they present themselves to her.

A similar pattern of "theological" reflection appears again and again in all of Thérèse's great "discoveries." Regarding the "little way," for example, frustrated by the failure of her aspirations to become a great saint, Thérèse *reasons* that God "could not inspire unrealizable desires," and that therefore if she cannot "grow up" by her own efforts, the God of Merciful Love must lower himself to her level, if only she knows how to remain truly a "little one" (Ms C 2v-3r); she turns to Scripture to find confirmation of her insight.[79] Or again, perplexed by the disparity between the limitations of her circumstances and her "desires and longings which reach even unto infinity," desires to serve God even as "warrior, priest, apostle, doctor, and martyr," Thérèse once more turns to Scripture, discovering her solution in a creative synthesis of Pauline themes (concerning the church as Christ's body and charity as the "higher gift" which embraces and sustains all the others): "in the heart of the Church, my Mother, I shall be Love. Thus I shall be everything, and thus my dream will be realized."[80] Or again, pondering the "new commandment" of Jesus at the Last Supper to "love one another as I have loved you" in the light of her struggles to live charitably in community, she *reasons* once

---

[79] Ibid., 207-208.
[80] Ibid., 192-194.

more that the Lord does not "command the impossible," and that therefore, "never would I be able to love my Sisters as You love them, unless *You*, my Jesus, *loved them in me.*" In other words, she reaches the profound insight that the perfection of Christian charity is not a human accomplishment but consists in allowing God to love in and through us, with God's own love.[81] Or yet again, facing a premature death which threatened to frustrate all her hopes to continue working for the salvation of souls, she draws upon traditional Catholic doctrine for an original and creative solution:

> I really count on not remaining inactive in heaven.
> My desire is to work still for the Church and for souls. I
> am asking God for this and I am certain He will answer
> me. Are not the angels continually occupied with us
> without their ever ceasing to see the divine Face and to
> lose themselves in the Ocean of Love without shores?
> Why would Jesus not allow me to imitate them?
> ...What attracts me to the homeland of heaven is
> the Lord's call, the hope of loving Him finally as I have
> so much desired to love Him, and the thought that I shall
> be able to make Him loved by a multitude of souls who
> will bless Him eternally. (LT 254)[82]

In short, what we find here and elsewhere in Thérèse may not be systematically organized syllogisms with all the premises

---

[81] Ibid., 220-221.

[82] See Thérèse of Lisieux, *General Correspondence*, 2: 1142. Compare the famous text from the "Yellow Notebook" for 17 July 1897: "I feel that I'm about to enter my rest. But I feel especially that my mission is about to begin, my mission of making God loved as I love Him, of giving my little way to souls. If God answers my desires, my heaven will be spent on earth until the end of the world. Yes, I want to spend my heaven in doing good on earth. This isn't impossible, since from the bosom of the beatific vision, the angels watch over us.... I can't rest as long as there are souls to be saved." See Thérèse of Lisieux, *Her Last Conversations*, 102.

explicitly presented,[83] but they are logically patterned inferences where Thérèse is carefully thinking through issues that are at once personal and doctrinal. Like a medical researcher testing a new serum on herself, Thérèse attends closely to her own experiences and reactions but for the sake of sharing what she learns with others. Her biography and message are inextricably intertwined, because Thérèse's teaching arises out of deep reflection, in the light of Scripture, on the work of grace in her life. But from what she discovers, she draws conclusions applicable to all "little souls" like herself.

In that sense, even if her writings "are not of the same nature as those of theologians," they are "theological" in their implications. If she is "intuitive" in her approach, hers are not the "intuitions" of an ecstatic or visionary receiving dictated messages from beyond. Indeed, it has been suggested that Thérèse makes a better candidate for the doctorate precisely because her contribution is rooted in continual reflection on the Word of God and the ordinary experiences of life, rather than in the private revelations that so many Catholics today study with unhealthy fascination.[84] What might be called "intuition" in Thérèse is perhaps better described as her unerring instinct for the elements from Scripture or Tradition that most effectively address her concerns; seen from a faith perspective, this could also be called her "particular charism of wisdom for the good of the church."

Certainly Thérèse offers no programmatic remarks on theological methodology, and no one has asserted that professional theologians should mimic her very personal and unsystematic

---

[83] For example, when invoking her principle that "God would not inspire unrealizable desires," Thérèse simply assumes that her desires are in fact inspired by God, and are not mere selfish whims. Perhaps this is a justifiable assumption given that she "ambitions" only God's love, but she does not spell it out or defend it.

[84] See Jesús Castellano Cervera, "'Eminens Doctrina': Un requisito necesario para ser Doctor de la Iglesia," *Teresianum* 46 (1995): 18.

style. Still, in this regard she offers more than simply a reminder, as one theological expert in the process suggests, that theologians should practice intellectual humility and avoid "pretentious, cold rationalizing."[85] In her own unpolished way, Thérèse models a style of "theological" reflection that remains very close to its biblical and experiential sources, something many contemporary theologians consider worth striving for. We might even say that, in a broad sense, Thérèse engages in a theologizing rooted in "liberating praxis." Though her reflections are not informed by modern sociological and political analyses, she is in her own way concerned with, and directly involved in, the "emancipatory transformation" of all human society in the light of God's merciful love.[86] And her insights into the primacy of merciful love offer theologians new perspectives to explore regarding a variety of traditional theological areas and themes, as we will now indicate.

Thérèse in Relation to Particular Areas and Topics of Theology

Thérèse's main insights, as has often been noted, are all closely interrelated. As a result, her "doctrine" offers many points of entry; one can begin virtually anywhere and find connecting threads to all her other themes.[87] In fact, pursuing these connec-

---

[85] Pinckaers, "Thérèse of the Child Jesus, Doctor of the Church," *Josephinum Journal of Theology* 5 (Winter/Spring 1998): 37; see also the same remarks, in French, in the *Positio*, 907.

[86] See Rebecca C. Chopp, "Praxis," in *The New Dictionary of Catholic Spirituality*, 756-764.

[87] In a recent article, Thérèsian expert Bernard Bro seems to object to "compilations of Thérèsian 'themes'," since Thérèse never used the word and dealt in *realities* rather than themes. See Bernard Bro, "Le doctorat de Thérèse interroge la théologie," *Vie thérèsienne* 39 (1999): 51. Here, however, we are using the word "themes" simply for expository purposes, to help unpack and discuss various facets of Thérèse's teaching, without implying that she herself thought in terms of "themes." On the contrary, one of our points here is that Thérèse's "doctrine" is all of a piece.

tions is crucial, for it allows a more balanced reading of certain texts which could be easily misinterpreted when considered in isolation.

Merciful Love and the "Little Way"

Here let us begin with what is perhaps her most obvious theme, from which virtually all her other contributions flow, namely, her "rediscovery" in the Scriptures of the God of Merciful Love, before whom the only proper human stance is utter filial love and confidence. It is important for Thérèse that the human and divine elements here always be taken together and understood reciprocally; otherwise the stress on merciful love can sound merely abstract, and the emphasis on humility and "littleness" can seem mere pious affectation. As Thérèse herself found, the surrender to a God who is "nothing but mercy and love" goes hand in hand with the realization of our own radical poverty as creatures. We mentioned above that Thérèse came to her "rediscovery," described twice in *Story of a Soul,* through a long and painful personal process of lived experience and contemplative reflection on that experience.[88] After several years in religious life Thérèse finally realized that not only was she still weak but that in fact she would *never* by her own efforts reach the perfection to which she aspired since childhood. Yet she was convinced that God would not inspire unrealizable desires. And so, as she famously recounts, she searched the Scriptures for a solution and found it in the words of Proverbs and Isaiah: "Whoever is a little one, let him come to me" and "As one whom a mother caresses, so will I comfort you; you shall be carried at the breasts, and upon

---

[88] For a masterful analysis of Thérèse's discovery of the "little way," see Conrad De Meester, *The Power of Confidence: Genesis and Structure of the "Way of Spiritual Childhood" of Saint Thérèse of Lisieux* (Staten Island, NY: Alba House, 1998).

the knees they shall caress you" (Ms C 3r).[89] What she came to understand is that it is our very imperfection and helplessness, coupled with utter dependence and trust, that places the greatest claim on God's compassion and gives us the greatest assurance of God's help.

This is the essence of her "little way." All we need do is remain like "little children," in the Gospel sense of that expression, relying not on our own virtues or accomplishments but solely on the infinite mercy of the One who loves us and seeks only our love. In his famous work on the spirituality of liberation, *We Drink From Our Own Wells*, Gustavo Gutierrez has written that "spiritual childhood is required for entering the world of the poor—those for whom the God of the kingdom has a preferential love," and that "spiritual childhood is one of the most important concepts in the gospel, for it describes the outlook of the person who accepts the gift of divine filiation and responds to it by building fellowship."[90] For Thérèse, the honest recognition of our own imperfection and poverty leads paradoxically not to fear of God's wrath, as her contemporaries had thought, but to confidence in God's mercy:

> I understand that it is only love that makes us acceptable to God, that this love is the only good I ambition. Jesus deigned to show me the road that leads to this Divine Furnace, and this road is the *surrender* of the little child who sleeps without fear in its Father's arms. "Whoever is a *little one*, let him come to me."...
>
> ...Ah! if all weak and imperfect souls felt what the

---

[89] *Story of a Soul*, 208 (Ms C 3r). The texts are from Proverbs 9:4 and Isaiah 66:13, 12. It is one of the intriguing aspects of Thérèse's presentation that she does not here quote some of the Gospel texts that suggest themselves, on becoming "like a little child" or on the Father revealing himself "to the merest children."

[90] Gustavo Gutierrez, *We Drink From Our Own Wells: The Spiritual Journey of a People* (Maryknoll, NY: Orbis Books, 1985), 127.

least of souls feels, that is, the soul of your little Thérèse, not one would despair of reaching the summit of the mount of love. Jesus does not demand great actions from us but simply *surrender* and *gratitude*….

…See, then, all that Jesus lays claim to from us; He has no need of our works but only of our *love*…. (Ms B 1r–v)[91]

For Thérèse, this insight opened up fresh perspectives on virtually every aspect of her faith. Typical of Thérèse's rereading of her faith in light of her "discovery" is, for example, the way she reinterprets divine justice. She is well aware of devout souls who offer themselves as "victims of God's Justice in order to turn away the punishments reserved for sinners, drawing them upon themselves" (Ms B 84r).[92] Though admiring the generosity of such gestures, she is drawn instead to surrender herself to "Merciful Love," since what God most desires—even "needs," according to Thérèse—are those willing to be "set on fire" with his "infinite love."[93] This is the context for her well-known "Act of Oblation to Merciful Love," on which countless theological commentaries have been written. Thus, for Thérèse, the much feared attribute of divine justice takes on a different emphasis. "All of [God's] perfections," Thérèse writes, "appear to be resplendent *with love;* even His Justice (and perhaps this even more so than the others) seems to me clothed in *love*. What a sweet joy it is to think that God is *Just*, i.e., that He takes into account our weakness, that He is perfectly aware of our fragile nature" (Ms A 83v). As she would elsewhere explain to her missionary brother, Adolphe Roulland, God is all-merciful precisely *because* all-just

---

[91] *Story of a Soul*, 188-189.
[92] Ibid., 180.
[93] Ibid., 180-181.

and all-knowing; God understands our weakness.[94] She, therefore, scarcely ever considers the possibility of damnation and is blissfully unconcerned about purgatory, which she views in any case in terms of love rather than punishment.[95]

Thérèse never attempted to construct any new theological "system" based on her insights. But as Cardinal Schönborn suggests in the *Positio*, she may in a sense have helped inaugurate a change in the whole modern theological climate[96] and offered a different approach to a host of traditional theological concerns.

Thérèse, Christ, and the Trinity

Several consultors in the doctoral process, as we noted, claim that what we find in Thérèse is not a "Christology" in the strict sense but rather a "Christocentrism." Certainly she does not present her thoughts on Christ in any systematic way. Nonetheless, the role of Jesus in her "doctrine" is clearly central and has generated significant recent interest among theologians. In this regard we have already considered the contributions of the various theological experts and consultors in the canonical process, especially those of François-Marie Léthel, whose chapter in the

---

[94] See LT 226 (May 9, 1997) to P. Roulland, *General Correspondence*, 2:1093: "I know one must be very pure to appear before the God of Holiness, but I know, too, that the Lord is infinitely just; and it is this justice which frightens so many souls that is the object of my joy and confidence. To be just is not only to exercise severity in order to punish the guilty; it is also to recognize right intentions and to reward virtue. I expect as much from God's justice as from His mercy. It is because He is just that 'He is compassionate and filled with gentleness, slow to punish, and abundant in mercy, for he knows our frailty....'"

[95] See, for example, *Story of a Soul*, 180-181 (A 84r-v), and LT 221 in *General Correspondence*, vol. II, 1072. For further discussion of Thérèse's views on purgatory, see Jean Guitton, *The Spiritual Genius of Saint Thérèse of Lisieux* (Liguori, MO: Liguori/Triumph, 1997), 39-44; and Philippe de la Trinité, *Il purgatorio? Che ne pensa S. Teresa di Lisieux* (Rome: Teresianum, 1972). The latter is an expanded version of Philippe de la Trinité's booklet, *La doctrine de Sainte Thérèse de l'Enfant-Jésus sur le purgatoire* (Paris: Libraire du Carmel, 1950).

[96] *Positio*, 829. This "vote" is not signed, as we mentioned, but other consultors refer to its author by name.

Informatio on "the theology of Thérèse of Lisieux" is a virtual reprise of his book, *L'amour de Jésus: La christologie de sainte Thérèse de l'Enfant-Jésus* (Paris: Desclée, 1997). We need not repeat their remarks here, except to recall that, for Thérèse, Jesus is the most perfect expression of God's merciful love toward creatures. The divine infancy, in Thérèse's view, reveals a God so desirous of our love as to give himself completely into our hands in the form of a helpless child. Her devotion to the Holy Face similarly focuses not on reparation for offenses but on infinite love revealed in the face of the Suffering Servant, "veiled" and "hidden" by the wounds his creatures have inflicted, "thirsting" desperately for their love from the cross.[97] Thérèse included both elements in her religious name: "of the Infant Jesus and the Holy Face." As the commentators have noted, for her the crèche and cross are never separated but conjoined in a balance that avoids the extremes of either an over-sentimentalization of the infancy or a morbid preoccupation with the physical agonies of the Passion. Drawing upon authors from the French School of Spirituality, William M. Thompson has argued for a retrieval of the theology of childhood in Christology and presents Thérèse's teaching on the divine infancy as an excellent example of what he is proposing:

---

[97] In 1896 Thérèse consecrated herself solemnly to the Holy Face, just as she had done to Merciful Love the preceding year, as if the former were an extension of the latter. See the important text of this "Consecration to the Holy Face" (Pri 12)—with its references to Christ's "thirst" for love, his "veiled gaze," and Thérèse's desire for "souls," especially of "apostles and martyrs," in order to "inflame poor sinners with your Love"—in *The Prayers of Saint Thérèse of Lisieux*, trans. Aletheia Kane (Washington, DC: ICS Publications, 1997), 91-92. On the Holy Face, see also her poem "My Heaven on Earth" (PN 20) and her second "pious recreation," entitled "The Angels at the Crib of Jesus." Thérèse's sister Céline writes that "in our appraisal of her devotional life in Carmel, we must recognize, in the interests of objective truth, that her devotion to the Holy Face of Jesus transcended—or more accurately embraced—all the other attractions of her spiritual life"; see Sister Geneviève of the Holy Face, *A Memoir of My Sister St. Thérèse* (New York: P.J. Kenedy & Sons, 1959), 111. On Christ's "thirst" for love, see, for example, *Story of a Soul*, 189: "Jesus is *parched*, for He meets only the ungrateful and indifferent among His disciples in the world, and... alas, He finds few hearts who surrender to Him without reservations, who understand the real tenderness of His infinite Love" (Ms B 1v); see also ibid., 99 (Ms A 45v) and the many references in her letters.

So far as I can tell it is a remarkable, original, and fresh expression of the varied dimensions of childhood we have tried to sound out in these pages. And it is far from childish.... But to remove any doubt in this regard, she also takes the name of the "Holy Face," calling to mind the shroud-like suffering of Jesus on the way of the cross. Womb/crib and cross are united in her religious name.... Perhaps each intensifies elements of the other, the child bringing out the cross's fructifying freshness, and the cross bringing out the Christian child's nonchildish maturity....

...She is a cloistered Carmelite, but she is a special means of the birthing of many new Christians. She can only be this if she profoundly "swims" in the womb of grace. And that means being child.

...The child Jesus conformed this child into the form of the Christian child. Readers of her story will remember her many sufferings....

...Not surprisingly, then, Thérèse widens our imaginations with respect to the suffering and the victimized in history.... But her sensitivity to the Child God creates in her a sensitivity which does not miss the voiceless.[98]

Thus, according to Thompson, Thérèsian devotion to the infancy is "fresh, creative, original, and playful" but "light years away from anything childish."[99] It implies, rather, a profound identification with Jesus, incarnate love, as he identifies with the poor and

---

[98] William M. Thompson, *The Struggle for Theology's Soul: Contesting Scripture in Theology* (New York: Crossroad, 1996), 227-228. In an earlier work, Thompson suggests that the very structure of *Story of a Soul* mirrors "this fascinating interplay between Jesus' childhood and Holy Face"; see William M. Thompson, *Christology and Spirituality* (New York: Crossroad, 1991), 127-130. Thompson speaks here of Thérèse's "narrative Christology."

[99] Thompson, *The Struggle for Theology's Soul*, 229.

marginalized, those who "count for nothing," among whom the world's children are disproportionately represented.

More recently, theologian Mark A. McIntosh has begun to develop a Christology and theology of the Trinity drawn from mystical texts, according to which "God is God precisely because God chooses to *be* God by giving Godself away," and "we become who we are as Christ came to be who he is, by giving self away freely in love."[100]

> ...[T]he self only comes to know and love itself truly (to *be* in a more than provisional sense), by being known and loved in God, by being drawn into the deepest basis of our own being within the trinitarian life of God.
>
> It is not that there is a substance called 'selfhood' here, infinite in God and doled out in finite quantities to human persons. The idea is rather that the divine activity of being God, namely the infinite self-bestowal of the trinitarian persons one to another, is the eternal mutual activity of 'selving' which alone sustains particular identity. It is this activity that evokes human identity in the first place, and it is by ever-less obstructed participation in this activity that human identity flourishes.
>
> So the reality we call human selfhood is constituted by its basis in the infinite self-giving of the trinitarian life.... In the eternal play of the trinitarian life this absolute renunciation of the self on behalf of the other may be an infinite event of bliss and joy, but in the broken shards of human moral history the very same event may necessarily be enacted in painfully sacrificial terms.[101]

---

[100] Mark A. McIntosh, *Mystical Theology: The Integrity of Spirituality and Theology* (Malden, MA: Blackwell Publishers, 1998), 159, 208.

[101] Ibid., 238-239.

We need not pursue the details of McIntosh's dense exposition here, and he does not explicitly mention Thérèse in this context. Nonetheless, there appear to be many possible points of contact with the Saint of Lisieux, who famously said, for example, that "to love is to give everything and to give oneself" (*aimer c'est tout donner et se donner soi-même*).[102] At the end of her life she sent a final card to her missionary brother, Maurice Bellière, with the inscription: "I cannot fear a God who made himself so little for me…. I love him, for he is nothing but love and mercy."[103] If "the core of her message is actually the mystery itself of God-Love," as Pope John Paul II contends, and "the merciful love of the three Divine Persons" stands "at the summit, as source and goal," Thérèse would seem to offer valuable resources for this kind of theological project.[104]

Thérèse and Sacramental Theology

For the most part, Thérèse's comments on the sacraments are relatively sketchy and usually in relation to particular receptions of the sacraments by herself or friends. In *Story of a Soul*, for example, she recounts the experience of her first confession, first communion, and confirmation; she describes her own religious profession in spousal terms (as was typical in women's religious communities of the time). One might be able to piece to-

---

[102] See stanza 22 of "Why I Love You, O Mary!" (PN 54) in *The Poetry of Saint Thérèse of Lisieux*, 219.

[103] See the note to LT 266 in the NEC version of the *Correspondance générale*, 2: 1281. Unfortunately, the English language ICS edition provides only the text that Thérèse wrote on the back of this, the last picture that she painted: "Last souvenir of a soul, sister of your own soul. Thérèse of the Child Jesus"; see *General Correspondence*, 2: 1181. The picture itself bore the title, "L'Hostie de Noël."

[104] *Divini Amoris Scientia*, no. 8. In an earlier work on von Balthasar's Christology, McIntosh does incorporate Thérèse somewhat but primarily from von Balthasar's perspective rather than in her own right. See Mark A. McIntosh, *Christology from Within: Spirituality and the Incarnation in Hans Urs von Balthasar* (Notre Dame, IN: University of Notre Dame Press, 1996), 60-62, 65, 79-81, 101-104.

gether a "Thérèsian" theology of marriage, for example, but it would require a great deal of excavation of (and extrapolation from) scattered remarks by and about her.

More extensive, however, are her reflections on the eucharist and the sacrament of orders. It is clear that Thérèse gave a great deal of thought to priests and the ordained priesthood throughout her life, a fact hardly surprising given the pious Catholic environment in which she was raised. Indeed, her trip to Rome had convinced her that priests, despite the "dignity" of their calling, were "nevertheless weak and fragile men" (Ms A 56r). In the canonical examination before her profession, when asked her reasons for entering Carmel, she responded, "I came to save souls and especially to pray for priests" (Ms A 69v).[105] This was the very reason why, as she understood it, Teresa of Avila had inaugurated the life of the Discalced Carmelite nuns in the first place. This is also the reason why many individual priests and priests' associations have adopted Thérèse as a special patron.

Thérèse understood the ordained priesthood, however, less in terms of *office* than in terms of *service* to others, preaching the Gospel (like her two "missionary brothers") and providing the sacramental presence of Christ in the eucharist. In describing her own "desires and longings" for the priesthood in Manuscript B, for example, she exclaims: "With what love, O Jesus, I would carry You in my hands when, at my voice, You would come down from heaven. And with what love I would give You to souls!" (Ms B 2v). For Thérèse, ordained ministry, along with that of the apostle, martyr, and doctor, is another (albeit privileged) instrument and expression of God's merciful love toward the "little ones." William Thompson sees in Thérèse's texts a radical challenge to the church "to rethink its definition of its various ministries, particu-

---

[105] Thérèse of Lisieux, *Story of a Soul*, 122, 149.

larly that of priesthood—away from all tinge of exclusivity, and toward a ministry which nourishes love because it embodies an inclusivistic love."[106]

What of Thérèse's own attraction to the priesthood? It is true that she writes, in the same famous passage from Manuscript B, that "while desiring to be a *Priest,* I admire and envy the humility of St. Francis of Assisi and I feel the *vocation* of imitating him in refusing the sublime dignity of the *Priesthood.*" It is true that she writes to her sister Céline: "Is not the apostolate of prayer, so to speak, more elevated than that of the word? Our mission as Carmelites is to form evangelical workers who will save thousands of souls whose mothers we shall be.... I find that our share is really beautiful, what have we to envy in priests?" (LT 135).[107] It is true, finally, that she finds the fulfillment of her "desires and longings" in the vocation to be "love in the heart of the church, my mother," since it is love which makes all the other particular ecclesial vocations possible. Nowhere does she advocate a change in the current policy of limiting sacramental orders to males. Still, neither does she ever suggest that this "feeling within herself the vocation of the priest" is merely a selfish or misguided dream. As Thompson remarks, "there is perhaps more of a critical 'sting' in the Theresian charism than we have yet come to realize."[108]

Regarding the eucharist, Thérèse simply accepted without question the traditional Catholic understanding of "real presence" she was taught in her catechism classes as a child. Where she broke

---

[106] William M. Thompson, *Fire and Light: The Saints and Theology* (New York: Paulist Press, 1987), 173.

[107] Thérèse of Lisieux, *General Correspondence,* 2: 753. In her poem "Sacristans of Carmel" (PN 40), Thérèse describes herself and her sisters as "hosts" transformed into other Christs through the eucharist, and thereby made partakers in the "sublime mission of the priest" as they "help the apostles by our prayers, our love"; see *The Poetry of Saint Thérèse of Lisieux,* 170-171.

[108] Thompson, *Fire and Light: The Saints and Theology,* 173.

new ground, however, was in moving beyond the prevalent attitude that reception of the eucharist should be rare and reserved only for those "worthy." Though influenced by the "prisoner of the tabernacle" spirituality of her times,[109] Thérèse famously observes: "It is not to remain in a golden ciborium that He comes to us *each day* from heaven; it's to find another heaven...: the heaven of our soul, made to His image, the living temple of the adorable Trinity" (Ms A 48v).[110] But Thérèse does not stop there. For her, the purpose of the eucharist is not simply to give Christ another kind of "tabernacle" in which to be imprisoned but to transform this "living temple" into another Christ, to spread the Gospel and serve others.[111] Thérèse advises her scrupulous cousin that sacraments are intended by God to be loving helps for sinners, not as rewards for sinlessness.[112] Pope Piux X, who called Thérèse "the greatest saint of modern times" before she was ever canonized, praised her for advocating frequent (even daily) communion, something she unfortunately never lived to see in Carmel.[113]

---

[109] See, for example, her poems "My Desires Near Jesus Hidden in His Prison of Love" (PN 25) and "The Atom of Jesus-Host" (PN 19), in *The Poetry of Saint Thérèse of Lisieux*, 106-107, 133-135, as well as the "Prayer to Jesus in the Tabernacle" (Pri 7) in *The Prayers of Saint Thérèse of Lisieux*, 75-76. To be sure, some of these texts were written at the request of other sisters, so it is not always clear to what extent the sentiments expressed are identical with Thérèse's own.

[110] Thérèse of Lisieux, *Story of a Soul*, 104.

[111] Compare the words of the "Act of Oblation to Merciful Love" (Pri 6), "remain in me as in a tabernacle," in *The Prayers of Saint Thérèse of Lisieux*, 54, with the sentiments expressed in her poem, "The Sacristans of Carmel" (PN 40), described in note 86 above.

[112] See Letter 92 (May 30, 1889) to Marie Guérin, in *General Correspondence*, vol. I, 567-569.

[113] See Pierre Descouvemont and Raymond Zambelli, "Thérèse's Universal Influence," in *Saint Thérèse of Lisieux: Her Life, Times, and Teaching* (Washington, DC: ICS Publications, 1997), 262. Céline remarks that in Carmel Thérèse prayed "that there might be a liberalizing change in this traditional legislation" restricting frequent communion, and "predicted... that it would not be long after her death before we, at Carmel, should enjoy the privilege of daily communion." "This prophecy," she says, "was verified to the letter"; see *A Memoir of My Sister St. Thérèse*, 116.

Thérèse, Mary, and the Saints

In an era which often stressed Mary's special privileges and promoted Marian devotions often based on private revelations and apocryphal stories, Thérèse returned to the Mary of the Gospel and of ordinary experience: "I must see her real life, not her imagined life," she said. "I'm sure that her real life was very simple. They show her to us as unapproachable, but they should present her to us as imitable.... We know very well that the Blessed Virgin is Queen of heaven and earth, but she is more Mother than Queen."[114] The pope himself has noted how Thérèse in many respects anticipated the Mariology of Vatican II in chapter 8 of *Lumen Gentium* and his own teaching in *Redemptoris Mater*.[115]

Thérèse herself had a lively devotion to Mary and the saints, and a keen sense of connectedness with the whole Mystical Body, living and dead. No doubt she would have welcomed the current revival of interest among theologians in the traditional symbol of the "communion of saints." In his recent book, *Love in the Heart of the Church*, Carmelite theologian Christopher O'Donnell argues that "by placing the communion of saints at the centre of [Thérèse's] concerns, we are in a position to develop a new kind of ecclesiology," and fresh perspective on suffering, mission, charism, and a host of other themes.[116] In her latest book, *Friends of God and Prophets*, without explicitly referring to Thérèse, Elizabeth Johnson presents a "feminist theological reading of the communion of saints." After many pages on the history of this "symbol," its misuse and present neglect, Johnson begins her detailed feminist retrieval of the communion of saints, and arrives at what she presents as an important rediscovery:

---

[114] St. Thérèse of Lisieux, *Her Last Conversations*, trans. John Clarke, 161.

[115] *Divini Amoris Scientia*, no. 8.

[116] Christopher O'Donnell, *Love in the Heart of the Church: The Mission of Thérèse of Lisieux* (Dublin: Veritas, 1997), 216.

The arena where holiness flourishes is everyday life which itself has a sacred character. The term "heroic sanctity," used in official church language as a criterion for those whose cases are tested for canonization, reflects a value given to a certain kind of spiritual achievement, attained by intrepid acts and buttressed by miracle. It customarily points to such deeds as witnessing to the point of bloody martyrdom, or engaging in the white martyrdom of stringent asceticism.... Traditional "lives of the saints" are filled with such titanic acts. Noble they may be, but their telling within a tradition of holiness interpreted along lines of hierarchical dualism serves to reinforce the "unsaintliness" of those who do not measure up to these epic proportions. Reading the communion of saints as a company of the friends of God and prophets reclaims the ordinary milieu of virtue and the nobility of struggle despite failure and defeat, locating holiness not only or even chiefly in mighty, ideal deeds but in creative fidelity in the midst of everyday life.[117]

Take away the academic phraseology and sociological analysis, however, and we are close to what Thérèse already taught a century ago in contrasting the way of "great souls" with the "little way" of holiness in the circumstances of everyday life.

Thérèse, Grace, and Eschatology

Without any formal theological training or detailed exposure to Reformation disputes, Thérèse presents in simple language a carefully nuanced understanding of the relationship between

---

[117] Elizabeth A. Johnson, *Friends of God and Prophets: A Feminist Theological Reading of the Communion of Saints* (New York: Crossroad, 1999), 229. For further reflections on the difficulties raised by the "heroic" model of sanctity, see Lawrence S. Cunningham, *The Meaning of Saints* (San Francisco: Harper & Row, 1980).

God's grace and human works. Within her own thoroughly Catholic context Thérèse nevertheless was able to move beyond the "mercenary spirituality" of her childhood, and its preoccupation with tallying up merits, to go to God "with empty hands," as she famously put it.[118] Hans Urs von Balthasar has said that in her own way, without consciously intending to do so, Thérèse responds to Luther and Calvin point by point and even goes beyond them on the issue of faith and works.[119]

And as for eschatology, Thérèse boldly recasts even the traditional Christian understanding of eternal life. Instead of wanting endless rest in heaven, she hopes instead for unending activity on earth, helping to extend Jesus' salvific work. As we have seen, invoking a familiar Thérèsian principle, she reasons that the God of Merciful Love could not have inspired her desire for a great posthumous mission without intending to satisfy it, and that if the angels can be ceaselessly active without ever losing the beatific vision, so can she. Indeed, she is firmly convinced that her evangelical mission will be far more fruitful *after* her death than before.[120] And history seems to have proven her right! She offers us a dynamic vision of a resurrected life in Christ that does not sepa-

---

[118] The expression "with empty hands" comes from Thérèse's "Act of Oblation to Merciful Love" (Pri 6). See *The Prayers of Saint Thérèse of Lisieux*, 54: "After earth's exile, I hope to go and enjoy you in the Fatherland, but I do not want to lay up merits for Heaven. I want to work for your Love alone.... In the evening of this life, I shall appear before you with empty hands, for I do not ask you, Lord, to count my merits. All our justice is stained in your eyes. I wish, then, to be clothed in your own Justice and to receive from your Love the eternal possession of Yourself." For Thérèse's understanding of "merits," see De Meester, *The Power of Confidence*, 299-303.

[119] Hans Urs von Balthasar, *Two Sisters in the Spirit: Thérèse of Lisieux and Elizabeth of the Trinity* (San Francisco, CA: Ignatius Press, 1992), 283-284.

[120] See, for example, LT 254 to P. Roulland, in *General Correspondence*, 2: 1141-1142: "When you receive this letter, no doubt I shall have left this earth. The Lord in His infinite mercy will have opened His kingdom to me, and I shall be able to draw from His treasures in order to grant them liberally to the souls who are dear to me.... I shall be more useful to you in heaven than on earth."

rate us from ongoing care for the earth and the human family which gave us birth.

Other Areas

Space does not permit detailed discussion of the many other areas of Thérèse's "doctrine" that have attracted the attention of theologians, except to list a few of them briefly. We have already said something about Thérèse's contribution to the contemporary understanding of *mission* and the apostolic dimension of every Christian calling by virtue of baptism. In analyzing Thérèse's understanding of *vocation*, Hans Urs von Balthasar credits her with finally overcoming the age-old dichotomizing of contemplation and action, by recognizing that a contemplative loving is itself the most fruitful action on behalf of the church and the world.[121] Regarding *ecclesiology*, William Thompson has argued that the well-known passage in Manuscript B that ends with "In my heart of the Church, my mother, I shall be Love," is not merely about the personal discovery of her own vocation, but also sketches out a whole vision of the church, an "ecclesiology of love," where structure and hierarchy are all preserved but are subordinated to the Gospel message of confidence in God's merciful love.[122] Thompson also characterizes Thérèse's reflections on her own *trial of faith* as a rich source for Christology and soteriology.[123] In a recent essay, theologian Mary Frohlich goes so far as to claim that Thérèse's trial of faith "may open up new vistas for theology and ecclesial practice in the postmodern era.... I suggest that our newest Doc-

---

[121] Hans Urs von Balthasar, *Two Sisters in the Spirit: Thérèse of Lisieux and Elizabeth of the Trinity*, 196-197.

[122] Thompson, *Fire and Light: The Saints and Theology*, 171 ff. Many of the "Thérèsian themes" already treated above, such as ordained ministry, the sacraments, and the communion of saints, are ultimately ecclesiological in their implications.

[123] Ibid., 89-93.

tor of the Church points us in this direction because her final trial of faith is, all at once, a radical transcendence of intentional consciousness, a heroic exemplification of the kenosis of Jesus Christ, and an unreserved act of solidarity with those most abandoned to nothingness."[124] The list of suggestions regarding fruitful Thérèsian threads for theologians to follow could be extended indefinitely.

Reflections

These, then, are but a few areas where Thérèse seems to have made important contributions, for others to explore and develop. If today we take some of them for granted, that only shows, I think, how much her ideas have already been absorbed by the church of our time. They were by no means commonplace in her own day. For example, though she is never mentioned in *Lumen Gentium*, Thérèse is often credited as one of the major forces behind the Second Vatican Council's emphasis on the "universal call to holiness," which is hardly conceivable without the changes she helped bring about in the modern understanding of sanctity. And although she was by no means the only influence at work in 20th-century Catholicism's return to the Scriptures, she was certainly ahead of her time in this respect, and the popularity of her biblically rooted spirituality surely helped paved the way for this development. Even today, major theologians are still "rediscovering," often without realizing it, points which Thérèse had made over a century ago.

To what extent all of this proves Thérèse's "doctrinal eminence" and suitability for doctrinal honors is perhaps still debat-

---

[124] Mary Frohlich, "Desolation and Doctrine in Thérèse of Lisieux," *Theological Studies* 61 (June 2000): 279.

able. Those who insist that only theologians with a "doctrinal corpus" should be named "doctors of the universal church," or only patristic authors and medieval *magistri*, will not be convinced by anything said here that Thérèse deserves the title. What I have tried to suggest in this chapter, however, is that, at least from the perspective of the Magisterium, which bestows this title and interprets its meaning, Thérèse does fit the present criteria as they have evolved over time. We have seen that, in naming her a "doctor," John Paul II made no pretence of equating her with the "great" doctors in terms of systematic theological achievements; he linked her with those among the previously named doctors who could be characterized primarily as "masters of the spiritual life." Nonetheless, he clearly indicates that Thérèse's "spiritual message" arises out of living experience of the truths of Christian doctrine and has doctrinal implications; he insists that it can serve in some sense as a "reference point" for theologians, especially in such areas as Christology, ecclesiology, Mariology, and so on. This is not to say that Thérèse is now *the* standard against which theological positions must be judged. It would certainly go too far to claim that a thorough knowledge of Thérèse is indispensable for modern theologians. But her teaching is a "reference point" at least in the same sense as a "religious classic," from which theologians and others can continue to learn, and in which they will continue to find fresh insights. Whatever title one prefers, this is certainly a special gift to the church over and above the example of a holy life, and deserves its own acknowledgment. Thérèse was already a "doctor *in* the church" long before she was officially named a "doctor *of* the church."[125]

---

[125] This phrase is borrowed from Philippe de la Trinité; see his *Thérèse de Lisieux, la sainte de l'enfance spirituelle, relecture des textes d'A. Combes* (Paris: P. Lethielleux, 1980), 124.

CONCLUSION

The preceding pages have attempted to offer some insight into St. Thérèse's doctorate when viewed within the context of the church's evolving understanding of the nature and significance of its "doctors." I have focused especially on the official documents related to her canonical process, because they are as yet little known and because they provide the best evidence of how this ecclesiastical event came about and what the Magisterium intended in declaring Thérèse a "doctor of the universal church." In the first chapter I reviewed the history of the title, from its biblical roots to the curial discussions of its meaning and scope just prior to the choice of Thérèse for this honor. In the second chapter I outlined Thérèse's life and message, particularly as these pertained to questions raised about her suitability for the doctorate, and I described the growing efforts since the early decades of the 20th century to have her declared a doctor. Chapter 3 contained a close reading of the actual *Positio* prepared for the canonical process, including the official "vota" of the experts and theologians asked for their opinion on Thérèse's qualifications, particularly with respect to "eminence of doctrine." In chapter 4 I examined the pope's careful efforts—in his Apostolic Letter *Divini Amoris Scientia* and related statements and events—to situate and explain the significance of formally bestowing the title on the saint of Lisieux. I then attempted to describe briefly how the doctorate of Thérèse has so far been received and to indicate some areas in which she seemed to offer a positive contribution, not only to the church in general, but to theological endeavors in particular.

There is no denying that the church's understanding of its διδάσκαλοι and their ecclesiastical role has undergone significant development since New Testament times. As we have seen, until the 16th century the term *doctor ecclesiae* was generally reserved for patristic authors alone. By such a standard, not even Thomas Aquinas and Bonaventure would have qualified. The decisions of Pius V and Sixtus V (in 1567 and 1588 respectively) to include these two giants of medieval theology among the ranks of the doctors, then, already represented a certain broadening of the category to incorporate saints whose "eminent doctrine" was presented in a style differing from that of the Church Fathers. Similarly, Pius IX's choice of Alphonsus Liguori in 1871 proved that figures of the modern era could also be doctors, just as his recognition of Francis de Sales in 1877 demonstrated that those who were known primarily as great preachers and spiritual writers could also qualify. Indeed, most of those declared "doctors of the universal church" during the past 100 years are not remembered for any global perspective on theology as a whole but for their contribution to the development of a particular theological field or issue.

We can understand, then, why the Congregation for the Causes of Saints and other curial groups have had such a difficult time clarifying the requirements for a candidate to be named a "doctor of the church." On the one hand, there is an obvious desire to preserve the seriousness of the title, by continuing to insist especially on the importance of the second of the three traditional requirements: holiness of life, eminence of doctrine, and formal declaration by a pope or council. Throughout the canonical process for Thérèse, we have seen the fear expressed that too broad a notion of "doctrinal eminence" would open the category of "doctor" to virtually any saint and empty the title of all significance. On the other hand, those involved in the process are well aware that the traditional understanding of "doctrinal eminence" has changed over time and must continue to change if the title is to have more than merely antiquarian interest and if the church is to recognize that the charism of "doctors" did not cease with the patristic or medieval period.[1]

Here, as in so many other areas, Thérèse seems to represent both continuity with the past and also a new departure. When viewed from a more traditional interpretation of "eminent doctrine" as requiring a "doctrinal corpus," she clearly does not qualify for doctrinal honors, as several of the consultors in the process point out. She is not a professional theologian, and her presentation can hardly be called "systematic," as this is usually understood.

Yet on the other hand, when compared with other doctors, she seems no less "systematic" than Catherine of Siena, for example, and her message is better known and more influential than that of many others on whom the title has been bestowed.[2] One can make a strong case, as we have seen, that she amply fulfills the six "Norms and Criteria" for judging doctrinal eminence which were first elaborated by the Congregation for the Doctrine of the Faith, subsequently approved by the pope in November

---

[1] After all, there are only a finite number of Church Fathers and medieval *magistri* who would count as plausible candidates. Thus to interpret the requirement of "eminent doctrine" too narrowly and traditionally would seem to mean that "doctor of the church" would eventually become a closed category, once all the viable candidates had been so designated.

[2] As Lawrence Cunningham remarks of another "doctor of the universal church," for example: "Even Saint Anthony of Padua (1195–1231), about whom we do know a good deal, is popularly venerated less for his person and his apostolate and more for his reputation as a miracle worker.... Anthony is called upon as the saint who will cause lost things to be found." See Lawrence S. Cunningham, *The Meaning of Saints* (San Francisco: Harper & Row, 1980), 148.

1996 and finally given to the experts and consultors in Thérèse's canonical process.[3] Whether these "Norms and Criteria" are themselves adequate is a further question. In one sense, the haste to have Thérèse named a doctor of the church during the centenary of her death seems to have preempted the more careful study that Paul VI had called for when he suspended further concessions of the title in 1972. Many aspects of the requirement of "eminent doctrine" still need further clarification, and the choice of Thérèse as a doctor has only raised them more vividly.

Ultimately, the debate over Thérèse's particular qualifications should perhaps be seen as part of a much larger issue, concerning how the church understands, identifies, and celebrates those of its members entrusted by the Holy Spirit with a special doctrinal mission. One might compare the situation to the long evolution in the church's understanding of what constitutes authentic martyrdom, from the clear early cases of those deliberately killed (in "odium fidei") by Roman authorities for explicitly professing their faith, to more recent cases such as Maximilian Kolbe, who simply volunteered to take the place of another prisoner in Dachau condemned to die, or Edith Stein, who was rounded up and sent to Auschwitz along with many other Catholics of Jewish descent in retaliation for a statement of the Dutch bishops against the Nazis.[4] The church continues to clarify what it means in the changing situations of human history to give "witness" to one's faith in Christ to the point of shedding blood and recognizes that the "hatred of the faith" traditionally required may

---

[3] I am referring here, of course, to the as yet unpublished curial document discussed at length in previous chapters, namely, "Norme di procedure e criteri dottrinali per il giudizio circa la 'Eminens Doctrina' dei santi propositi come 'Dottori della Chiesa'."

[4] For a discussion of the evolving requirements for recognition as a martyr, see chapter 4 in Kenneth L. Woodward, *Making Saints: How the Catholic Church Determines Who Becomes a Saint, Who Doesn't, and Why* (New York: Simon & Schuster, Touchstone Books, 1990, 1996), 127-155.

not always be explicitly stated by those responsible for the martyr's death. No doubt it can be argued that some of those recently recognized as martyrs represent an unwarranted broadening of the concept, to the point that they run the risk of reducing the title's traditional importance. Yet perhaps we should rather say that the Congregation for the Causes of Saints is simply trying to take account of what the faithful have long recognized, namely, that those believers whose Christian commitment to charity and social justice led to their deaths are just as truly "martyrs" as the figures listed in the ancient martyrologies and may offer a more inspiring witness of what it means to "lay down one's life" with Christ today.

Similarly, some might argue that the choice of Thérèse represents the *reductio ad absurdum* of the trend in recent centuries to broaden the category of "doctors of the church" and that it is high time to raise the bar again. Yet at a time when the humanities are attempting to broaden the "canon" of classic texts in various fields to include previously marginalized voices, at a time when Catholic theology is no longer a monolithic discipline, at a time when many are trying to heal the long standing split between spirituality and systematic theology, perhaps Thérèse is an especially providential choice for doctoral honors. Certainly among modern saints she is one of those most strongly identified with a particular *teaching* for the sake of the church, a teaching, moreover, which has not only been widely studied by theologians but has received enthusiastic reception among the faithful.[5] In declaring her a doctor of the church, John Paul II has made it clear that he is not presenting her as a *magistra in sacra pagina* or systematic theologian but rather as a "master of the spiritual life." Just as

---

[5] On the significance of "reception" as a theological principle, see the article "Reception" in Christopher O'Donnell's *Ecclesia: A Theological Encyclopedia of the Church* (Collegeville, MN: Liturgical Press, 1996), 400-402. The article includes a very useful bibliography on this theme.

clearly, however, he indicates that "spiritual life" here is not to be understood as an area of private devotion divorced from other aspects of the Christian vocation but rather as a totality of Spirit-led action and reflection rooted in the same fundamental Christian mysteries that theologians explore. In a most powerful way, Thérèse both *shows* us what it means to live the truths of the faith and *teaches* us what she has learned by doing so. Her "doctrine" is all the more convincing, because she has first put it into practice herself. Thus, as Pope John Paul II suggests, she may be a doctor particularly well suited to our times, which demands that words be confirmed by deeds.

Whither Thérèse and the doctorate? I have already outlined, in the fourth chapter, a few areas in which Thérèse might be able to serve theologians as a "reference point," as Pope John Paul II has said. Some theologians have already begun exploring the implications of her message for various questions in contemporary theology. Perhaps her formal recognition as a "doctor of the universal church" may encourage others to do likewise or make theological journals and publishing houses more receptive to serious Thérèsian studies. Only time will tell.

Will Thérèse's doctorate open the floodgates to a host of other candidates? In the concluding chapter of his recent book on the *doctores ecclesiae*, Bernard McGinn asks "What is the future of the doctors of the church?" and proposes a long list of possible candidates for future doctoral honors, including a number of figures not yet canonized (for example, Boethius and Julian of Norwich) and even some (like Isaac of Nineveh and Martin Luther) who lie beyond the bounds of the Roman Catholic tradition as it is normally understood.[6] It seems unlikely that the traditional understanding of "doctor of the church" will become

---

[6] Bernard McGinn, *The Doctors of the Church: Thirty-Three Men and Women Who Shaped Christianity* (New York: Crossroad, 1999).

so ecumenically broad any time soon, especially since orthodoxy, at least in terms of the standards of the candidate's own times, is still considered a necessary component of eminent doctrine. Still, given how far the concept of "doctor" has evolved over the centuries, perhaps we cannot altogether rule out some future developments in the direction McGinn suggests.

What about the suggestion of some consultors to inaugurate a new liturgical and ecclesiastical category of "spiritual teachers" for those who, like Thérèse, are reliable guides for Christian living but lack a doctrinal corpus? Such a proposal would perhaps have the pedagogical and catechetical advantage of allowing the church to formally identify a certain "canon" of spiritual masters. However, I suspect the strongest objection to this idea is that it might further exacerbate the unfortunate split between theology and spirituality. The greatest doctors of the church, after all, span both categories; doctrine and spirituality are as inseparable in Augustine as they are in Thérèse.

What of the multitude of other saints and blesseds suggested by the consultors and others as candidates also worthy of doctoral honors, such as Irenaeus of Lyons, Francis of Assisi, Hildegard of Bingen, Gertrude of Helfta, Ignatius of Loyola, Louis-Marie Grignion de Montfort, John Vianney, Elizabeth of the Trinity, and Edith Stein? What about a future doctorate for the present pope himself, whom some admirers are already calling "John Paul the Great"? The possibility of another "doctor-pope" raises special questions, as Betti points out, because although Gregory the Great and Leo the Great are already numbered among the 33 officially recognized "doctors of the universal church," it is not yet clear what magisterial weight a doctoral declaration adds to what papal texts already enjoy.[7]

---

[7] Umberto Betti, "A proposito del conferimento del titolo di Dottore della Chiesa," *Antonianum* 63 (1988): 289, n. 39.

Regarding the other names mentioned, certainly no candidate is likely to be named a doctor before some formal recognition as a saint, if the requirement of outstanding holiness of life is to be preserved. The traditional strictures against choosing martyrs, which would have eliminated Irenaeus of Lyons and Edith Stein, appear likely to be lifted. In that case, Irenaeus would seem to be an excellent choice from the patristic era. Edith Stein, a figure in whom there is now much interest, does offer voluminous writings and something approaching a "doctrinal corpus," but she is currently admired more for her heroic life than for her systematic teaching, which has not yet been sufficiently studied and appropriated by the larger church. The spiritual doctrines of Francis of Assisi[8] and Ignatius of Loyola have had incalculable influence within and even beyond the bounds of Roman Catholicism, but the number of texts offered in each case is even more limited than that of Thérèse. As for John Vianney, interest in his message seems to have waned, although it is sobering to realize that Hans Urs von Balthasar identifies him along with Thérèse as "the only two perfectly evident instances in the nineteenth century of a primarily theological mission."[9] One suspects that Pope John Paul would be happy to bestow doctoral honors on Elizabeth of the Trinity and Louis-Marie Grignion de Montfort, since he is known to be an admirer of their writings. However Eliza-

---

[8]   In an article from the Catholic News Service at the time of the declaration of Thérèse's doctorate, author Cindy Wooden asks "whether Pope John Paul has broadened the understanding of doctor of the church in a way that will lead to new requests for saints never before considered eligible." "A prime example may be the co-patron of Italy, St. Francis of Assisi," she suggests; "while not a trained theologian, not even an ordained priest, his spirituality continues to influence individuals and religious orders 771 years after his death." See Cindy Wooden, "St. Thérèse of Lisieux, Doctor of the Church: Not a Divine Ph.D.," Catholic News Service, 7 November 1997. However, one suspects that the most significant objection to Francis as doctor would be that his influence rests primarily on his example and the importance of the movement he started, not on his writings, which are very few.

[9]   Hans Urs von Balthasar, *Two Sisters in the Spirit: Thérèse of Lisieux and Elizabeth of the Trinity* (San Francisco: Ignatius Press, 1992), 28.

beth is, if anything, less "systematic" than Thérèse, and officially embracing de Montfort's "high" Mariology might seem ecumenically insensitive at this moment in history (as would, perhaps, bestowing doctoral honors on Hildegard of Bingen, some of whose writings have an anti-Semitic tone). In many respects the simplest and easiest next choice would be Bernardine of Siena, since his process is already complete and awaits only a papal proclamation. But, short of a new resurgence of devotion to the Holy Name, there seems to be no pressing reason to name him soon.

Indeed, one suspects that for Pope John Paul II the pastoral advantage and timeliness of a potential doctoral declaration are at least as important a consideration as the quantity and theological depth of a candidate's writings, or the presence of a doctrinal corpus. After all, the Vatican must select "doctors of the universal church" not from abstract models but from concrete individuals, and few candidates are equally strong in every area enumerated by the "Criteria and Norms." Despite her "lack of a doctrinal corpus," Thérèse certainly has the advantage of being widely known for a set of writings and a message whose riches continue to be mined by theologians and the ordinary faithful alike. With the celebration of her centenary, and the obvious interest in her doctorate expressed by so many episcopal conferences and private individuals, no doubt Pope John Paul II viewed the declaration of Thérèse as a "doctor of the church" as a positive response to the "signs of the times."

What impact Thérèse's doctorate will have in the long run remains to be seen. Interest in the saint of Lisieux has certainly not waned. If anything, the crowds for the recent visit of her relics to the United States were much larger than for any of the events held during her centenary in 1997, including those commemorating her doctorate. This might suggest that her declaration as "doctor of the universal church" has so far had little impact on the faithful as a whole, and indeed the ceremonies in

Rome on 19 October 1997 garnered far less attention than the funeral of Mother Teresa several months before. Still, it was striking that at nearly every stop on the recent tour of her relics, local news coverage mentioned not only the circumstances of Thérèse's life but also the fact that she had recently been named the 33rd "doctor of the universal church," the youngest in this category, the one closest to our own time, and only the third woman to be so honored. Moreover, in nearly every report ordinary Catholics were able to speak eloquently of Thérèse's "message," her "little way," and her emphasis on the God of Merciful Love. Clearly Thérèse has already been "received" by the faithful as a reliable teacher of God's truth and a sure guide to "ordinary holiness," whatever importance they may attach to her new title.

Surely much more could be said about the significance of doctors of the universal church and of Thérèse's doctorate. The preceding pages have simply offered a few pointers for other researchers to explore in greater depth. My hope is that theologians may find in Thérèse both a companion in their search for truth and also a source of helpful insights and perspectives in their particular fields. Yet whatever changes may eventually come in the understanding of the doctorate and in the analysis of Thérèse's message, one thing remains certain: that the Holy Spirit will continue to bless the people of God with faithful teachers manifesting "a particular charism of wisdom for the good of the church."

BIBLIOGRAPHY

I. Primary Sources for Thérèse's Life and "Doctrine"

A. Writings by Thérèse

La Bible avec Thérèse de Lisieux: Textes de Sainte Thérèse de l'Enfant-Jésus et de la Sainte-Face. Paris: Editions du Cerf/Desclée de Brouwer, 1979.

General Correspondence. Translated by John Clarke. 2 vols., Washington, DC: ICS Publications, 1982, 1988.

Her Last Conversations. Translated by John Clarke. Washington, DC: ICS Publications, 1977.

Histoire d'une âme de Sainte Thérèse de Lisieux selon la disposition originale des autographes novellement établie par Conrad De Meester. Moerzeke, Belgium: Carmel-Edit, 1999.

Manuscrits autobiographiques. 3 vols. + facsimiles. Edited by François de Sainte-Marie. Lisieux: Carmel de Lisieux, 1956.

Les mots de Sainte Thérèse de L'Enfant-Jésus et de la Sainte-Face: Concordance générale. Établie par Soeur Geneviève, O.P., de Clairefontaine, Soeur Cécile, O.C.D., du Carmel de Lisieux, et Jacques Lonchampt. Paris: Éditions du Cerf, 1996.

Oeuvres complètes. 8 vols. Nouvelle édition du centenaire. Paris: Éditions du Cerf/Desclée de Brouwer, 1996.

Oeuvres complètes (textes et dernières paroles). Édition du centenaire. Paris: Éditions du Cerf/Desclée de Brouwer, 1998.

The Poetry of Saint Thérèse of Lisieux. Translated by Donald Kinney. Washington, DC: ICS Publications, 1996.

The Prayers of Saint Thérèse of Lisieux. Translated by Aletheia Kane. Washington, DC: ICS Publications, 1997.

Saint Thérèse of Lisieux, the Little Flower of Jesus. Translated by Thomas Taylor. New York: P.J. Kenedy & Sons, 1927.

Six, Jean-François, ed. *Thérèse de Lisieux par elle-même.* 3 vols. Paris: Bernard Grasset and Desclée de Brouwer, 1997.

Story of a Soul: The Autobiography of St. Thérèse of Lisieux. Translated by John Clarke, 3d ed. Washington, DC: ICS Publications, 1996.

B. Thérèse by Those Who Knew Her

Ahern, Patrick V. *Maurice and Thérèse: The Story of a Love.* New York: Doubleday, 1998.

Descouvemont, Pierre. *Thérèse of Lisieux and Marie of the Trinity: The Transformative Relationship of St. Thérèse of Lisieux and Her Novice Sister Marie of the Trinity.* Translated by Alexandra Plettenberg-Serban. Staten Island, NY: Alba House, 1997.

François de Sainte-Marie. *Visage de Thérèse de Lisieux.* 2 vols. Lisieux: Office de Lisieux, 1961.

Geneviève de la Sainte-Face. *Conseils et souvenirs.* Paris: Éditions du Cerf/Desclée de Brouwer, 1973.

Geneviève of the Holy Face. *A Memoir of My Sister St. Thérèse.* New York: P.J. Kenedy & Sons, 1959.

Martin, Zélie. *Correspondance familiale 1863-1877.* Lisieux: Carmel de Lisieux, 1958.

The Photo Album of St. Thérèse of Lisieux. Commentary by François de Sainte-Marie. Translated by Peter-Thomas Rohrbach. New York: P.J. Kenedy & Sons, 1962.

Procès de béatification et canonisation de sainte Thérèse de l'Enfant-Jésus et de la Sainte-Face. 2 vols. Rome: Teresianum, 1973, 1986.
Vol. 1: *Procès informatif ordinaire.*
Vol. 2: *Procès apostolique.*

St. Thérèse of Lisieux by Those Who Knew Her. Translated by Christopher O'Mahony. Dublin: Veritas, 1975.

II. Biographical and Historical Studies Related to Issues Raised about Thérèse's "Doctrine"

Baudouin-Croix, Marie. *Léonie Martin: A Difficult Life.* Dublin: Veritas, 1993.

De Meester, Conrad, ed. *Saint Thérèse of Lisieux: Her Life, Times, and Teachings.* Washington, DC: ICS Publications, 1997.

Descouvemont, Pierre, and Helmuth Nils Loose. *Thérèse and Lisieux.* Toronto, Ontario: Novalis, 1996.

Dowling, Matthew James. "The Evolution of a Modern Pilgrimage: Lisieux, 1897-1939." Ph.D. diss., Yale University, 1995.

Emert, Joyce R. *Louis Martin: Father of a Saint.* Staten Island, NY: Alba House, 1983.

Furlong, Monica. *Thérèse of Lisieux.* New York: Virago/Pantheon, 1987.

Gaucher, Guy. *The Passion of Thérèse of Lisieux.* New York: Crossroad, 1990.

———. *The Story of a Life.* San Francisco, CA: HarperSanFrancisco, 1987.

Goerres, Ida F. *The Hidden Face: A Study of St. Thérèse of Lisieux.* New York: Pantheon, 1959.

O'Connor, Patricia. *Thérèse of Lisieux: A Biography.* Huntington, IN: Our Sunday Visitor, 1983.

Piat, Stéphane-Joseph. *Céline, Sister Geneviève of the Holy Face: Sister and Witness of Saint Thérèse of Lisieux.* Translated by the Carmelite Sisters of the Eucharist. San Francisco: Ignatius Press, 1997.

———. *The Story of a Family: The Home of The Little Flower.* Translated by a Benedictine of Stanbrook Abbey. New York: P.J. Kenedy & Sons, 1947.

Robo, Etienne. *Two Portraits of St. Teresa of Lisieux*. Revised and enlarged ed. Westminster, MD: Newman Press, 1957.

Rohrbach, Peter-Thomas. *The Search for Saint Thérèse*. Garden City, NY: Hanover House, Doubleday & Co., 1961.

Six, Jean-François. *Light of the Night: The Last Eighteen Months in the Life of Thérèse of Lisieux*. Notre Dame, IN: University of Notre Dame Press, 1998.

_____. *Thérèse de Lisieux au Carmel*. Paris: Éditions du Seuil, 1973.

_____. *Lisieux au temps de Thérèse*. Preface by Yvette Roudy. Paris: Desclée de Brouwer, 1997.

_____. *La véritable enfance de Thérèse de Lisieux: névrose et sainteté*. Paris: Éditions du Seuil, 1972.

Vinatier, Jean. *Mère Agnès de Jesus: Pauline Martin, soeur aînée et "petite Mère" de sainte Thérèse de l'Enfant-Jesus*. Paris: Éditions du Cerf, 1993.

III. Official Documents Regarding the Declaration of Thérèse as "Doctor of the Church"

Cappella papale presieduta dal Santo Padre Giovanni Paolo II per la proclamazione a "Dottore della Chiesa" di Santa Teresa di Gesù Bambino e del Santo Volto. Vatican City: Tipografia Vaticana, 1997.

Congregatio de Causis Sanctorum (Prot. N. 2168). *Urbis et Orbis. Concessionis tituli Doctoris Ecclesiae universalis S. Teresiae Iesu Infante et a Sacro Vultu, moniali professae Ordinis Carmelitarum Discalceatorum (1873-1897)*. 2 vols.

Vol. 1 (Pp. ix + 964): Includes *Positio* and votes of five theological consultors. Cabellione: Rogeri Rimbaud, 1997.

Vol. 2 (Pp. 158): Includes votes of theological consultors. Roma: Tipografia Guerra, 1997.

John Paul II, "Divini Amoris Scientia: Apostolic Letter." *Origins* 27 (20 November 1997): 390-396.

_____. "St Theresa of Child Jesus To Be Proclaimed Doctor of the Church (World Youth Day: Sunday Angelus Meditation)." *L'Osservatore Romano*, English language edition, 27 August 1997, 1, 12.

_____. "St. Thérèse of Lisieux Proclaimed a Doctor of the Church: Homily." *Origins* 27 (6 November 1997): 349, 351-352.

_____. "St Thérèse Lived Filial Abandonment to Mary (Sunday Angelus: 19 October)." *L'Osservatore Romano*, English language edition, 22 October 1997, 1, 4.

_____. "Thérèse: Model of a Life Offered to God." *L'Osservatore Romano*, English language edition, 29 October 1997, 2.

IV. Secondary Works on Thérèse's "Doctrine" and Doctorate

Ahern, Patrick V. "The Case for St. Thérèse as a Doctor of the Church." *America* 169 (August 28 - September 4, 1993): 12-13.

_____. "Thérèse, Doctor of the Church." *Origins* 27 (4 September 1994): 193-195.

_____. "A Teacher for Today: Why St. Thérèse Should be Named a Doctor of the Church." *Spiritual Life* 40 (Summer 1994): 118-120.

Azcuy, Virginia R. and Eduardo de la Serna. "Vida teologal y ciencia teológica de Teresa de Lisieux: Aportes a una causa doctoral." *Teresianum* 48 (1997): 3-51.

Baudry, Joseph, ed. *Thérèse et ses théologiens: Colloque organisé par l'Institut Catholique de Toulouse et les Carmes de Toulouse*. Versailles: Éditions Saint Paul, 1998.

Bernard, Charles André. "Actualité et modernité de Thérèse de Lisieux," *Didaskalia* 27(1997): 3-21.

_____. "L'amour sauveur dans la vie de sainte Thérèse de Lisieux: essai sur son itinéraire spirituel," *Revue d'ascétique et mystique* 32 (1956): 297-328, 420-449.

_____. *Le Dieu des mystiques, tome II: La conformation au Christ.* Paris: Éditions du Cerf, 1988.

Bro, Bernard. "Le doctorat de Thérèse interroge la théologie." *Vie thérèsienne* 39 (1999): 22-69.

_____. *The Little Way: The Spirituality of Thérèse of Lisieux.* Westminster, MD: Christian Classics, 1980.

Bryden, Mary. "Saints and Stereotypes: The Case of Thérèse of Lisieux." *Literature and Theology* 13 (March 1999): 1-16.

Caprioli, Mario. "I Papi del secolo XX e S. Teresa di Lisieux." *Teresianum* 46(1995): 323-366.

Casarella, Peter. "Sisters in Doing the Truth: Dorothy Day and St. Thérèse of Lisieux." *Communio* 24 (Fall 1997): 468-498.

Castellano Cervera, Jesús. "El doctorado de Santa Teresa del Niño Jesus." *Revista de Espiritualidad* 226-227 (1998): 77-111.

Collins, Mary. "Daughters of the Church: The Four Theresas." In *Women—Invisible in Theology and Church.* Edited by Elisabeth Schüssler Fiorenza and Mary Collins, *Concilium* 182. Edinburgh: T. & T. Clark, 1985, 17-26.

Combes, André. *The Heart of Saint Thérèse.* New York: P.J. Kenedy & Sons, 1951.

_____. *The Spirituality of St. Thérèse (An Introduction).* New York: P.J. Kenedy & Sons, 1950.

_____. *Saint Thérèse and Her Mission: The Basic Principles of Theresian Spirituality.* Translated by Alastair Guinan. New York: P.J. Kenedy & Sons, 1955.

Conn, Joann Wolski. "A Feminist View of Thérèse." In *Carmelite Studies V: Experiencing St. Thérèse Today,* edited by John Sullivan, 119-139, 201-203. Washington, DC: ICS Publications, 1990.

_____. "Thérèse of Lisieux from a Feminist Perspective." *Spiritual Life* 28 (1982): 233-239.

De Meester, Conrad. "De la cellule de Thérèse de Lisieux." In *Thérèse et ses theologiens: Colloque organisé par l'Institut Catholique de Toulouse et les Carmes de Toulouse*, 13-51. Edited by Joseph Baudry. Versailles: Éditions Saint Paul, 1998.

_____. *The Power of Confidence: Genesis and Structure of the "Way of Spiritual Childhood" of St. Thérèse of Lisieux*. Staten Island, NY: Alba House, 1999.

_____. *With Empty Hands: The Message of Thérèse of Lisieux*. Revised ed. Washington, DC: ICS Publications, 2000.

Droulers, Paul. "Le doctorat de Sainte Thérèse de Lisieux propose en 1932." *Ephemerides Carmeliticae* 24 (1973): 86-129.

Faber, Eva Maria. "Chemin de kénose: la réponse de sainte Thérèse à l'héroïsme de ses contemporains d'après le Père Erich Przywara, S.J." In *Thérèse et ses theologiens: Colloque organisé par l'Institut Catholique de Toulouse et les Carmes de Toulouse*, 95-108. Edited by Joseph Baudry. Versailles: Éditions Saint Paul, 1998.

Frohlich, Mary. "Desolation and Doctrine in Thérèse of Lisieux." *Theological Studies* 61 (June 2000).

Gaucher, Guy. *Jean et Thérèse: Flammes d'amour*. Paris: Éditions du Cerf, 1996.

_____. *John of the Cross and Thérèse of Lisieux: Flames of Love*. Translated by Alexandra Plettenberg-Serban. Staten Island, NY: Alba House, 1998.

_____. "Le père Desbuquois et le doctorat de Thérèse." *Carmel* (1998): 43-53.

Gauthier, Jacques. "La théologie pratique de Thérèse de Lisieux, Doctor de l'Église." *Pastoral Sciences* 16 (1997): 105-133.

Gouley, Bernard, Rémi Mauger, and Emmanuelle Chevalier. *Thérèse de Lisieux ou La grande saga d'une petite soeur, 1897-1997*. Paris: Fayard, 1997.

Graham, William C. "Is There a Case against Saint Thérèse as

Doctor of the Church?" *Sisters Today* 67 (January 1995): 56-58.

———. "My Response to Father Russell." *Sisters Today* 69 (1997): 13-14.

Guitton, Jean. *The Spiritual Genius of Saint Thérèse of Lisieux.* Liguori, MO: Liguori/Triumph, 1997.

Jamart, François. *Complete Spiritual Doctrine of St. Thérèse of Lisieux.* Translated by Walter van de Putte. Staten Island, NY: Alba House, 1961.

Jean-Gabriel de l'Enfant Jesus. "L'éminence de la doctrine de Thérèse dans la Positio." *Carmel* (1998): 69-86.

Krauthauser, Carl. "The Doctor of Merciful Love: Saint Thérèse of Lisieux." *Eastern Churches Journal* 1997 (4): 89-110.

———. "Doctor of Merciful Love: St Thérèse of Lisieux in Light of the Mystical Theology of the Eastern Church." *Diakonia* 30 (1997): 38-56.

Lamoureaux, Françoise Thérèse. "L'antigiansenismo di Teresa di Lisieux." *Rivista di scienze dell'educazione* 34 (1996): 257-264.

———. Teresa di Lisieux e l'amore del prossimo." *Rivista di vita spirituale* 50 (1996): 493-510.

Langlois, Claude. "L'abbé Combes, théologien et historien de Thérèse." In *Thérèse et ses théologiens: Colloque organisé par l'Institut Catholique de Toulouse et les Carmes de Toulouse,* 133-160. Edited by Joseph Baudry. Versailles: Éditions Saint Paul, 1998.

Laurentin, René. *Thérèse de Lisieux: Mythes et réalité.* 2d ed., rev. Paris: Beachesne, 1972.

Léthel, François-Marie. "L'amour de Jesus." In *Thérèse de l'Enfant-Jésus, Docteur de l'Amour: Rencontre théologique et spirituelle, 1990,* 113-155. Venasque: Éditions du Carmel, 1990.

———. *L'amour de Jésus: La christologie de sainte Thérèse de l'Enfant-Jésus.* Paris: Desclée, 1997.

"Lettre du Père Yves Congar à Mgr. Gaucher." *La Documentation Catholique* 2040 (15 December 1991): 1088.

Likoudis, James, ed. *St. Thérèse of Lisieux: Doctor of the Church?* New Rochelle, NY: Catholics United for the Faith, 1992.

Maccise, Camilo. "Influence de sainte Thérèse sur la vie spirituelle du monde moderne." In *Une sainte pour le troisième millénaire: Actes du colloque internationale pour le centenaire de la mort de sainte Thérèse de l'Enfant-Jésus de la Saint-Face, Lisieux 30 septembre - 4 octobre 1996, 59-80.* Venasque: Éditions du Carmel, 1997.

Maccise, Camilo and Joseph Chalmers. *A Doctor for the Third Millenium: Letter from the O.C.D. and O.Carm. General Superiors on the Occasion of the Doctorate of Saint Thérèse of Lisieux.* Rome: Casa Generalizia O.C.D., 1997.

Marcil, Ivan. "La kénose du Christ chez Thérèse de l'Enfant-Jésus et de la Sainte-Face." *Teresianum* 48 (1997): 451-520.

Marie-Eugene of the Child-Jesus. *Under the Torrent of His Love: Thérèse of Lisieux, a Spiritual Genius.* Staten Island, NY: Alba House, 1995.

Mattei, Giampaolo. "Quella 'sorpresa' in Piazza san Pietro." *L'Osservatore Romano,* Lunedi-Martedi 20-21 Ottobre 1997, 7.

Miller, Frederick L. *The Trial of Faith of St. Thérèse of Lisieux.* Staten Island, NY: Alba House, 1998.

Mitescu, Adriana. "S. Thérèse de l'Enfant-Jésus et de la S. Face: La Sainte Face, le point de jonction de l'Église latine avec l'Orient de la lumière sophianique." *Teresianum* 47 (1996): 3-55.

O'Donnell, Christopher. *Love in the Heart of the Church: The Mission of Thérèse of Lisieux.* Dublin: Veritas, 1997.

_____. "Thérèse Among the Doctors of the Church." *Milltown Studies* 45 (Summer 2000): 112-138.

Petitot, Hyacinthe. *Saint Teresa of Lisieux: A Spiritual Renascence.*

Translated by the Benedictines of Stanbrook Abbey. New York: Benziger Brothers, 1927.

_____. *Sainte Thérèse de Lisieux, Une renaissance spirituelle*. Paris: Desclée, Éditions de la Revue des Jeunes, 1925.

Philipon, M.M. *The Message of Thérèse of Lisieux*. Translated by E.J. Ross. Westminster, MD: Newman Press, 1954.

Philippe de la Trinité. *Il purgatorio? Che ne pensa S. Teresa di Lisieux*. Rome: Teresianum, 1972.

_____. *La doctrine de Sainte Thérèse de l'Enfant-Jesus sur le purgatoire*. Paris: Libraire du Carmel, 1950.

_____. *Thérèse de Lisieux, la sainte de l'enfance spirituelle: Une relecture des textes d'André Combes*. Paris: P. Lethielleux, 1980.

Pinckaers, Servais. "Thérèse of the Child Jesus, Doctor of the Church." *Josephinum Journal of Theology* 5 (Winter/Spring 1998): 26-40.

Russell, John F. "St. Thérèse of Lisieux: Doctor of the Church?" *America* 167 (October 10, 1992): 250-251.

_____. "St. Thérèse of Lisieux: Doctor of the Church?" *Sisters Today* 69 (January 1997): 7-12.

Une sainte pour le troisième millénaire: Actes du colloque international pour le centenaire de la mort de sainte Thérèse de l'Enfant-Jésus de la Sainte-Face, Lisieux, 30 septembre-octobre 1996. Venasque: Editions du Carmel, 1997.

Saint Chamas, Loys de. *Sainte Thérèse de l'Enfant-Jésus: Dieu à l'oeuvre*. Venasque: Éditions du Carmel, 1998.

Schmitt, Thomas. "John Paul II and Thérèse of Lisieux." *Communio* 24 (Fall 1997): 541-549.

Sicari, Antonio. *La teologia di S. Teresa di Lisieux, Dottore della Chiesa*. Rome: Edizioni OCD; Milan: Editorale Jaca Book, 1997.

Thérèse au milieux des Docteurs: Colloque avec Thérèse de l'Enfant-Jésus. Ed. Centre Notre Dame de Vie. Venasque: Éditions du Carmel, 1998.

Thérèse de l'Enfant-Jésus, Docteur de l'Amour: Rencontre théologique et spirituelle, 1990. Venasque: Éditions du Carmel, 1990.

Thompson, William M. "Thérèse of Lisieux: A Challenge for Doctrine and Theology—Forerunner of Vatican II." In *Carmelite Studies V: Experiencing St. Thérèse Today,* edited by John Sullivan, 176-190, 206-209. Washington, DC: ICS Publications, 1990.

Valabek, Redemptus Mary. "St. Thérèse of Lisieux, Doctor of the Church." *Carmel in the World* 37 (1998): 37-63.

Von Balthasar, Hans Urs. *Two Sisters in the Spirit: Thérèse of Lisieux and Elizabeth of the Trinity.* San Francisco: Ignatius Press, 1992.

_____. *Thérèse of Lisieux: The Story of a Mission.* New York: Sheed and Ward, 1954.

_____. "The Timeliness of Lisieux." In *Carmelite Studies I: Spiritual Direction,* edited by John Sullivan, 103-121. Washington, DC: ICS Publications, 1980.

Welch, John. "Saint Thérèse's Discovery of Merciful Love." In *Master of the Sacred Page: Essays and Articles in Honor of Roland E. Murphy, O. Carm., on the Occasion of his Eightieth Birthday,* edited by Keith J. Egan and Craig E. Morrison, 389-401. Washington, DC: Carmelite Institute, 1997.

Wiseman, James. "The Spirituality of St. Thérèse of Lisieux as Seen in Her Poetry." *Communio* 24 (Fall 1997): 529-540.

Wooden, Cindy. "St. Thérèse of Lisieux, Doctor of the Church: Not a Divine Ph.D." Catholic News Service, 7 November 1997.

V. On the History and Theological Role of Saints and Doctors of the Church

Betti, Umberto. "A proposito del conferimento del titolo di Dottore della Chiesa." *Antonianum* 63 (1988): 278-291.

_____. "Preserve the True Meaning of the Canonical Requisites." *L'Osservatore Romano*, English language edition (29 June 1981): 3.

Boniface VIII. *Gloriosus Deus*. In *Corpus Iuris Canonici*, Pars Secunda: *Decretalium Collectiones*, cols. 1059-1060. Edited by Aemelius Friedberg. Ex Officina Bernhardi Tauchnitz: Leipzig, 1922.

Bouyer, Louis. *Women Mystics: Hadewijch of Antwerp, Teresa of Avila, Thérèse of Lisieux, Elizabeth of the Trinity, Edith Stein*. San Francisco, CA: Ignatius Press, 1993.

Castellano, Jesús. "'Eminens doctrina': un requisito necesario para ser Doctor de la Iglesia." *Teresianum* 46 (1995): 3-21.

Cunningham, Lawrence S. "A Decade of Research on the Saints, 1980-1990." *Theological Studies* 53 (1992): 517-533.

_____. *The Meaning of Saints*. San Francisco: Harper & Row, 1980.

_____. "Saints and Martyrs: Some Contemporary Considerations." *Theological Studies* 60 (1999): 529-537.

Egan, Keith J. "The Significance for Theology of the Doctor of the Church: Teresa of Avila." In *The Pedagogy of God's Image: Essays on Symbol and the Religious Imagination*. The Annual Publication of the College Theology Society, 153-171. Chico, CA: Scholars Press, 1982.

Ellsberg, Robert. "Saints for Today." *New Theology Review* 12 (May 1999): 17-22.

Galot, Jean. "Recognize the Charism in its Specific Value." *L'Osservatore Romano*, English language edition (29 June 1981): 2-3.

Gherardini, Bruno. "Eminence of Doctrine and Holiness of Life." *L'Osservatore Romano*, English language edition, 29 June 1981, 2-3.

Huscenot, Jean. *Les docteurs de l'Eglise*. Paris: Médiaspaul, 1997.

Johnson, Elizabeth A. *Friends of God and Prophets: A Feminist Theo-*

logical Reading of the Communion of Saints. New York: Continuum, 1998.

Lesage, Robert. "Docteurs de l'Église." In *Catholicisme: Hier, aujourd'hui, demain,* 3 cols. 936-937. Paris: Letouzey et Ané, 1952.

Léthel, François-Marie. *Connaître l'amour du Christ qui surpasse toute connaissance. La théologie des saints.* Venasque: Éditions du Carmel, 1989.

_____. *Théologie de l'amour de Jésus: Écrits sur la théologie des saints.* Venasque: Éditions du Carmel, 1996.

Madoz, J. "'Doctor ecclesiae'." *Estudios eclesiasticos* 11 (January 1932): 26-43.

McGinn, Bernard. *The Doctors of the Church: Thirty-Three Men and Women Who Shaped Christianity.* New York: Crossroad, 1999.

McIntosh, Mark A. *Christology from Within: Spirituality and the Incarnation in Hans Urs von Balthasar.* Notre Dame, IN: University of Notre Dame Press, 1996.

_____. *Mystical Theology: The Integrity of Spirituality and Theology.* Malden, MA: Blackwell Publishers, 1998.

Miscellanea in occasione del IV centenario della congregazione per le cause dei santi (1588-1988). Vatican City, 1988.

Palazzini, Pietro. "I quattrocento anni della Congregazione per le Cause dei Santi." *Divinitas* 35 (1991): 86-92.

Pugliese, Vincenzo, Giuseppe Löw, and Giovanni Carandente. "Dottori della Chiesa." In *Enciclopedia cattolica,* 1901-1907. Città del Vaticano, 1950.

Rahner, Hugo. "Kirchenlehrer." In *Lexicon für theologie und kirche,* 6: cols. 230-231. Edited by Michael Buchberger. Freiburg: Verlag Herder, 1961.

Rahner, Karl. "The Church of the Saints." In *Theological Investigations* 3, 91-105. Baltimore, MD: Helicon, 1966.

Sherry, Patrick. *Spirits, Saints, and Immortality.* Albany, NY: SUNY Press, 1984.

Smolinsky, Heribert. "Kirchenlehrer, Kirchenlehrerin." In *Lexicon für theologie und kirche*, 6: cols. 20-22. 3rd ed., rev. Edited by Walter Kaspar. Freiburg: Herder, 1997.

Sorrentino, Domenico. "Sulla 'Teologia dei santi' di Léthel." *Asprenas* 41 (1994): 389-404.

Thompson, William M. *Christology and Spirituality*. New York: Crossroad, 1991.

_____. *Fire and Light: The Saints and Theology*. New York: Paulist Press, 1987.

_____. *The Struggle for Theology's Soul: Contesting Scripture in Theology*. New York: Crossroad, 1996.

Trapé, Agostino. "Community and Peculiarity." *L'Osservatore Romano*, English language edition, 29 June 1981, 3.

von Balthasar, Hans Urs. "Saints in the Church." In *The Von Balthasar Reader*, edited by Medard Kehl and Werner Löser, 376-407. New York: Crossroad, 1982.

_____. "Theology and Sanctity." In *Word and Redemption: Essays in Theology*, 2, 49-86. New York: Herder and Herder, 1965.

Wilson, Stephen, ed. *Saints and Their Cults: Studies in Religious Sociology, Folklore, and History*. New York: Cambridge University Press, 1983.

Woodward, Kenneth L. *Making Saints: How the Catholic Church Determines Who Becomes a Saint, Who Doesn't, and Why*. New York: Simon & Schuster, Touchstone Books, 1990, 1996.

Wyschograd, Edith. *Saints and Postmodernism: Revisioning Moral Philosophy*. Chicago: University of Chicago Press, 1990.

VI. Other Works Cited

Agnew, Mary Barbara. "Sacrifice." In *The New Dictionary of Catholic Spirituality*, 845-846. Edited by Michael Downey. Collegeville, MN: Liturgical Press, 1993.

Augustine, Saint. *Against Julian*. Translated by Matthew A. Schumacher. New York: Fathers of the Church, 1957.

Chopp, Rebecca C. "Praxis." In *The New Dictionary of Catholic Spirituality*, 756-764. Edited by Michael Downey. Collegeville, MN: Liturgical Press, 1993.

Darricau, Raymond. "Margaret of the Most Holy Sacrament (Margaret Parigot, 1619-1648)." In *Saints of Carmel*, 187-194. Edited by Louis Saggi. Rome: Carmelite Institute, 1972.

Didache. In *The Apostolic Fathers*. Vol. 1, 303-333. Translated by Kirsopp Lake. Loeb Classical Library. Cambridge, MA: Harvard University Press; London: William Heinemann, 1977.

Downey, Michael. *Understanding Christian Spirituality*. New York: Paulist Press, 1997.

García-Rivera, Alex. *St. Martin de Porres: The "Little Stories" and the Semiotics of Culture*. Maryknoll, NY: Orbis Books, 1995.

The Golden Arrow: The Autobiography and Revelations of Sister Mary of St. Peter. Edited and translated by Emeric B. Scallan. New York: William-Frederick Press, 1954.

Gregory the Great. *Forty Gospel Homilies*. Translated by David Hurst. Cistercian Studies Series, no. 123. Kalamazoo, MI: Cistercian Publications, 1990.

Gutierrez, Gustavo. *We Drink From Our Own Wells: The Spiritual Journey of a People*. Maryknoll, NY: Orbis Books, 1985.

John Paul II. "Constitutio Apostolica de Romana Curia: Pastor Bonus." *Acta Apostolicae Sedis* 80 (28 June 1988): 841-923.

_____. "Youth, Meet the Lord." *The Pope Speaks* 42 (1997): 7-11.

Kapelrud, A.S. "lamad." In *Theological Dictionary of the Old Testament*. Edited by G. Johannes Botterweck, Helmer Ringgren, and Heinz-Josef Fabry. Translated by Douglas W. Scott. Vol. 8: lakad—mor. Grand Rapids, MI: Wm. B. Eerdmans Publishing Co., 1997.

Lambertini, Prospero (Benedict XIV). *De servorum Dei beatificatione et beatorum canonizatione*. 7 vols. Prati: Typographia Aldina, 1841.

Luciani, Albino. *Illustrissimi: Letters from Pope John Paul I*. Translated by William Weaver. Boston: Little, Brown and Co., 1978.

The Martyrdom of Polycarp. In *The Apostolic Fathers*. Vol. 2, 307-345. Translated by Kirsopp Lake. Loeb Classical Library. Cambridge, MA: Harvard University Press; London: William Heinemann, 1977.

O'Donnell, Christopher. "Reception." In *Ecclesia: A Theological Encyclopedia of the Church*, 400-402. Collegeville, MN: Liturgical Press, 1996.

Parker, Pierson. "Teacher." In *The Interpreter's Dictionary of the Bible*, 4: 522-523. George Arthur Buttrick, gen. ed. New York: Abingdon, 1962.

Paul VI. "Teresa of Avila: The Message of Prayer." *The Pope Speaks* 15 (1970): 218-222.

Pius V. *Mirabilis Deus*. In *Bullarum diplomatum et privilegiorum sanctorum Romanorum pontificum taurinensis editio*. Vol. 7: 564-565. Naples: Henrico Caporaso, 1882.

Professio fidei, Mansi, *Sacrorum conciliorum nova et amplissima collectio*. S. IX. Florentiae, 1759.

Rengstorf, Karl Heinrich. "διδάσκω," in *Theological Dictionary of the New Testament*. Edited by Gerhard Kittel and Gerhard Friedrich. Translated by Geoffrey W. Bromiley. Vol. II: Δ–H. Grand Rapids, MI: Wm. B. Eerdmans Publishing Co., 1968.

Sixtus V. *Triumphantis Hierusalem Gloriam*. In *Bullarum diplomatum et privilegiorum sanctorum Romanorum pontificum taurinensis editio*. Vol. 8: 1005-1012. Naples: Henrico Caporaso, 1883.